The Harvard Book of

CONTEMPORARY AMERICAN POETRY

The Harvard Book of

CONTEMPORARY AMERICAN POETRY

edited by
Helen Vendler

The Belknap Press of Harvard University Press
Cambridge, Massachusetts

Selection and editorial matter copyright © 1985
    by Helen Vendler
All rights reserved
Printed in the United States of America
10 9 8 7 6

This book is printed on acid-free paper, and its binding
materials have been chosen for strength and durability.

Library of Congress Cataloging in Publication Data
Main entry under title:

The Harvard book of contemporary American poetry.

    Includes indexes.
    1.   American poetry — 20th century.   I.   Vendler,
Helen Hennessy.
PS615.H37   1985   811.5′08   85-5473
ISBN 0-674-37340-5 (alk. paper)

Pages 425 – 430 constitute an extension of this
copyright page.

Designed by Gwen Frankfeldt

Contents

The Harvard Book of

CONTEMPORARY
AMERICAN
POETRY

Contemporary American Poetry

> But sometimes everything I write
> with the threadbare art of my eye
> seems a snapshot,
> lurid, rapid, garish, grouped,
> heightened from life,
> yet paralyzed by fact.
> All's misalliance.
> Yet why not say what happened?
>
> —Robert Lowell, "Epilogue"

The charm of poetry, the command of poetry, move us sometimes alternately, sometimes in unison. The intimate linguistic charm of poetry stops at the frontiers of its original language; the intellectual and moral command of poetry survives translation. This anthology of American poetry will be able to extend its charm only to those who genuinely know the American language — by now a language separate, in accent, intonation, discourse, and lexicon, from English. But the poems collected here can extend their command to anyone able to read English. And just as European and Asian and African writing has entered into the bloodstream of American literature, so the poems in these pages may have a second, transformed life in new poems in Chinese or Bengali or Hebrew.

It is tempting to represent poetry, with its oral origins, as a chorus of voices rising from the abyss of history. Our greatest American poet, Walt Whitman, urges us to understand poetry through that vocal model. But against the ear, the eye makes its case — for the jagged edges of a Berryman dream song, for the minimalist shapeliness of an Ammons stanza, for the weighty block of a Lowell sonnet. These signs of writing construct poetry too; and the play of light and shadow in the

text — now a haunting voice, now a calligraphic curve —
awakens part of the nameless happiness of reading. Poetry is
the most speaking of written signs; it is the most designed of
spoken utterances; it inhabits, and makes us travelers in, a
place where every phrase of the spoken language would be as
outlined as an urn, and where each sentence of the written
language would ring like "church bells beyond the starres
heard." Such a place exists nowhere in life. In life, most
written language is deliberately processed into neutrality so as
to be forgotten as fast as possible in favor of the deposit of
information it leaves behind; and the spoken language melts
into air, unshaped and unremembered — except by writers.
Only the ear of the writer is, as Keats said, "open like a greedy
shark" to catch the tunings of historical language. Though no
writer ends there, that is where all writers begin.

This collection preserves, then, some of the American
language of the twentieth century. It is a language that has
assimilated the syncopation of jazz, the stylishness of
advertising, the technicalities of psychoanalysis, the simplicities
of rural speech, the discourse of the university disciplines, the
technology of the engineer, the banalities of journalism. These
have been recorded in our novels too, where the vernacular
thrives and where the rhythms of American life — urgent and
noisy and irregular in the cities, more long-breathed in the
countryside — have found a place. But poetry offers us
something different from the novel, because it engages
constantly in a strange process of self-interruption, its pause at
the end of each line.

While the novel, unstoppable, wants to keep reeling us into
its labyrinth, the unjustified margin of poetry pulls us up,
even if gently, at the end of each line. (Even the prose poem,
by its sheer density, forces an interruption on us at the end of
each sentence, a practice that would be fatal to a novel.) In the
perpetual self-halting of poetry must lie the ground of its
peculiar attraction. It insists on a spooling, a form of
repetition, the reinscribing of a groove, the returning upon an
orbit already traced. Lyric poetry — for all its plot, its logic, its
conclusions — is profoundly unlinear. It does not advance.
(Perhaps it does not advance even in the way Coleridge thought
it did, like a snake doubling back on itself at each motion.)
Poetry, instead, looks — and looks again. Its second look may

be different from the first, but it looks again at the same thing. It does not progress to a new vista. Every poem is, in Wallace Stevens' phrase, "one last look at the ducks."

In this way, poetry is at odds with the optimistic American dream of an ever-unrolling frontier, of "a land still vaguely realizing westward / But still unstoried, artless, unenhanced, / Such as she was, such as she would become" (Frost, "The Gift Outright"). That epic dream of realizing westward opposes the lyric poet's calling — to look over and over at the one place where the eye or the mind alights: to read "a text, albeit done in plant," with the same stubbornness as Frost's exemplary mountain climber. Stevens' version of poetic intensity of regard appears in "Credences of Summer": "Let's see the thing itself and nothing else . . . Burn everything not part of it to ash."

The optic concentration announced by Stevens and other modernists becomes a general duty in the latter half of the twentieth century. Stevens and Williams had taken as their model the visual concentration of painters; but as photography put into question the illusionistic values expressed in painting, the snapshot (rather than the art-photograph) began to seem a necessary, if threatening, model for the poet. And the cultural skepticism first taken as total subject by Stevens pervades the work of his successors. For them, Wordsworth's two axiomatic points of beginning — perception and memory — have become two points of suspicion. They become points of annihilation, even, in the writing of poets who insist on the degree to which perception is socially conditioned and who refuse the nostalgias of memory.

The poets of the second half of the century cannot quite take the work of the great modernists for granted. For personal and sometimes political reasons, they must repeat in their own poetry the experiments of their predecessors — experiments in perception, in memory, in language. Replication of the great modernists — in homage, in quarrel — marks the poetry of these later poets. Yeats reappears in Roethke and Berryman, Moore in Ammons, Auden in Merrill, Williams in Rich, Stevens in Ashbery, Eliot in Lowell. The list could be rewritten, equally truly, in different ways: we can see Auden in Berryman, Williams in Ammons, Stevens in Merrill, Frost in Rich, Eliot in Ashbery, Pound in Lowell. (And a comparable

set of lists could be made for the younger poets: we can find
Lowell in Bidart, Bishop in Graham, Hayden in Harper,
Winters in Pinsky.)

The areas of intersection between generations are both
partial and multiple. And the history of the rewriting of the
modernists by their successors sheds light on each half of the
juncture. One can imagine Ammons (trained in the sciences)
thinking of Frost: "Yes, he noticed natural things; but why did
he not want to know their inner laws? If instead of Calvinist
design, one thought in terms of inner biological and physical
design, how would one respond to nature, what would one say
about it?" This is of course not how poets write poems. Still,
if in Ammons one sees a Frost thoroughly secularized, one
sees both poets more clearly. Lowell — to take a second
case — was as interested in history as Pound was. But Pound
thought of himself an archaeologist reassembling shards of
culture, while Lowell took on the role of a chronicler in whom
the past assumes the integral form of a single psyche.
Implicitly, Lowell's project calls into question the artificial
helplessness of Pound before the pieces of the past, and
suggests that we cannot avoid, even against our will, forming
a gestalt of what we inherit. Pound is all nominal phrases;
Lowell is all syntax. When the history of the relation between
the two halves of the twentieth century is written, the second
half will be seen, as in these cases of Ammons and Lowell, to
be a long critique of the first, as well as a long absorption of it.

This formulation is both true and false when we apply it to
poets who are women. Bishop, Plath, Sexton, Rich, Clampitt
— and such later poets as Glück, Graham, and Dove — have,
as notable predecessors who were women, only Dickinson and
Moore. One tradition against which poets of our century have
rebelled is the "woman's voice" as it took acceptable
conventional form. Poetry written by women was limited both
in subject (love, God, children, death) and in expression
(self-deprecatory, whimsical, supplicatory, resigned). Modern
poets had no models to speak of in writing about being
mothers, daughters, or wives. They had scarcely any models for
political expression. Their aim, topically speaking, was to
chart the unexplored territory of untouched subjects. Their
aim, expressively speaking, was to find new tones of voice. A
certain satire on previous tones, and on social expectations,

was necessary to clear the air: Sylvia Plath and Anne Sexton were savagely satiric toward the voice of the "nice girl"; Elizabeth Bishop coolly took on a "man's subject"— exploration and discovery of foreign lands; Adrienne Rich assumed a "man's role"—the denunciation of social and political evil. As a result of the expansion of topic and expression achieved by these women, later poets feel free to speak in wide-ranging voices. Art, race relations, cultural mythology, metaphysics—written about without self-deprecation or apology—are now available subjects for any younger woman.

Though of course influenced by predecessors, each of the writers here has found an uninhabited place in the zodiac of poetry and has printed a new sign there. It may help to mention how, in some notable cases, that work has been done. The staking out of an imaginative claim is the single most interesting act by each powerful poet. Elizabeth Bishop, as I have said, staked out travel, in all its symbolic reaches of pilgrimage, exile, homelessness, exploration, exhaustion, colonializing, mapping, and being lost. Travel is not an unusual topic—but because it had been considered a Byronic narrative subject rather than a lyrical one, Bishop had a free hand and an open field. Lowell, to take another example, staked out history—again, not an uncommon preoccupation for epic or narrative, but less common in lyric (traditionally a private, not a public, genre). Because his ancestors the Lowells, the Starks, and the Winslows had helped to make American history, history had, for Lowell, a right to appear in the privacy of lyric. He is also the first American poet of the family romance—not the Freudian archetype unadorned, but that archetype tethered by the infinitely many fetters of particular occasions. Whereas Freud had summoned up detail only to reach the Oedipal shape beneath, Lowell, accepting the primal scheme, delighted in reanimating it within the triviality and absurdity of its manifestation in family life. A worldly irony tinges Lowell's history, where the superego always betrays the id.

But in Berryman—to take yet another example of the imaginative claim to a personal territory—the id is the subject of real interest. Berryman gives it a voice, and names it Henry; it sings, in his *Dream Songs,* its plaintive, outraged, impetuous, suicidal, childlike, and harrowing desires. The superego still does the writing (and has its unnamed and reproachful minstrel-show black-face voice in the *Dream Songs*), but it cannot accomplish its writing without quoting the id. It argues, implicitly, that any writing that does not quote the id is concealing its darker twin. Berryman learned the language of the id from Roethke; but Roethke, after his astonishing discovery of that language, repudiated it. As a ghost of himself, he lived out his life imitating Yeats in bad poems.

Ginsberg provides another example of new subject matter. In seeking out an authentic voice for himself (after a youthful period of imitating Marvell and Donne), he found with exhilaration the proletarian ground cleared by Williams, the first American poet after Whitman to treat the urban poor in a language technically appropriate to the subject. But Ginsberg had a new area to claim as his own — the Jewish milieu, already well represented in the novel but as yet without a memorable poetry of its own. In the long elegy for his mother, "Kaddish," Ginsberg made a founding gesture comparable to that made in the black vernacular by Langston Hughes. Through the work of such poets, the poetry of the second half of this century begins to be ethnically representative.

But originality in poetry makes for difficulty. It is the vice of distinctiveness, as Hopkins once remarked, to become queer, and original authors may at first sound odd or look odd on the page. Memorable language, in Roland Barthes's terms, is always in some way "writerly" rather than "readerly." Stevens said that the poem "must resist the intelligence almost successfully," and he encountered that resistance in his readers almost from the beginning. To a colleague who complained that he could not understand Stevens' poetry, Stevens replied, "It isn't necessary that you understand my poetry or any poetry. It's only necessary that the writer understand it." If writing is genuine, and genuinely talented, it will eventually be understood.

While the new writing is transgressing the current codes for the understanding of art, it will bring the reader up short. But mystery, obliquity, allusion, linguistic play, and the assumption of new roles for the spirit, once accepted, buoy the reader into another, headier atmosphere, one proper to the modern vista the author offers us. When language and vision coalesce in poetry, a new attitude is born. What do such new attitudes look like? To Moore, writing the poem "Poetry," they resemble nothing so much as the unforgettable and distinctive gestures of animals: "the bat / holding on upside down or in quest of something to / eat, elephants pushing, a wild horse taking a roll, a tireless wolf under / a tree." Thousands of people have written verse putting ideas into statement; but inept verse has none of the excess of distinctive manner ("elephants pushing, a wild horse taking a roll") common to all remarkable poetry.

That excess of manner can be minimalist (minimalism is a form of excess in concision) or maximalist (a form of excess beyond informational necessity). This brilliance of manner — even, and perhaps especially, in the art that conceals art — is the sign of verse that is on its way to becoming poetry. It is this excess which is the sign of the aesthetic dynamic in the poem, as form struggles into articulation — the brilliance of the surreal in Plath, of the nonchalant in Ammons, of the tragicomic in Ginsberg, of the unearthly in Glück, of the intense in Bidart. Though it is easy to find a feeling to express or a cause to espouse, it is next to impossible to find a stylization that succeeds: only a few poets in each century have done it. These are the poets who are elevated to canonical status by the envy and admiration of their fellow poets. As Hugh Kenner reminds us, it is poets — and not anthologists or professors — who eventually decide which poets are read after their own generation has disappeared. All poets envy that authority of style on the page which says, even in a few lines, "Milton" or "Tennyson," in the way that a few bars of music will say "Mozart" or "Wagner." It is perhaps too early to tell which American poets will belong, hundreds of years from now, to the common music of our century and which ones will survive as major figures. Both destinies are honorable ones.

Each of our poets preserves some part of culture that would lapse unrecorded were it not for art. The social genres — drama and the novel — preserve our life with others; the private genre, lyric, preserves our inner life. In that sense, poetry has a historical function; it is, as Wordsworth said, the history of feeling. But his definition is ampler than that:

poetry is, he said, the history *and science* of feeling. Poetry is analytic as well as expressive; it distinguishes, reconstructs, and redescribes what it discovers about the inner life. The poet accomplishes the analytic work of poetry chiefly by formal means. A poem composed of only two stanzas, for instance, is almost always occupied with binary terms — choice, contrast, comparison. It would falsify the subject of such a poem to have more than two stanzas; the two-stanza form insists that one must occupy one room or the other of the poem. (See Stevens' "The Emperor of Ice-Cream," where one room holds concupiscence, the other, death.) A poem full of appositions suggests that its subject is one that must be incremental, qualified, explained; a poem full of lists announces formally that its subject is plenitude, good or bad; a poem presenting a tale within a tale suggests the ever-receding planes of truth in life. In the best poems, there is no such thing as separable form or content; form is content-as-arranged, or content is form-as-exemplified. No proposition in poetry is detachable from its functional expression.

In what Richard Wilbur has called the "mad *instead*" of poetry, things have their meaning only in the context of the world that they there create. The world of the poem is analogous to the existential world, but not identical with it. In a famous created world of Blake's, for instance, there is a rose doomed to mortal illness by the love of a flying worm who is invisible. We do not experience such a poem by moving it piecemeal into our world, deciding what the rose "symbolizes" and what the worm "stands for." On the contrary, we must move ourselves into its ambience, into a world in which a dismayed man can converse with his beloved rose and thrust upon her, in his anguished jealousy, diagnosis and fatal prognosis in one sentence:

> O Rose thou art sick.
> The invisible worm
> That flies in the night,
> In the howling storm:
>
> Has found out thy bed
> Of crimson joy:
> And his dark secret love
> Does thy life destroy.

After living in Blake's world for the space of eight lines, we return to our own world, haunted and accused.

This truth — that we live in the poem's world, not it in ours — applies not only to "symbolic" poems. One can equally well inhabit, and be haunted by, the world of 91 Revere Street where Lowell lived as a boy, a house seen through the myopic and baleful lens of the Freudian memory. Or one can live in the ignited air of Plath's "Lady Lazarus"; or in the somber bus ride from New York to Ohio in Clampitt's "Procession at Candlemas," where the poet reviews the cultural images of femaleness from Athena to Mary. A successful poem is, as Williams said, a machine made out of words; if it is properly constructed it cannot fail to perform its function, which is so to control its reader, by its selective and stylized processional means, that the reader "cannot choose but hear." A reader enters and joins — like Keats's spectator of the urn — the procession of forms that give access to an imagined plane of projected existence.

Of course every accomplished poem has both an illusionistic and a self-conscious status; it is both imagined and made. It could not attain its illusionistic ends — that this is "a cry from the heart" or "a diary entry" or "a letter to the world" — without shaping its language to convey spontaneity, intimacy, a heart laid bare. When we first read a poem we read it illusionistically; later we may see its art; and these remain as figure and ground, each to the other, constructing part of the chiaroscuro of poetry.

These qualities are to be found in all poetry. But there are national differences among poetries as well as linguistic differences, and American poetry has added something new to the store of poetry in the world. The mixed poverty and riches of the United States have brought into being a poetry that differs from that of England. In England — a tiny country, agriculturally cultivated for centuries, architecturally and historically rich, uninvaded in battle since 1066, with a small, homogeneous educated class — a coherent poetry was possible for a number of centuries. In America — an enormous wilderness only recently settled, educationally and ethnically diverse, made and remade by waves of immigrants — poetry was bound to be diffuse, heterogeneous, and, vis-à-vis England, defensive. Although the victories won by American

modernists were indisputable, they were won chiefly by
Americans who had Europeanized themselves with a
vengeance. Pound and Eliot became expatriates; Frost went
deliberately to England for three years and published his first
book there; Stevens said that French and English constitute a
single language. And Williams made himself so pointedly
American only because he was by birth and education so
European (his father was English, his mother Puerto Rican,
and he had been educated in part in Switzerland). In spite of
their American origins, each of these authors had to come to
terms in some way with Europe.

For our second-generation modernists, a less embattled
relation with Europe — and consequently with America — was
possible. American poetry was for poets writing after 1940 a
splendid present reality, not (as it had been for the early
modernists) a luminous possibility. Younger poets turned
away from England and France, and found poetic models in
South America, Italy, Germany, Poland. Robert Bly's journal
The Fifties (later *The Sixties*) brought Neruda, Machado,
Vallejo, and others into American writing; Montale was
translated by Lowell and Charles Wright; Rilke and Trakl
from Germany, Herbert and Milosz from Poland, have
suggested new structures, tones, and procedures to American
poets. The practice of translation was given further impetus by
Lowell's powerful and idiosyncratic example in *Imitations*
(1961) and *Near the Ocean* (1967). By rewriting poets from
Horace to Pasternak in his own irregular, idiomatic, and
forceful American voice, Lowell announced that American
poetry henceforth would possess the past in a commanding,
not subordinate, manner.

As the high tension of American modernism subsided,
other tensions, of a different sort, replaced it. The poets
included here write — as the earlier modernists did not — from
a Freudian culture, one in which a vaguely Freudian model of
the soul has replaced an older Christianized Hellenic model.
In the Freudian world, motives are doubted, the unreliability
of memory (with its self-servingness) is taken for granted, the
significance of peripheral detail is magnified, and truths of
human relation and human frailty take on an unlovely
explicitness. These poets also, many of them, write within a
post-Marxist clouding of the American self-image: voices of

protest rise from women (Plath, Sexton, Rich), from blacks (Hayden, Harper, Dove), from the dispossessed (James Wright), from the counterculture (Snyder), from self-declared homosexuals and lesbians (Ginsberg, Rich), from Americans in opposition to American foreign policy (Lowell, Merwin). Finally, all of these poets write within a culture in which physical science has replaced metaphysics as the model of the knowable. The epistemological shift toward scientific models of verification has caused the usual throes of fundamentalist reaction in American culture, as elsewhere; but there is no significant poet whose work does not mirror, both formally and in its preoccupations, the absence of the transcendent.

It is the social consciousness of American lyric (from Whitman to the present) that perhaps strikes the foreign reader most strongly. Pound's great failed effort in the *Cantos* — to turn the lyric radically toward historic and social reality — has borne results in all our recent poets, no matter how un-Poundian their style. The inner life can no longer be insulated from the political and social life of the state: World War II ended, perhaps forever, any hope that the American continent could ignore Europe and Asia, and the Vietnam War ended any delusion that America could claim a permanent moral superiority to the "Old World." Even our most inward poets — Stevens, Bishop, Merwin, Merrill, Graham — find themselves drawn into the social vortex, as Stevens confronts the Depression, as Bishop writes about the poor in Rio or the sins of the Conquistadors, as Merwin protests the Vietnam War, as Merrill composes fantasies of nuclear disaster, as Graham thinks about Buchenwald. In incorporating social reality, the lyric repossesses — especially in the work of our most socially detailed poets, Lowell and Ginsberg — much of the terrain of the novel, continuing that historical consciousness in lyric begun in this century, in English, by Yeats.

The lyric poet has had to evolve new strategies of representation in order to become a social voice. Ginsberg revived the Blakean prophetic voice that confirmed the psalms and prophecies of his Jewish upbringing; Lowell borrowed the Poundian heaping up of detail but marshaled it within a magisterial categorical system; Rich turned to the voice of Protestant homiletic so native to American sermons and political exhortations but less familiar in lyric; Hayden and

Goldbarth (among others) learned from Pound an allusiveness that takes for granted a common possession of historical narrative; Nemerov returned to the voice of Latin social epigram, jaunty and morose at once; Bidart revived the dramatic monologue, putting his own voice at the service of historical figures from Ellen West to Nijinsky. These ventures strain the capacities of lyric almost beyond its own strengths. When these poets lose control, it is sometimes because their unwieldy social material has overwhelmed the single sensibility bearing it. The poem diffuses its strength into randomness and multiplicity of detail. Or, in a different error, the poet, intimidated by the sheer mass of social and historical freight, subjects it too readily to a single political or moral view.

The poem that best sums up the aesthetic predicament of our present poets is Lowell's great "Epilogue," the last poem in his last book, a conscious envoy to his lifelong poetic effort. There, the poet, no longer an illusionistic painter in oils, no longer a poet of "plot and rhyme" (Lowell had forgone these in his last book), must confront the frightening randomness of the moving camera lens that is now his own eye.

> Those blessèd structures, plot and rhyme —
> why are they no use to me now
> I want to make
> something imagined, not recalled?
> I hear the noise of my own voice:
> *The painter's vision is not a lens,*
> *it trembles to caress the light.*
> But sometimes everything I write
> with the threadbare art of my eye
> seems a snapshot,
> lurid, rapid, garish, grouped,
> heightened from life,
> yet paralyzed by fact.
> All's misalliance.

The poem collapses, helpless. But then it gains a second wind by saying, rebelliously (as Lowell rebukes those critics who accused him of cannibalizing his life for his art, of lurid detailing of what should remain private), "Yet why not say what happened?" This "accuracy with respect to the structure of reality" (Stevens' phrase) is for Lowell the saving motive

that unites all artists. Once he has found it, he can resuscitate
his poem with a single self-command:

> Yet why not say what happened?
> Pray for the grace of accuracy
> Vermeer gave to the sun's illumination
> stealing like the tide across a map
> to his girl solid with yearning.

The lurid snapshot of the post-modernist American poet and
the caressing vision of the seventeenth-century Dutch painter
have in common the wish to be accurate with respect to the
structure of reality. The poet knows that, without the accurate
record of art, people subside, as transient statistics, into the
anonymous census of history:

> We are poor passing facts,
> warned by that to give
> each figure in the photograph
> his living name.

Ending his poem, Lowell can call it not by the denigrating
name of "snapshot," but by the honorific name of
"photograph"—a writing with light. Its light is its accuracy.

All the poets included here attempt that accuracy—of
perception, of style—that makes a new poetry. When a new
reality is born and exerts its pressure on poets, their resisting
pressure of language and imagination generates a new poetic.
The reality our poets have found in America (in this century
as before) is, first and foremost, the American climate and
landscape, so various as to defeat expression entirely if one
were to use only the principal English vocabulary of lark,
primrose, and cottage farm. The second reality is the American
language, its dialects and regional rhythms; third, American
political ideals as they adjust to political reality (alternately
fulfilling and frustrating social hopes); fourth, the ambivalent
relation of Americans to their parent cultures and to European
history; and fifth, the various new readings of experience
suggested by contemporary science, psychology, and
anthropology. Some of these pressures are felt everywhere in
the world; some are peculiar to America. There are pressures
felt by poetry in other countries—the pressures of internal

war, invasion, famine — that American poetry has not felt, except in the person of its émigré poets like Simic (who, though he writes in English, remembers in his poetry the war years of his Yugoslavian childhood).

Some of our poets cite American pressures in a self-conscious and explicit way. But more often these physical and philosophical pressures simply underlie certain styles of utterance. John Ashbery's free-floating poems — long spirals of language on which we embark as on an ocean liner — simply assume, as givens, axioms of the infinity and relativity of time and space; of the indeterminacy of a life unguided by providence or will; of a demotic social world generating tireless banalities of language; of an interpenetration of media in which movies, television, phonographs, radios, newspapers, and books produce a cacophony out of which meaning can scarcely form before it redissolves; of a series of illusions deconstructing themselves even as pleasure is at work constructing new illusions to replace the old. Ashbery's decor is whimsically American and European by turns, but his sensibility — dégagé, knowledgeable, self-mocking, lyrical — is as recognizably American in one way as Lowell's — ironic, Calvinist, ambitious — is in another. They are, perhaps, these two poets, New York and Boston personified. As soon as one says that, another voice argues that Ginsberg is New York too, in his expressive tragicomedy, just as Bishop is Boston — discreet, plain-spoken, sharp.

As our cities find their embodiments and our countryside its voices (the bleak midwestern speech of James Wright, the passionately southern descriptiveness of Dave Smith, the spare west-coast rituals of Gary Snyder), the map of North America, once so empty of poetry except in the East, begins to be filled in. As the gaze reaches Ohio, it finds Clampitt and Dove; in Nova Scotia, Bishop and Strand; in Virginia, Dave Smith; in Minnesota, James Wright; in Tennessee, Charles Wright; in Connecticut, Stevens and Merrill; in New York City, O'Hara; in Ithaca, Ammons; on the west coast, Roethke and Snyder and Bidart; in Chicago, Goldbarth; in St. Louis, Nemerov. (I give only a few instances, which could be multiplied.) This scanning would not have been so well rewarded fifty years ago; the map would have been largely blank. Of course, even what we have is not enough. The aim of poetry is to saturate every terrain, every city, every village, so that every American child might find a native landscape invested with language. This was, after all, the normal condition for the European child. The *genius loci* lives only where poetry creates it.

The Boston State House, the Shaw Memorial, Beacon Street, the Boston Common, the Public Garden, the King's Chapel Burying Ground — to speak only of places in one city — are different now because they are wreathed, invisibly but powerfully, in Lowell's lines. Stonington is peopled by Merrill's ghosts, summoned up in his recent trilogy, *The Changing Light at Sandover.* Clampitt's poetry makes a glowing atmosphere around the Maine coast. What painters — John Marin, Georgia O'Keeffe, Charles Sheeler — and photographers like Ansel Adams have done for the American landscape in this century, the poets must do in their turn, so that there will be no American landscape that does not speak in words as well as in line and color.

Every poet feels a despair that so much goes unrecorded. An adequate written language is, as Yeats said, "gradual time's last gift"; and a great deal that has happened in America has not had its adequate expression in verse. Slavery had only its spirituals. To stand for the whole of the Civil War, we have only a few poems by Melville and Whitman. Our recent Hispanic and Asian migrations are merely the newest pressures of a social reality demanding a responsive counterpressure from artists.

More subtly present than American social changes — whether occasioned by immigration, feminism, the therapeutic hour, nuclear fission, or anything else — are those modern seismic shifts of consciousness which are usually tracked only by hindsight. These occur, for the artist, as formal problems: if a line sounds wrong, "fixed," "pat," "complacent," it is because it is phrased in a language or cadence not true to present sensibility. One of the most interesting of recent formal changes is the alteration that has taken place in the way poets end poems. Resounding closure — like the providential teleology of which it is the formal counterpart — no longer seems "true." A diffuseness and "evenness" of aura tends to spread round the close of poems, which dissolve rather than end. A tentativeness of gesture corresponds to what must be, in a pluralistic society, an inevitable pluralism of view. When the

gesture toward pluralism is not made by discretion or
tentativeness, it is made by sheer aggregation — Lowell will
put everything into his sonnets rather than keep any part of
history or mentality out.

An immense amount of verse, most of it not rising to a
memorable level, is printed every year in the United States.
This anthology can be nothing more than a sampling of what
seems to my taste satisfying in that massive unrolling of
printed pages. I have preferred to choose fewer poets, and
represent them by more poems, rather than have more poets
with fewer poems each. In this way, readers can see the poets
whole. I have had to leave out many poets whose aims were
admirable but whose poems seemed thin (whatever their past
historical effect). This collection opens with the poetry of
Stevens, since he flowered late and came into his own only
after the 1955 publication of the *Collected Poems;* he is the
chief link between the earlier high modernists (Eliot, Pound,
Williams, Crane, Moore) and the later poets. Thinking
especially of foreign readers, I have added brief biographies.
Though the artist who writes is not that "bundle of accidents
and incoherence that sits down to breakfast" (Yeats), both
artist and person inhabit the same body, in the same place,
and that identity is not irrelevant. According to Stevens,
"Reality is only the base. But it is the base."

In a late poem, called simply "Poem," Elizabeth Bishop
traces the stages by which we enter a work of art (in this case,
an unremarkable painting by her great-uncle). First, we regard
it idly, with indifference. Next, we recognize some generic
feature of its content (Bishop decides that the scene resembles
her childhood Nova Scotia) or some process in its making
("fresh-squiggled from the tube"), but we remain observers,
outside the scene. Then, insensibly, we begin to enter the
work: "The air is fresh and cold; cold early spring." And we
are rewarded for our imaginative participation by a sudden
moment of recognition, as some detail strikes us as pertaining
directly to ourselves: "Heavens, I recognize the place, I know
it!" After that, our responses may continue to be sometimes
technical ("titanium white, one dab"), sometimes visual ("the
hint of steeple"), but they will also contain the personal, the
moral, the ratified ("the little of our earthly trust. Not

much."). At the end, we regret having to leave the scene—"the yet-to-be dismantled elms"—but even as we take our leave the work seems, because we have entered and recognized it, perpetually ours, vividly alive:

> Life and the memory of it cramped,
> dim, on a piece of Bristol board,
> dim, but how live, how touching in detail
> —the little that we get for free,
> the little of our earthly trust. Not much.
> About the size of our abidance
> along with theirs: the munching cows,
> the iris, crisp and shivering, the water
> still standing from spring freshets,
> the yet-to-be-dismantled elms, the geese.

No one can rise to the occasion in every encounter with a poem: but I trust that readers of this book will find among these poems many that will provoke that sharp and relieving pang—"Heavens, I recognize the place, I know it!" It is the effect every poet hopes for; and, to be complete, it must be followed by that other, estranging effect which tells us, by style, that the elms in the poem are, by their placement in the virtual world of language, already dismantled and gone.

The symbolic strength of poetry consists in giving presence, through linguistic signs, to absent realities, while insisting, by the very brilliance of poetic style, on the linguistic nature of its own being and the illusionistic character of its effects. The poem stands before us brilliantly photographic and brilliantly verbal at once. If it were not also (to paraphrase Lowell) a shape solid with yearning and written in light, a shape formed by both heart and mind, it would expend its mimetic and verbal energies in vain. "The poetry of a people," said T. S. Eliot, "takes its life from the people's speech and in turn gives life to it; and represents its highest point of consciousness, its greatest power and its most delicate sensibility." The poems in this volume represent American speech brought to that mastery and endowed with that life.

> Helen Vendler
> Cambridge, 1985

WALLACE STEVENS

(1879 – 1955)

Sunday Morning

I

Complacencies of the peignoir, and late
Coffee and oranges in a sunny chair,
And the green freedom of a cockatoo
Upon a rug mingle to dissipate
The holy hush of ancient sacrifice.
She dreams a little, and she feels the dark
Encroachment of that old catastrophe,
As a calm darkens among water-lights.
The pungent oranges and bright, green wings
Seem things in some procession of the dead,
Winding across wide water, without sound.
The day is like wide water, without sound,
Stilled for the passing of her dreaming feet
Over the seas, to silent Palestine,
Dominion of the blood and sepulchre.

II

Why should she give her bounty to the dead?
What is divinity if it can come
Only in silent shadows and in dreams?
Shall she not find in comforts of the sun,
In pungent fruit and bright, green wings, or else
In any balm or beauty of the earth,
Things to be cherished like the thought of heaven?
Divinity must live within herself:
Passions of rain, or moods in falling snow;
Grievings in loneliness, or unsubdued
Elations when the forest blooms; gusty
Emotions on wet roads on autumn nights;

All pleasures and all pains, remembering
The bough of summer and the winter branch.
These are the measures destined for her soul.

III

Jove in the clouds had his inhuman birth.
No mother suckled him, no sweet land gave
Large-mannered motions to his mythy mind.
He moved among us, as a muttering king,
Magnificent, would move among his hinds,
Until our blood, commingling, virginal,
With heaven, brought such requital to desire
The very hinds discerned it, in a star.
Shall our blood fail? Or shall it come to be
The blood of paradise? And shall the earth
Seem all of paradise that we shall know?
The sky will be much friendlier then than now,
A part of labor and a part of pain,
And next in glory to enduring love,
Not this dividing and indifferent blue.

IV

She says, "I am content when wakened birds,
Before they fly, test the reality
Of misty fields, by their sweet questionings;
But when the birds are gone, and their warm fields
Return no more, where, then, is paradise?"
There is not any haunt of prophecy,
Nor any old chimera of the grave,
Neither the golden underground, nor isle
Melodious, where spirits gat them home,
Nor visionary south, nor cloudy palm
Remote on heaven's hill, that has endured
As April's green endures; or will endure
Like her remembrance of awakened birds,
Or her desire for June and evening, tipped
By the consummation of the swallow's wings.

V

She says, "But in contentment I still feel
The need of some imperishable bliss."
Death is the mother of beauty; hence from her,
Alone, shall come fulfilment to our dreams
And our desires. Although she strews the leaves
Of sure obliteration on our paths,
The path sick sorrow took, the many paths
Where triumph rang its brassy phrase, or love
Whispered a little out of tenderness,
She makes the willow shiver in the sun
For maidens who were wont to sit and gaze
Upon the grass, relinquished to their feet.
She causes boys to pile new plums and pears
On disregarded plate. The maidens taste
And stray impassioned in the littering leaves.

VI

Is there no change of death in paradise?
Does ripe fruit never fall? Or do the boughs
Hang always heavy in that perfect sky,
Unchanging, yet so like our perishing earth,
With rivers like our own that seek for seas
They never find, the same receding shores
That never touch with inarticulate pang?
Why set the pear upon those river-banks
Or spice the shores with odors of the plum?
Alas, that they should wear our colors there,
The silken weavings of our afternoons,
And pick the strings of our insipid lutes!
Death is the mother of beauty, mystical,
Within whose burning bosom we devise
Our earthly mothers waiting, sleeplessly.

VII

Supple and turbulent, a ring of men
Shall chant in orgy on a summer morn
Their boisterous devotion to the sun,
Not as a god, but as a god might be,

Naked among them, like a savage source.
Their chant shall be a chant of paradise,
Out of their blood, returning to the sky;
And in their chant shall enter, voice by voice,
The windy lake wherein their lord delights,
The trees, like serafin, and echoing hills,
That choir among themselves long afterward.
They shall know well the heavenly fellowship
Of men that perish and of summer morn.
And whence they came and whither they shall go
The dew upon their feet shall manifest.

VIII

She hears, upon that water without sound,
A voice that cries, "The tomb in Palestine
Is not the porch of spirits lingering.
It is the grave of Jesus, where he lay."
We live in an old chaos of the sun,
Or old dependency of day and night,
Or island solitude, unsponsored, free,
Of that wide water, inescapable.
Deer walk upon our mountains, and the quail
Whistle about us their spontaneous cries;
Sweet berries ripen in the wilderness;
And, in the isolation of the sky,
At evening, casual flocks of pigeons make
Ambiguous undulations as they sink,
Downward to darkness, on extended wings.

Thirteen Ways of Looking at a Blackbird

I

Among twenty snowy mountains,
The only moving thing
Was the eye of the blackbird.

II

I was of three minds,
Like a tree
In which there are three blackbirds.

III

The blackbird whirled in the autumn winds.
It was a small part of the pantomime.

IV

A man and a woman
Are one.
A man and a woman and a blackbird
Are one.

V

I do not know which to prefer,
The beauty of inflections
Or the beauty of innuendoes,
The blackbird whistling
Or just after.

VI

Icicles filled the long window
With barbaric glass.
The shadow of the blackbird
Crossed it, to and fro.
The mood
Traced in the shadow
An indecipherable cause.

VII

O thin men of Haddam,
Why do you imagine golden birds?
Do you not see how the blackbird
Walks around the feet
Of the women about you?

VIII

I know noble accents
And lucid, inescapable rhythms;
But I know, too,
That the blackbird is involved
In what I know.

IX

When the blackbird flew out of sight,
It marked the edge
Of one of many circles.

X

At the sight of blackbirds
Flying in a green light,
Even the bawds of euphony
Would cry out sharply.

XI

He rode over Connecticut
In a glass coach.
Once a fear pierced him,
In that he mistook
The shadow of his equipage
For blackbirds.

XII

The river is moving.
The blackbird must be flying.

XIII

It was evening all afternoon.
It was snowing
And it was going to snow.
The blackbird sat
In the cedar-limbs.

Anecdote of the Jar

I placed a jar in Tennessee,
And round it was, upon a hill.
It made the slovenly wilderness
Surround that hill.

The wilderness rose up to it,
And sprawled around, no longer wild.
The jar was round upon the ground
And tall and of a port in air.

It took dominion everywhere.
The jar was gray and bare.
It did not give of bird or bush,
Like nothing else in Tennessee.

The Paltry Nude Starts on a Spring Voyage

But not on a shell, she starts,
Archaic, for the sea.
But on the first-found weed
She scuds the glitters,
Noiselessly, like one more wave.

She too is discontent
And would have purple stuff upon her arms,
Tired of the salty harbors,
Eager for the brine and bellowing
Of the high interiors of the sea.

The wind speeds her,
Blowing upon her hands
And watery back.
She touches the clouds, where she goes
In the circle of her traverse of the sea.

Yet this is meagre play
In the scrurry and water-shine,
As her heels foam —
Not as when the goldener nude
Of a later day

Will go, like the centre of sea-green pomp,
In an intenser calm,
Scullion of fate,
Across the spick torrent, ceaselessly,
Upon her irretrievable way.

The Snow Man

One must have a mind of winter
To regard the frost and the boughs
Of the pine-trees crusted with snow;

And have been cold a long time
To behold the junipers shagged with ice,
The spruces rough in the distant glitter

Of the January sun; and not to think
Of any misery in the sound of the wind,
In the sound of a few leaves,

Which is the sound of the land
Full of the same wind
That is blowing in the same bare place

For the listener, who listens in the snow,
And, nothing himself, beholds
Nothing that is not there and the nothing that is.

The Emperor of Ice-Cream

Call the roller of big cigars,
The muscular one, and bid him whip
In kitchen cups concupiscent curds.
Let the wenches dawdle in such dress
As they are used to wear, and let the boys
Bring flowers in last month's newspapers.
Let be be finale of seem.
The only emperor is the emperor of ice-cream.

Take from the dresser of deal,
Lacking the three glass knobs, that sheet
On which she embroidered fantails once
And spread it so as to cover her face.
If her horny feet protrude, they come
To show how cold she is, and dumb.
Let the lamp affix its beam.
The only emperor is the emperor of ice-cream.

The Idea of Order at Key West

She sang beyond the genius of the sea.
The water never formed to mind or voice,
Like a body wholly body, fluttering
Its empty sleeves; and yet its mimic motion
Made constant cry, caused constantly a cry,
That was not ours although we understood,
Inhuman, of the veritable ocean.

The sea was not a mask. No more was she.
The song and water were not medleyed sound
Even if what she sang was what she heard,
Since what she sang was uttered word by word.
It may be that in all her phrases stirred
The grinding water and the gasping wind;
But it was she and not the sea we heard.

For she was the maker of the song she sang.
The ever-hooded, tragic-gestured sea
Was merely a place by which she walked to sing.
Whose spirit is this? we said, because we knew
It was the spirit that we sought and knew
That we should ask this often as she sang.

If it was only the dark voice of the sea
That rose, or even colored by many waves;
If it was only the outer voice of sky
And cloud, of the sunken coral water-walled,
However clear, it would have been deep air,
The heaving speech of air, a summer sound

Repeated in a summer without end
And sound alone. But it was more than that,
More even than her voice, and ours, among
The meaningless plungings of water and the wind,
Theatrical distances, bronze shadows heaped
On high horizons, mountainous atmospheres
Of sky and sea.

                It was her voice that made
The sky acutest at its vanishing.
She measured to the hour its solitude.
She was the single artificer of the world
In which she sang. And when she sang, the sea,
Whatever self it had, became the self
That was her song, for she was the maker. Then we,
As we beheld her striding there alone,
Knew that there never was a world for her
Except the one she sang and, singing, made.

Ramon Fernandez, tell me, if you know,
Why, when the singing ended and we turned
Toward the town, tell why the glassy lights,
The lights in the fishing boats at anchor there,
As the night descended, tilting in the air,
Mastered the night and portioned out the sea,
Fixing emblazoned zones and fiery poles,
Arranging, deepening, enchanting night.

Oh! Blessed rage for order, pale Ramon,
The maker's rage to order words of the sea,
Words of the fragrant portals, dimly-starred,
And of ourselves and of our origins,
In ghostlier demarcations, keener sounds.

A Postcard from the Volcano

Children picking up our bones
Will never know that these were once
As quick as foxes on the hill;

And that in autumn, when the grapes
Made sharp air sharper by their smell
These had a being, breathing frost;

And least will guess that with our bones
We left much more, left what still is
The look of things, left what we felt

At what we saw. The spring clouds blow
Above the shuttered mansion-house,
Beyond our gate and the windy sky

Cries out a literate despair.
We knew for long the mansion's look
And what we said of it became

A part of what it is . . . Children,
Still weaving budded aureoles,
Will speak our speech and never know,

Will say of the mansion that it seems
As if he that lived there left behind
A spirit storming in blank walls,

A dirty house in a gutted world,
A tatter of shadows peaked to white,
Smeared with the gold of the opulent sun.

Arrival at the Waldorf

Home from Guatemala, back at the Waldorf.
This arrival in the wild country of the soul,
All approaches gone, being completely there,

Where the wild poem is a substitute
For the woman one loves or ought to love,
One wild rhapsody a fake for another.

You touch the hotel the way you touch moonlight
Or sunlight and you hum and the orchestra
Hums and you say "The world in a verse,

A generation sealed, men remoter than mountains,
Women invisible in music and motion and color,"
After that alien, point-blank, green and actual Guatemala.

No Possum, No Sop, No Taters

He is not here, the old sun,
As absent as if we were asleep.

The field is frozen. The leaves are dry.
Bad is final in this light.

In this bleak air the broken stalks
Have arms without hands. They have trunks

Without legs or, for that, without heads.
They have heads in which a captive cry

Is merely the moving of a tongue.
Snow sparkles like eyesight falling to earth,

Like seeing fallen brightly away.
The leaves hop, scraping on the ground.

It is deep January. The sky is hard.
The stalks are firmly rooted in ice.

It is in this solitude, a syllable,
Out of these gawky flitterings,

Intones its single emptiness,
The savagest hollow of winter-sound.

It is here, in this bad, that we reach
The last purity of the knowledge of good.

The crow looks rusty as he rises up.
Bright is the malice in his eye . . .

One joins him there for company.
But at a distance, in another tree.

from *The Auroras of Autumn*

II

Farewell to an idea . . . A cabin stands,
Deserted, on a beach. It is white,
As by a custom or according to

An ancestral theme or as a consequence
Of an infinite course. The flowers against the wall
Are white, a little dried, a kind of mark

Reminding, trying to remind, of a white
That was different, something else, last year
Or before, not the white of an aging afternoon,

Whether fresher or duller, whether of winter cloud
Or of winter sky, from horizon to horizon.
The wind is blowing the sand across the floor.

Here, being visible is being white,
Is being of the solid of white, the accomplishment
Of an extremist in an exercise . . .

The season changes. A cold wind chills the beach.
The long lines of it grow longer, emptier,
A darkness gathers though it does not fall

And the whiteness grows less vivid on the wall.
The man who is walking turns blankly on the sand.
He observes how the north is always enlarging the change,

With its frigid brilliances, its blue-red sweeps
And gusts of great enkindlings, its polar green,
The color of ice and fire and solitude.

III

Farewell to an idea . . . The mother's face,
The purpose of the poem, fills the room.
They are together, here, and it is warm,

With none of the prescience of oncoming dreams.
It is evening. The house is evening, half dissolved.
Only the half they can never possess remains,

Still-starred. It is the mother they possess,
Who gives transparence to their present peace.
She makes that gentler that can gentle be.

And yet she too is dissolved, she is destroyed.
She gives transparence. But she has grown old.
The necklace is a carving not a kiss.

The soft hands are a motion not a touch.
The house will crumble and the books will burn.
They are at ease in a shelter of the mind

And the house is of the mind and they and time,
Together, all together. Boreal night
Will look like frost as it approaches them

And to the mother as she falls asleep
And as they say good-night, good-night. Upstairs
The windows will be lighted, not the rooms.

A wind will spread its windy grandeurs round
And knock like a rifle-butt against the door.
The wind will command them with invincible sound.

VI

It is a theatre floating through the clouds,
Itself a cloud, although of misted rock
And mountains running like water, wave on wave,

Through waves of light. It is of cloud transformed
To cloud transformed again, idly, the way
A season changes color to no end,

Except the lavishing of itself in change,
As light changes yellow into gold and gold
To its opal elements and fire's delight,

Splashed wide-wise because it likes magnificence
And the solemn pleasures of magnificent space.
The cloud drifts idly through half-thought-of forms.

The theatre is filled with flying birds,
Wild wedges, as of a volcano's smoke, palm-eyed
And vanishing, a web in a corridor

Or massive portico. A capitol,
It may be, is emerging or has just
Collapsed. The denouement has to be postponed . . .

This is nothing until in a single man contained,
Nothing until this named thing nameless is
And is destroyed. He opens the door of his house

On flames. The scholar of one candle sees
An Arctic effulgence flaring on the frame
Of everything he is. And he feels afraid.

VII

Is there an imagination that sits enthroned
As grim as it is benevolent, the just
And the unjust, which in the midst of summer stops

To imagine winter? When the leaves are dead,
Does it take its place in the north and enfold itself,
Goat-leaper, crystalled and luminous, sitting

In highest night? And do these heavens adorn
And proclaim it, the white creator of black, jetted
By extinguishings, even of planets as may be,

Even of earth, even of sight, in snow,
Except as needed by way of majesty,
In the sky, as crown and diamond cabala?

It leaps through us, through all our heavens leaps,
Extinguishing our planets, one by one,
Leaving, of where we were and looked, of where

We knew each other and of each other thought,
A shivering residue, chilled and foregone,
Except for that crown and mystical cabala.

But it dare not leap by chance in its own dark.
It must change from destiny to slight caprice.
And thus its jetted tragedy, its stele

And shape and mournful making move to find
What must unmake it and, at last, what can,
Say, a flippant communication under the moon.

World Without Peculiarity

The day is great and strong—
But his father was strong, that lies now
In the poverty of dirt.

Nothing could be more hushed than the way
The moon moves toward the night.
But what his mother was returns and cries on his breast.

The red ripeness of round leaves is thick
With the spices of red summer.
But she that he loved turns cold at his light touch.

What good is it that the earth is justified,
That it is complete, that it is an end,
That in itself it is enough?

It is the earth itself that is humanity . . .
He is the inhuman son and she,
She is the fateful mother, whom he does not know.

She is the day, the walk of the moon
Among the breathless spices and, sometimes,
He, too, is human and difference disappears

And the poverty of dirt, the thing upon his breast,
The hating woman, the meaningless place,
Become a single being, sure and true.

Puella Parvula

Every thread of summer is at last unwoven.
By one caterpillar is great Africa devoured
And Gibraltar is dissolved like spit in the wind.

But over the wind, over the legends of its roaring,
The elephant on the roof and its elephantine blaring,
The bloody lion in the yard at night or ready to spring

From the clouds in the midst of trembling trees
Making a great gnashing, over the water wallows
Of a vacant sea declaiming with wide throat,

Over all these the mighty imagination triumphs
Like a trumpet and says, in this season of memory,
When the leaves fall like things mournful of the past,

Keep quiet in the heart, O wild bitch. O mind
Gone wild, be what he tells you to be: *Puella.*
Write *pax* across the window pane. And then

Be still. The *summarium in excelsis* begins . . .
Flame, sound, fury composed . . . Hear what he says,
The dauntless master, as he starts the human tale.

Angel Surrounded by Paysans

One of the countrymen:

                                           There is
   A welcome at the door to which no one comes?

The angel:
   I am the angel of reality,
   Seen for a moment standing in the door.

   I have neither ashen wing nor wear of ore
   And live without a tepid aureole,

   Or stars that follow me, not to attend,
   But, of my being and its knowing, part.

   I am one of you and being one of you
   Is being and knowing what I am and know.

   Yet I am the necessary angel of earth,
   Since, in my sight, you see the earth again,

   Cleared of its stiff and stubborn, man-locked set,
   And, in my hearing, you hear its tragic drone

   Rise liquidly in liquid lingerings,
   Like watery words awash; like meanings said

   By repetitions of half-meanings. Am I not,
   Myself, only half of a figure of a sort,

A figure half seen, or seen for a moment, a man
Of the mind, an apparition apparelled in

Apparels of such lightest look that a turn
Of my shoulder and quickly, too quickly, I am gone?

Final Soliloquy of the Interior Paramour

Light the first light of evening, as in a room
In which we rest and, for small reason, think
The world imagined is the ultimate good.

This is, therefore, the intensest rendezvous.
It is in that thought that we collect ourselves,
Out of all the indifferences, into one thing:

Within a single thing, a single shawl
Wrapped tightly round us, since we are poor, a warmth,
A light, a power, the miraculous influence.

Here, now, we forget each other and ourselves.
We feel the obscurity of an order, a whole,
A knowledge, that which arranged the rendezvous,

Within its vital boundary, in the mind.
We say God and the imagination are one . . .
How high that highest candle lights the dark.

Out of this same light, out of the central mind,
We make a dwelling in the evening air,
In which being there together is enough.

The Plain Sense of Things

After the leaves have fallen, we return
To a plain sense of things. It is as if
We had come to an end of the imagination,
Inanimate in an inert savoir.

It is difficult even to choose the adjective
For this blank cold, this sadness without cause.
The great structure has become a minor house.
No turban walks across the lessened floors.

The greenhouse never so badly needed paint.
The chimney is fifty years old and slants to one side.
A fantastic effort has failed, a repetition
In a repetitiousness of men and flies.

Yet the absence of the imagination had
Itself to be imagined. The great pond,
The plain sense of it, without reflections, leaves,
Mud, water like dirty glass, expressing silence

Of a sort, silence of a rat come out to see,
The great pond and its waste of the lilies, all this
Had to be imagined as an inevitable knowledge,
Required, as a necessity requires.

The Planet on the Table

Ariel was glad he had written his poems.
They were of a remembered time
Or of something seen that he liked.

Other makings of the sun
Were waste and welter
And the ripe shrub writhed.

His self and the sun were one
And his poems, although makings of his self,
Were no less makings of the sun.

It was not important that they survive.
What mattered was that they should bear
Some lineament or character,

Some affluence, if only half-perceived,
In the poverty of their words,
Of the planet of which they were part.

The River of Rivers in Connecticut

There is a great river this side of Stygia,
Before one comes to the first black cataracts
And trees that lack the intelligence of trees.

In that river, far this side of Stygia,
The mere flowing of the water is a gayety,
Flashing and flashing in the sun. On its banks,

No shadow walks. The river is fateful,
Like the last one. But there is no ferryman.
He could not bend against its propelling force.

It is not to be seen beneath the appearances
That tell of it. The steeple at Farmington
Stands glistening and Haddam shines and sways.

It is the third commonness with light and air,
A curriculum, a vigor, a local abstraction . . .
Call it, once more, a river, an unnamed flowing,

Space-filled, reflecting the seasons, the folk-lore
Of each of the senses; call it, again and again,
The river that flows nowhere, like a sea.

Not Ideas about the Thing but the Thing Itself

At the earliest ending of winter,
In March, a scrawny cry from outside
Seemed like a sound in his mind.

He knew that he heard it,
A bird's cry, at daylight or before,
In the early March wind.

The sun was rising at six,
No longer a battered panache above snow . . .
It would have been outside.

It was not from the vast ventriloquism
Of sleep's faded papier-mâché . . .
The sun was coming from outside.

That scrawny cry — It was
A chorister whose c preceded the choir.
It was part of the colossal sun,

Surrounded by its choral rings,
Still far away. It was like
A new knowledge of reality.

The Course of a Particular

Today the leaves cry, hanging on branches swept by wind,
Yet the nothingness of winter becomes a little less.
It is still full of icy shades and shapen snow.

The leaves cry . . . One holds off and merely hears the cry.
It is a busy cry, concerning someone else.
And though one says that one is part of everything,

There is a conflict, there is a resistance involved;
And being part is an exertion that declines:
One feels the life of that which gives life as it is.

The leaves cry. It is not a cry of divine attention,
Nor the smoke-drift of puffed-out heroes, nor human cry.
It is the cry of leaves that do not transcend themselves,

In the absence of fantasia, without meaning more
Than they are in the final finding of the ear, in the thing
Itself, until, at last, the cry concerns no one at all.

Of Mere Being

The palm at the end of the mind,
Beyond the last thought, rises
In the bronze decor,

A gold-feathered bird
Sings in the palm, without human meaning,
Without human feeling, a foreign song.

You know then that it is not the reason
That makes us happy or unhappy.
The bird sings. Its feathers shine.

The palm stands on the edge of space.
The wind moves slowly in the branches.
The bird's fire-fangled feathers dangle down.

LANGSTON HUGHES
(1902–1967)

The Negro Speaks of Rivers

I've known rivers:
I've known rivers ancient as the world and older than the flow
  of human blood in human veins.

My soul has grown deep like the rivers.

I bathed in the Euphrates when dawns were young.
I built my hut near the Congo and it lulled me to sleep.
I looked upon the Nile and raised the pyramids above it.
I heard the singing of the Mississippi when Abe Lincoln went
  down to New Orleans, and I've seen its muddy bosom turn
  all golden in the sunset.

I've known rivers:
Ancient, dusky rivers.

My soul has grown deep like the rivers.

I, Too

I, too, sing America.

I am the darker brother.
They send me to eat in the kitchen
When company comes,
But I laugh,
And eat well,
And grow strong.

Tomorrow,
I'll be at the table
When company comes.

Nobody'll dare
Say to me,
"Eat in the kitchen,"
Then.

Besides,
They'll see how beautiful I am
And be ashamed—

I, too, am America.

Dream Boogie

Good morning, daddy!
Ain't you heard
The boogie-woogie rumble
Of a dream deferred?

Listen closely:
You'll hear their feet
Beating out and beating out a—

> *You think*
> *It's a happy beat?*

Listen to it closely:
Ain't you heard
something underneath
like a—

> *What did I say?*

Sure,
I'm happy!
Take it away!

> *Hey, pop!*
> *Re-bop!*
> *Mop!*

> *Y-e-a-h!*

What don't bug
them white kids
sure bugs me:
We knows everybody
ain't free!

Some of these young ones is cert'ly bad —
One batted a hard ball right through my window
and my gold fish et the glass.

What's written down
for white folks
ain't for us a-tall:
"Liberty And Justice —
Huh — For All."

Oop-pop-a-da!
Skee! Daddle-de-do!
Be-bop!

Salt'peanuts!

De-dop!

Preference

I likes a woman
six or eight and ten years older'n myself.
I don't fool with these young girls.
Young girl'll say,
     Daddy, I want so-and-so.
     I needs this, that, and the other.
But a old woman'll say,
     Honey, what does YOU need?
     I just drawed my money tonight
     and it's all your'n.
That's why I likes a older woman
who can appreciate me:
When she conversations you
it ain't forever, *Gimme!*

Ballad of the Landlord

Landlord, landlord,
My roof has sprung a leak.
Don't you 'member I told you about it
Way last week?

Landlord, landlord,
These steps is broken down.
When you come up yourself
It's a wonder you don't fall down.

Ten Bucks you say I owe you?
Ten Bucks you say is due?
Well, that's Ten Bucks more'n I'll pay you
Till you fix this house up new.

What? You gonna get eviction orders?
You gonna cut off my heat?
You gonna take my furniture and
Throw it in the street?

Um-huh! You talking high and mighty.
Talk on — till you get through.
You ain't gonna be able to say a word
If I land my fist on you.

Police! Police!
Come and get this man!
He's trying to ruin the government
And overturn the land!

Copper's whistle!
Patrol bell!
Arrest.

Precinct Station.
Iron cell.
Headlines in press:

MAN THREATENS LANDLORD

TENANT HELD NO BAIL

JUDGE GIVES NEGRO 90 DAYS IN COUNTY JAIL

Cafe: 3 A.M.

Detectives from the vice squad
with weary sadistic eyes
spotting fairies.

> *Degenerates,*
> some folks say.

> But God, Nature,
> or somebody
> made them that way.

Police lady or Lesbian
over there?

> *Where?*

Theme for English B

The instructor said,

> *Go home and write*
> *a page tonight.*
> *And let that page come out of you —*
> *Then, it will be true.*

I wonder if it's that simple?

I am twenty-two, colored, born in Winston-Salem.
I went to school there, then Durham, then here
to this college on the hill above Harlem.
I am the only colored student in my class.
The steps from the hill lead down into Harlem,
through a park, then I cross St. Nicholas,
Eighth Avenue, Seventh, and I come to the Y,
the Harlem Branch Y, where I take the elevator
up to my room, sit down, and write this page:

It's not easy to know what is true for you or me
at twenty-two, my age. But I guess I'm what
I feel and see and hear. Harlem, I hear you:
hear you, hear me — we two — you, me, talk on this page.
(I hear New York, too.) Me — who?

Well, I like to eat, sleep, drink, and be in love.
I like to work, read, learn, and understand life.
I like a pipe for a Christmas present,
or records — Bessie, bop, or Bach.
I guess being colored doesn't make me *not* like
the same things other folks like who are other races.

So will my page be colored that I write?
Being me, it will not be white.
But it will be
a part of you, instructor.
You are white —
yet a part of me, as I am a part of you.
That's American.
Sometimes perhaps you don't want to be a part of me.
Nor do I often want to be a part of you.
But we are, that's true!
As I learn from you,
I guess you learn from me —
although you're older — and white —
and somewhat more free.

This is my page for English B.

High to Low

God knows
We have our troubles, too —
One trouble is you:
you talk too loud,
cuss too loud,
look too black,
don't get anywhere,
and sometimes it seems
you don't even care.
The way you send your kids to school
stockings down,
(not Ethical Culture)
the way you shout out loud in church,
(not St. Phillips)

and the way you lounge on doorsteps
just as if you were down South,
(not at 409)
the way you clown —
the way, in other words,
you let me down —
me, trying to uphold the race
and you —
well, you can see,
we have our problems,
too, with you.

World War II

What a grand time was the war!
    Oh, my, my!
What a grand time was the war!
    My, my, my!

In wartime we had fun,
Sorry that old war is done!
What a grand time was the war,
    My, my!

Echo:

    Did
    Somebody
    Die?

Harlem

What happens to a dream deferred?

    Does it dry up
    like a raisin in the sun?
    Or fester like a sore—
    And then run?
    Does it stink like rotten meat?
    Or crust and sugar over—
    like a syrupy sweet?

    Maybe it just sags
    like a heavy load.

    Or does it explode?

Island

Between two rivers,
North of the park,
Like darker rivers
The streets are dark.

Black and white,
Gold and brown—
Chocolate-custard
Pie of a town.

Dream within a dream,
Our dream deferred.

Good morning, daddy!

Ain't you heard?

THEODORE ROETHKE

(1908 – 1963)

Cuttings

Sticks-in-a-drowse droop over sugary loam,
Their intricate stem-fur dries;
But still the delicate slips keep coaxing up water;
The small cells bulge;

One nub of growth
Nudges a sand-crumb loose,
Pokes through a musty sheath
Its pale tendrilous horn.

Cuttings

(later)

This urge, wrestle, resurrection of dry sticks,
Cut stems struggling to put down feet,
What saint strained so much,
Rose on such lopped limbs to a new life?

I can hear, underground, that sucking and sobbing,
In my veins, in my bones I feel it, —
The small waters seeping upward,
The tight grains parting at last.
When sprouts break out,
Slippery as fish,
I quail, lean to beginnings, sheath-wet.

Weed Puller

Under the concrete benches,
Hacking at black hairy roots, —
Those lewd monkey-tails hanging from drainholes, —
Digging into the soft rubble underneath,
Webs and weeds,
Grubs and snails and sharp sticks,
Or yanking tough fern-shapes,
Coiled green and thick, like dripping smilax,
Tugging all day at perverse life:
The indignity of it! —
With everything blooming above me,
Lilies, pale-pink cyclamen, roses,
Whole fields lovely and inviolate, —
Me down in that fetor of weeds,
Crawling on all fours,
Alive, in a slippery grave.

My Papa's Waltz

The whiskey on your breath
Could make a small boy dizzy;
But I hung on like death:
Such waltzing was not easy.

We romped until the pans
Slid from the kitchen shelf;
My mother's countenance
Could not unfrown itself.

The hand that held my wrist
Was battered on one knuckle;
At every step you missed
My right ear scraped a buckle.

You beat time on my head
With a palm caked hard by dirt,
Then waltzed me off to bed
Still clinging to your shirt.

Dolor

I have known the inexorable sadness of pencils,
Neat in their boxes, dolor of pad and paper-weight,
All the misery of manilla folders and mucilage,
Desolation in immaculate public places,
Lonely reception room, lavatory, switchboard,
The unalterable pathos of basin and pitcher,
Ritual of multigraph, paper-clip, comma,
Endless duplication of lives and objects.
And I have seen dust from the walls of institutions,
Finer than flour, alive, more dangerous than silica,
Silt, almost invisible, through long afternoons of tedium,
Dropping a fine film on nails and delicate eyebrows,
Glazing the pale hair, the duplicate grey standard faces.

The Minimal

I study the lives on a leaf: the little
Sleepers, numb nudgers in cold dimensions,
Beetles in caves, newts, stone-deaf fishes,
Lice tethered to long limp subterranean weeds,
Squirmers in bogs,
And bacterial creepers
Wriggling through wounds
Like elvers in ponds,
Their wan mouths kissing the warm sutures,
Cleaning and caressing,
Creeping and healing.

The Lost Son

1. The Flight

At Woodlawn I heard the dead cry:
I was lulled by the slamming of iron,
A slow drip over stones,
Toads brooding in wells.

All the leaves stuck out their tongues;
I shook the softening chalk of my bones,
Saying,
Snail, snail, glister me forward,
Bird, soft-sigh me home,
Worm, be with me.
This is my hard time.

Fished in an old wound,
The soft pond of repose;
Nothing nibbled my line,
Not even the minnows came.

Sat in an empty house
Watching shadows crawl,
Scratching.
There was one fly.

Voice, come out of the silence.
Say something.
Appear in the form of a spider
Or a moth beating the curtain.

Tell me:
Which is the way I take;
Out of what door do I go,
Where and to whom?

     Dark hollows said, lee to the wind,
     The moon said, back of an eel,
     The salt said, look by the sea,
     Your tears are not enough praise,
     You will find no comfort here,
     In the kingdom of bang and blab.

     Running lightly over spongy ground,
     Past the pasture of flat stones,
     The three elms,
     The sheep strewn on a field,
     Over a rickety bridge
     Toward the quick-water, wrinkling and rippling.

     Hunting along the river,
     Down among the rubbish, the bug-riddled foliage,

By the muddy pond-edge, by the bog-holes,
By the shrunken lake, hunting, in the heat of summer.

The shape of a rat?
    It's bigger than that.
    It's less than a leg
    And more than a nose,
    Just under the water
    It usually goes.

    Is it soft like a mouse?
    Can it wrinkle its nose?
    Could it come in the house
    On the tips of its toes?

    Take the skin of a cat
    And the back of an eel,
    Then roll them in grease, —
    That's the way it would feel.

    It's sleek as an otter
    With wide webby toes
    Just under the water
    It usually goes.

2. *The Pit*

Where do the roots go?
    Look down under the leaves.
Who put the moss there?
    These stones have been here too long.
Who stunned the dirt into noise?
    Ask the mole, he knows.
I feel the slime of a wet nest.
    Beware Mother Mildew.
Nibble again, fish nerves.

3. *The Gibber*

At the wood's mouth,
By the cave's door,
I listened to something
I had heard before.

Dogs of the groin
Barked and howled,
The sun was against me,
The moon would not have me.

The weeds whined,
The snakes cried,
The cows and briars
Said to me: Die.

What a small song. What slow clouds. What dark water.
Hath the rain a father? All the caves are ice. Only the snow's here.
I'm cold. I'm cold all over. Rub me in father and mother.
Fear was my father, Father Fear.
His look drained the stones.

> What gliding shape
> Beckoning through halls,
> Stood poised on the stair,
> Fell dreamily down?

> From the mouths of jugs
> Perched on many shelves,
> I saw substance flowing
> That cold morning.

> Like a slither of eels
> That watery cheek
> As my own tongue kissed
> My lips awake.

Is this the storm's heart? The ground is unstilling itself.
My veins are running nowhere. Do the bones cast out their fire?
Is the seed leaving the old bed? These buds are live as birds.
Where, where are the tears of the world?
Let the kisses resound, flat like a butcher's palm;
Let the gestures freeze; our doom is already decided.
All the windows are burning! What's left of my life?
I want the old rage, the lash of primordial milk!
Goodbye, goodbye, old stones, the time-order is going,
I have married my hands to perpetual agitation,
I run, I run to the whistle of money.

> Money money money
> Water water water

How cool the grass is.
Has the bird left?
The stalk still sways.
Has the worm a shadow?
What do the clouds say?

These sweeps of light undo me.
Look, look, the ditch is running white!
I've more veins than a tree!
Kiss me, ashes, I'm falling through a dark swirl.

4. *The Return*

The way to the boiler was dark,
Dark all the way,
Over slippery cinders
Through the long greenhouse.

The roses kept breathing in the dark.
They had many mouths to breathe with.
My knees made little winds underneath
Where the weeds slept.

There was always a single light
Swinging by the fire-pit,
Where the fireman pulled out roses,
The big roses, the big bloody clinkers.

Once I stayed all night.
The light in the morning came slowly over the white
Snow.
There were many kinds of cool
Air.
Then came steam.

Pipe-knock.

Scurry of warm over small plants.
Ordnung! ordnung!
Papa is coming!

A fine haze moved off the leaves;
Frost melted on far panes;
The rose, the chrysanthemum turned toward the light.
Even the hushed forms, the bent yellowy weeds
Moved in a slow up-sway.

5. *"It was beginning winter"*

It was beginning winter,
An in-between time,
The landscape still partly brown:
The bones of weeds kept swinging in the wind,
Above the blue snow.

It was beginning winter,
The light moved slowly over the frozen field,
Over the dry seed-crowns,
The beautiful surviving bones
Swinging in the wind.

Light traveled over the wide field;
Stayed.
The weeds stopped swinging.
The mind moved, not alone,
Through the clear air, in the silence.

> Was it light?
> Was it light within?
> Was it light within light?
> Stillness becoming alive,
> Yet still?

A lively understandable spirit
Once entertained you.
It will come again.
Be still.
Wait.

Elegy for Jane
My Student, Thrown by a Horse

I remember the neckcurls, limp and damp as tendrils;
And her quick look, a sidelong pickerel smile;
And how, once startled into talk, the light syllables leaped for her,
And she balanced in the delight of her thought,
A wren, happy, tail into the wind,
Her song trembling the twigs and small branches.

The shade sang with her;
The leaves, their whispers turned to kissing;
And the mold sang in the bleached valleys under the rose.

Oh, when she was sad, she cast herself down into such a pure
    depth,
Even a father could not find her:
Scraping her cheek against straw;
Stirring the clearest water.

My sparrow, you are not here,
Waiting like a fern, making a spiny shadow.
The sides of wet stones cannot console me,
Nor the moss, wound with the last light.

If only I could nudge you from this sleep,
My maimed darling, my skittery pigeon.
Over this damp grave I speak the words of my love:
I, with no rights in this matter,
Neither father nor lover.

The Waking

I wake to sleep, and take my waking slow.
I feel my fate in what I cannot fear.
I learn by going where I have to go.

We think by feeling. What is there to know?
I hear my being dance from ear to ear.
I wake to sleep, and take my waking slow.

Of those so close beside me, which are you?
God bless the Ground! I shall walk softly there,
And learn by going where I have to go.

Light takes the Tree; but who can tell us how?
The lowly worm climbs up a winding stair;
I wake to sleep, and take my waking slow.

Great Nature has another thing to do
To you and me; so take the lively air,
And, lovely, learn by going where to go.

This shaking keeps me steady. I should know.
What falls away is always. And is near.
I wake to sleep, and take my waking slow.
I learn by going where I have to go.

Heard in a Violent Ward

In heaven, too,
You'd be institutionalized.
But that's all right, —
If they let you eat and swear
With the likes of Blake,
And Christopher Smart,
And that sweet man, John Clare.

ELIZABETH BISHOP

(1911–1979)

The Monument

Now can you see the monument? It is of wood
built somewhat like a box. No. Built
like several boxes in descending sizes
one above the other.
Each is turned half-way round so that
its corners point toward the sides
of the one below and the angles alternate.
Then on the topmost cube is set
a sort of fleur-de-lys of weathered wood,
long petals of board, pierced with odd holes,
four-sided, stiff, ecclesiastical.
From it four thin, warped poles spring out,
(slanted like fishing-poles or flag-poles)
and from them jig-saw work hangs down,
four lines of vaguely whittled ornament
over the edges of the boxes
to the ground.
The monument is one-third set against
a sea; two-thirds against a sky.
The view is geared
(that is, the view's perspective)
so low there is no "far away,"
and we are far away within the view.
A sea of narrow, horizontal boards
lies out behind our lonely monument,
its long grains alternating right and left
like floor-boards — spotted, swarming-still,
and motionless. A sky runs parallel,
and it is palings, coarser than the sea's:
splintery sunlight and long-fibred clouds.
"Why does that strange sea make no sound?

Is it because we're far away?
Where are we? Are we in Asia Minor,
or in Mongolia?"
                    An ancient promontory,
an ancient principality whose artist-prince
might have wanted to build a monument
to mark a tomb or boundary, or make
a melancholy or romantic scene of it . . .
"But that queer sea looks made of wood,
half-shining, like a driftwood sea.
And the sky looks wooden, grained with cloud.
It's like a stage-set; it is all so flat!
Those clouds are full of glistening splinters!
What is that?"
                    It is the monument.
"It's piled-up boxes,
outlined with shoddy fret-work, half-fallen off,
cracked and unpainted. It looks old."
—The strong sunlight, the wind from the sea,
all the conditions of its existence,
may have flaked off the paint, if ever it was painted,
and made it homelier than it was.
"Why did you bring me here to see it?
A temple of crates in cramped and crated scenery,
what can it prove?
I am tired of breathing this eroded air,
this dryness in which the monument is cracking."

It is an artifact
of wood. Wood holds together better
than sea or cloud or sand could by itself,
much better than real sea or sand or cloud.
It chose that way to grow and not to move.
The monument's an object, yet those decorations,
carelessly nailed, looking like nothing at all,
give it away as having life, and wishing;
wanting to be a monument, to cherish something.
The crudest scroll-work says "commemorate,"
while once each day the light goes around it
like a prowling animal,
or the rain falls on it, or the wind blows into it.
It may be solid, may be hollow.

The bones of the artist-prince may be inside
or far away on even drier soil.
But roughly but adequately it can shelter
what is within (which after all
cannot have been intended to be seen).
It is the beginning of a painting,
a piece of sculpture, or poem, or monument,
and all of wood. Watch it closely.

Over 2000 Illustrations and a Complete Concordance

Thus should have been our travels:
serious, engravable.
The Seven Wonders of the World are tired
and a touch familiar, but the other scenes,
innumerable, though equally sad and still,
are foreign. Often the squatting Arab,
or group of Arabs, plotting, probably,
against our Christian Empire,
while one apart, with outstretched arm and hand
points to the Tomb, the Pit, the Sepulcher.
The branches of the date-palms look like files.
The cobbled courtyard, where the Well is dry,
is like a diagram, the brickwork conduits
are vast and obvious, the human figure
far gone in history or theology,
gone with its camel or its faithful horse.
Always the silence, the gesture, the specks of birds
suspended on invisible threads above the Site,
or the smoke rising solemnly, pulled by threads.
Granted a page alone or a page made up
of several scenes arranged in cattycornered rectangles
or circles set on stippled gray,
granted a grim lunette,
caught in the toils of an initial letter,
when dwelt upon, they all resolve themselves.
The eye drops, weighted, through the lines
the burin made, the lines that move apart
like ripples above sand,

dispersing storms, God's spreading fingerprint,
and painfully, finally, that ignite
in watery prismatic white-and-blue.

Entering the Narrows at St. Johns
the touching bleat of goats reached to the ship.
We glimpsed them, reddish, leaping up the cliffs
among the fog-soaked weeds and butter-and-eggs.
And at St. Peter's the wind blew and the sun shone madly.
Rapidly, purposefully, the Collegians marched in lines,
crisscrossing the great square with black, like ants.
In Mexico the dead man lay
in a blue arcade; the dead volcanoes
glistened like Easter lilies.
The jukebox went on playing "Ay, Jalisco!"
And at Volubilis there were beautiful poppies
splitting the mosaics; the fat old guide made eyes.
In Dingle harbor a golden length of evening
the rotting hulks held up their dripping plush.
The Englishwoman poured tea, informing us
that the Duchess was going to have a baby.
And in the brothels of Marrakesh
the little pockmarked prostitutes
balanced their tea-trays on their heads
and did their belly-dances; flung themselves
naked and giggling against our knees,
asking for cigarettes. It was somewhere near there
I saw what frightened me most of all:
A holy grave, not looking particularly holy,
one of a group under a keyhole-arched stone baldaquin
open to every wind from the pink desert.
An open, gritty, marble trough, carved solid
with exhortation, yellowed
as scattered cattle-teeth;
half-filled with dust, not even the dust
of the poor prophet paynim who once lay there.
In a smart burnoose Khadour looked on amused.

Everything only connected by "and" and "and."
Open the book. (The gilt rubs off the edges
of the pages and pollinates the fingertips.)

Open the heavy book. Why couldn't we have seen
this old Nativity while we were at it?
—the dark ajar, the rocks breaking with light,
an undisturbed, unbreathing flame,
colorless, sparkless, freely fed on straw,
and, lulled within, a family with pets,
—and looked and looked our infant sight away.

The Bight
On My Birthday

At low tide like this how sheer the water is.
White, crumbling ribs of marl protrude and glare
and the boats are dry, the pilings dry as matches.
Absorbing, rather than being absorbed,
the water in the bight doesn't wet anything,
the color of the gas flame turned as low as possible.
One can smell it turning to gas; if one were Baudelaire
one could probably hear it turning to marimba music.
The little ocher dredge at work off the end of the dock
already plays the dry perfectly off-beat claves.
The birds are outsize. Pelicans crash
into this peculiar gas unnecessarily hard,
it seems to me, like pickaxes,
rarely coming up with anything to show for it,
and going off with humorous elbowings.
Black-and-white man-of-war birds soar
on impalpable drafts
and open their tails like scissors on the curves
or tense them like wishbones, till they tremble.
The frowsy sponge boats keep coming in
with the obliging air of retrievers,
bristling with jackstraw gaffs and hooks
and decorated with bobbles of sponges.
There is a fence of chicken wire along the dock
where, glinting like little plowshares,
the blue-gray shark tails are hung up to dry
for the Chinese-restaurant trade.

Some of the little white boats are still piled up
against each other, or lie on their sides, stove in,
and not yet salvaged, if they ever will be, from the last bad storm,
like torn-open, unanswered letters.
The bight is littered with old correspondences.
Click. Click. Goes the dredge,
and brings up a dripping jawful of marl.
All the untidy activity continues,
awful but cheerful.

At the Fishhouses

Although it is a cold evening,
down by one of the fishhouses
an old man sits netting
his net, in the gloaming almost invisible
a dark purple-brown,
and his shuttle worn and polished.
The air smells so strong of codfish
it makes one's nose run and one's eyes water.
The five fishhouses have steeply peaked roofs
and narrow, cleated gangplanks slant up
to storerooms in the gables
for the wheelbarrows to be pushed up and down on.
All is silver: the heavy surface of the sea,
swelling slowly as if considering spilling over,
is opaque, but the silver of the benches,
the lobster pots, and masts, scattered
among the wild jagged rocks,
is of an apparent translucence
like the small old buildings with an emerald moss
growing on their shoreward walls.
The big fish tubs are completely lined
with layers of beautiful herring scales
and the wheelbarrows are similarly plastered
with creamy iridescent coats of mail,
with small iridescent flies crawling on them.
Up on the little slope behind the houses,
set in the sparse bright sprinkle of grass,

is an ancient wooden capstan,
cracked, with two long bleached handles
and some melancholy stains, like dried blood,
where the ironwork has rusted.
The old man accepts a Lucky Strike.
He was a friend of my grandfather.
We talk of the decline in the population
and of codfish and herring
while he waits for a herring boat to come in.
There are sequins on his vest and on his thumb.
He has scraped the scales, the principal beauty,
from unnumbered fish with that black old knife,
the blade of which is almost worn away.

Down at the water's edge, at the place
where they haul up the boats, up the long ramp
descending into the water, thin silver
tree trunks are laid horizontally
across the gray stones, down and down
at intervals of four or five feet.

Cold dark deep and absolutely clear,
element bearable to no mortal,
to fish and to seals . . . One seal particularly
I have seen here evening after evening.
He was curious about me. He was interested in music;
like me a believer in total immersion,
so I used to sing him Baptist hymns.
I also sang "A Mighty Fortress Is Our God."
He stood up in the water and regarded me
steadily, moving his head a little.
Then he would disappear, then suddenly emerge
almost in the same spot, with a sort of shrug
as if it were against his better judgment.
Cold dark deep and absolutely clear,
the clear gray icy water . . . Back, behind us,
the dignified tall firs begin.
Bluish, associating with their shadows,
a million Christmas trees stand
waiting for Christmas. The water seems suspended
above the rounded gray and blue-gray stones.
I have seen it over and over, the same sea, the same,

slightly, indifferently swinging above the stones,
icily free above the stones,
above the stones and then the world.
If you should dip your hand in,
your wrist would ache immediately,
your bones would begin to ache and your hand would burn
as if the water were a transmutation of fire
that feeds on stones and burns with a dark gray flame.
If you tasted it, it would first taste bitter,
then briny, then surely burn your tongue.
It is like what we imagine knowledge to be:
dark, salt, clear, moving, utterly free,
drawn from the cold hard mouth
of the world, derived from the rocky breasts
forever, flowing and drawn, and since
our knowledge is historical, flowing, and flown.

The Armadillo

For Robert Lowell

This is the time of year
when almost every night
the frail, illegal fire balloons appear.
Climbing the mountain height,

rising toward a saint
still honored in these parts,
the paper chambers flush and fill with light
that comes and goes, like hearts.

Once up against the sky it's hard
to tell them from the stars —
planets, that is — the tinted ones:
Venus going down, or Mars,

or the pale green one. With a wind,
they flare and falter, wobble and toss;
but if it's still they steer between
the kite sticks of the Southern Cross,

receding, dwindling, solemnly
and steadily forsaking us,
or, in the downdraft from a peak,
suddenly turning dangerous.

Last night another big one fell.
It splattered like an egg of fire
against the cliff behind the house.
The flame ran down. We saw the pair

of owls who nest there flying up
and up, their whirling black-and-white
stained bright pink underneath, until
they shrieked up out of sight.

The ancient owls' nest must have burned.
Hastily, all alone,
a glistening armadillo left the scene,
rose-flecked, head down, tail down,

and then a baby rabbit jumped out,
short-eared, to our surprise.
So soft! — a handful of intangible ash
with fixed, ignited eyes.

Too pretty, dreamlike mimicry!
O falling fire and piercing cry
and panic, and a weak mailed fist
clenched ignorant against the sky!

Filling Station

Oh, but it is dirty!
—this little filling station,
oil-soaked, oil-permeated
to a disturbing, over-all
black translucency.
Be careful with that match!

Father wears a dirty,
oil-soaked monkey suit
that cuts him under the arms,

and several quick and saucy
and greasy sons assist him
(it's a family filling station),
all quite thoroughly dirty.

Do they live in the station?
It has a cement porch
behind the pumps, and on it
a set of crushed and grease-
impregnated wickerwork;
on the wicker sofa
a dirty dog, quite comfy.

Some comic books provide
the only note of color —
of certain color. They lie
upon a big dim doily
draping a taboret
(part of the set), beside
a big hirsute begonia.

Why the extraneous plant?
Why the taboret?
Why, oh why, the doily?
(Embroidered in daisy stitch
with marguerites, I think,
and heavy with gray crochet.)

Somebody embroidered the doily.
Somebody waters the plant,
or oils it, maybe. Somebody
arranges the rows of cans
so that they softly say:
ESSO — SO — SO — SO
to high-strung automobiles.
Somebody loves us all.

Crusoe in England

A new volcano has erupted,
the papers say, and last week I was reading
where some ship saw an island being born:

at first a breath of steam, ten miles away;
and then a black fleck — basalt, probably —
rose in the mate's binoculars
and caught on the horizon like a fly.
They named it. But my poor old island's still
un-rediscovered, un-renamable.
None of the books has ever got it right.

Well, I had fifty-two
miserable, small volcanoes I could climb
with a few slithery strides —
volcanoes dead as ash heaps.
I used to sit on the edge of the highest one
and count the others standing up,
naked and leaden, with their heads blown off.
I'd think that if they were the size
I thought volcanoes should be, then I had
become a giant;
and if I had become a giant,
I couldn't bear to think what size
the goats and turtles were,
or the gulls, or the over-lapping rollers
— a glittering hexagon of rollers
closing and closing in, but never quite,
glittering and glittering, though the sky
was mostly overcast.

My island seemed to be
a sort of cloud-dump. All the hemisphere's
left-over clouds arrived and hung
above the craters — their parched throats
were hot to touch.
Was that why it rained so much?
And why sometimes the whole place hissed?
The turtles lumbered by, high-domed,
hissing like teakettles.
(And I'd have given years, or taken a few,
for any sort of kettle, of course.)
The folds of lava, running out to sea,
would hiss. I'd turn. And then they'd prove
to be more turtles.

The beaches were all lava, variegated,
black, red, and white, and gray;
the marbled colors made a fine display.
And I had waterspouts. Oh,
half a dozen at a time, far out,
they'd come and go, advancing and retreating,
their heads in cloud, their feet in moving patches
of scuffed-up white.
Glass chimneys, flexible, attenuated,
sacerdotal beings of glass . . . I watched
the water spiral up in them like smoke.
Beautiful, yes, but not much company.

I often gave way to self-pity.
"Do I deserve this? I suppose I must.
I wouldn't be here otherwise. Was there
a moment when I actually chose this?
I don't remember, but there could have been."
What's wrong about self-pity, anyway?
With my legs dangling down familiarly
over a crater's edge, I told myself
"Pity should begin at home." So the more
pity I felt, the more I felt at home.

The sun set in the sea; the same odd sun
rose from the sea,
and there was one of it and one of me.
The island had one kind of everything:
one tree snail, a bright violet-blue
with a thin shell, crept over everything,
over the one variety of tree,
a sooty, scrub affair.
Snail shells lay under these in drifts
and, at a distance,
you'd swear that they were beds of irises.
There was one kind of berry, a dark red.
I tried it, one by one, and hours apart.
Sub-acid, and not bad, no ill effects;
and so I made home-brew. I'd drink
the awful, fizzy, stinging stuff
that went straight to my head
and play my home-made flute
(I think it had the weirdest scale on earth)

and, dizzy, whoop and dance among the goats.
Home-made, home-made! But aren't we all?
I felt a deep affection for
the smallest of my island industries.
No, not exactly, since the smallest was
a miserable philosophy.

Because I didn't know enough.
Why didn't I know enough of something?
Greek drama or astronomy? The books
I'd read were full of blanks;
the poems — well, I tried
reciting to my iris-beds,
"They flash upon that inward eye,
which is the bliss . . ." The bliss of what?
One of the first things that I did
when I got back was look it up.

The island smelled of goat and guano.
The goats were white, so were the gulls,
and both too tame, or else they thought
I was a goat, too, or a gull.
Baa, baa, baa and *shriek, shriek, shriek,*
baa . . . *shriek* . . . *baa* . . . I still can't shake
them from my ears; they're hurting now.
The questioning shrieks, the equivocal replies
over a ground of hissing rain
and hissing, ambulating turtles
got on my nerves.

When all the gulls flew up at once, they sounded
like a big tree in a strong wind, its leaves.
I'd shut my eyes and think about a tree,
an oak, say, with real shade, somewhere.
I'd heard of cattle getting island-sick.
I thought the goats were.
One billy-goat would stand on the volcano
I'd christened *Mont d'Espoir* or *Mount Despair*
(I'd time enough to play with names),
and bleat and bleat, and sniff the air.
I'd grab his beard and look at him.
His pupils, horizontal, narrowed up

and expressed nothing, or a little malice.
I got so tired of the very colors!
One day I dyed a baby goat bright red
with my red berries, just to see
something a little different.
And then his mother wouldn't recognize him.

Dreams were the worst. Of course I dreamed of food
and love, but they were pleasant rather
than otherwise. But then I'd dream of things
like slitting a baby's throat, mistaking it
for a baby goat. I'd have
nightmares of other islands
stretching away from mine, infinities
of islands, islands spawning islands,
like frogs' eggs turning into polliwogs
of islands, knowing that I had to live
on each and every one, eventually,
for ages, registering their flora,
their fauna, their geography.

Just when I thought I couldn't stand it
another minute longer, Friday came.
(Accounts of that have everything all wrong.)
Friday was nice.
Friday was nice, and we were friends.
If only he had been a woman!
I wanted to propagate my kind,
and so did he, I think, poor boy.
He'd pet the baby goats sometimes,
and race with them, or carry one around.
—Pretty to watch; he had a pretty body.
And then one day they came and took us off.

Now I live here, another island,
that doesn't seem like one, but who decides?
My blood was full of them; my brain
bred islands. But that archipelago
has petered out. I'm old.
I'm bored, too, drinking my real tea,
surrounded by uninteresting lumber.
The knife there on the shelf—

it reeked of meaning, like a crucifix.
It lived. How many years did I
beg it, implore it, not to break?
I knew each nick and scratch by heart,
the bluish blade, the broken tip,
the lines of wood-grain on the handle . . .
Now it won't look at me at all.
The living soul has dribbled away.
My eyes rest on it and pass on.

The local museum's asked me to
leave everything to them:
the flute, the knife, the shrivelled shoes,
my shedding goatskin trousers
(moths have got in the fur),
the parasol that took me such a time
remembering the way the ribs should go.
It still will work but, folded up,
looks like a plucked and skinny fowl.
How can anyone want such things?
—And Friday, my dear Friday, died of measles
seventeen years ago come March.

Poem

About the size of an old-style dollar bill,
American or Canadian,
mostly the same whites, gray greens, and steel grays
—this little painting (a sketch for a larger one?)
has never earned any money in its life.
Useless and free, it has spent seventy years
as a minor family relic
handed along collaterally to owners
who looked at it sometimes, or didn't bother to.

It must be Nova Scotia; only there
does one see gabled wooden houses
painted that awful shade of brown.
The other houses, the bits that show, are white.

Elm trees, low hills, a thin church steeple
—that gray-blue wisp—or is it? In the foreground
a water meadow with some tiny cows,
two brushstrokes each, but confidently cows;
two minuscule white geese in the blue water,
back-to-back, feeding, and a slanting stick.
Up closer, a wild iris, white and yellow,
fresh-squiggled from the tube.
The air is fresh and cold; cold early spring
clear as gray glass; a half inch of blue sky
below the steel-gray storm clouds.
(They were the artist's specialty.)
A specklike bird is flying to the left.
Or is it a flyspeck looking like a bird?

Heavens, I recognize the place, I know it!
It's behind—I can almost remember the farmer's name.
His barn backed on that meadow. There it is,
titanium white, one dab. The hint of steeple,
filaments of brush-hairs, barely there,
must be the Presbyterian church.
Would that be Miss Gillespie's house?
Those particular geese and cows
are naturally before my time.

A sketch done in an hour, "in one breath,"
once taken from a trunk and handed over.
*Would you like this? I'll probably never
have room to hang these things again.
Your Uncle George, no, mine, my Uncle George,
he'd be your great-uncle, left them all with Mother
when he went back to England.
You know, he was quite famous, an R.A.*

I never knew him. We both knew this place,
apparently, this literal small backwater,
looked at it long enough to memorize it,
our years apart. How strange. And it's still loved,
or its memory is (it must have changed a lot).
Our visions coincided—"visions" is
too serious a word—our looks, two looks:
art "copying from life" and life itself,

life and the memory of it so compressed
they've turned into each other. Which is which?
Life and the memory of it cramped,
dim, on a piece of Bristol board,
dim, but how live, how touching in detail
—the little that we get for free,
the little of our earthly trust. Not much.
About the size of our abidance
along with theirs: the munching cows,
the iris, crisp and shivering, the water
still standing from spring freshets,
the yet-to-be-dismantled elms, the geese.

North Haven

In memoriam: R.T.S.L.

I can make out the rigging of a schooner
a mile off; I can count
the new cones on the spruce. It is so still
the pale bay wears a milky skin, the sky
no clouds, except for one long, carded, horse's-tail.

The islands haven't shifted since last summer,
even if I like to pretend they have
— drifting, in a dreamy sort of way,
a little north, a little south or sidewise,
and that they're free within the blue frontiers of bay.

This month, our favorite one is full of flowers:
Buttercups, Red Clover, Purple Vetch,
Hawkweed still burning, Daisies pied, Eyebright,
the Fragrant Bedstraw's incandescent stars,
and more, returned, to paint the meadows with delight.

The Goldfinches are back, or others like them,
and the White-throated Sparrow's five-note song,
pleading and pleading, brings tears to the eyes.
Nature repeats herself, or almost does:
repeat, repeat, repeat, revise, revise, revise.

Years ago, you told me it was here
(in 1932?) you first "discovered *girls*"
and learned to sail, and learned to kiss.
You had "such fun," you said, that classic summer.
("Fun" — it always seemed to leave you at a loss . . .)

You left North Haven, anchored in its rock,
afloat in mystic blue . . . And now — you've left
for good. You can't derange, or re-arrange,
your poems again. (But the Sparrows can their song.)
The words won't change again. Sad friend, you cannot change.

ROBERT HAYDEN

(1913 – 1980)

Sphinx

    If he could solve the riddle,
she would not leap
    from those gaunt rocks to her death,
but devour him instead.

    It pleasures her to hold
him captive there —
    to keep him in the reach of her
blood-matted paws.

    It is your fate, she has often
said, to endure
    my riddling. Your fate to live
at the mercy of my

    conundrum, which, in truth,
is only a kind
    of psychic joke. No, you shall
not leave this place.

    (Consider anyway the view from
here.) In time,
    you will come to regard my questioning
with a certain pained

    amusement; in time, get so
you would hardly find
    it possible to live without
my joke and me.

Homage to the Empress of the Blues

Because there was a man somewhere in a candystripe silk shirt,
gracile and dangerous as a jaguar and because a woman moaned
for him in sixty-watt gloom and mourned him Faithless Love
Twotiming Love Oh Love Oh Careless Aggravating Love,

> She came out on the stage in yards of pearls, emerging like
> a favorite scenic view, flashed her golden smile and sang.

Because grey laths began somewhere to show from underneath
torn hurdygurdy lithographs of dollfaced heaven;
and because there were those who feared alarming fists of snow
on the door and those who feared the riot-squad of statistics,

> She came out on the stage in ostrich feathers, beaded satin,
> and shone that smile on us and sang.

Mourning Poem for the Queen of Sunday

> Lord's lost Him His mockingbird,
> His fancy warbler;
> Satan sweet-talked her,
> four bullets hushed her.
> Who would have thought
> she'd end that way?

Four bullets hushed her. And the world a-clang with evil.
Who's going to make old hardened sinner men tremble now
and the righteous rock?
Oh who and oh who will sing Jesus down
to help with struggling and doing without and being colored
all through blue Monday?
Till way next Sunday?

> All those angels
> in their cretonne clouds and finery
> the true believer saw
> when she rared back her head and sang,
> all those angels are surely weeping.
> Who would have thought
> she'd end that way?

Four holes in her heart. The gold works wrecked.
But she looks so natural in her big bronze coffin
among the Broken Hearts and Gates-Ajar,
it's as if any moment she'd lift her head
from its pillow of chill gardenias
and turn this quiet into shouting Sunday
and make folks forget what she did on Monday.

> Oh, Satan sweet-talked her,
> and four bullets hushed her.
> Lord's lost Him His diva,
> His fancy warbler's gone.
> Who would have thought,
> who would have thought she'd end that way?

Those Winter Sundays

Sundays too my father got up early
and put his clothes on in the blueblack cold,
then with cracked hands that ached
from labor in the weekday weather made
banked fires blaze. No one ever thanked him.

I'd wake and hear the cold splintering, breaking.
When the rooms were warm, he'd call,
and slowly I would rise and dress,
fearing the chronic angers of that house,

Speaking indifferently to him,
who had driven out the cold
and polished my good shoes as well.
What did I know, what did I know
of love's austere and lonely offices?

Frederick Douglass

When it is finally ours, this freedom, this liberty, this beautiful
and terrible thing, needful to man as air,
usable as earth; when it belongs at last to all,

when it is truly instinct, brain matter, diastole, systole,
reflex action; when it is finally won; when it is more
than the gaudy mumbo jumbo of politicians:
this man, this Douglass, this former slave, this Negro
beaten to his knees, exiled, visioning a world
where none is lonely, none hunted, alien,
this man, superb in love and logic, this man
shall be remembered. Oh, not with statues' rhetoric,
not with legends and poems and wreaths of bronze alone,
but with the lives grown out of his life, the lives
fleshing his dream of the beautiful, needful thing.

RANDALL JARRELL
(1914 – 1965)

Losses

It was not dying: everybody died.
It was not dying: we had died before
In the routine crashes — and our fields
Called up the papers, wrote home to our folks,
And the rates rose, all because of us.
We died on the wrong page of the almanac,
Scattered on mountains fifty miles away;
Diving on haystacks, fighting with a friend,
We blazed up on the lines we never saw.
We died like aunts or pets or foreigners.
(When we left high school nothing else had died
For us to figure we had died like.)

In our new planes, with our new crews, we bombed
The ranges by the desert or the shore,
Fired at towed targets, waited for our scores —
And turned into replacements and woke up
One morning, over England, operational.
It wasn't different: but if we died
It was not an accident but a mistake
(But an easy one for anyone to make).
We read our mail and counted up our missions —
In bombers named for girls, we burned
The cities we had learned about in school —
Till our lives wore out; our bodies lay among
The people we had killed and never seen.
When we lasted long enough they gave us medals;
When we died they said, "Our casualties were low."
They said, "Here are the maps"; we burned the cities.

It was not dying — no, not ever dying;
But the night I died I dreamed that I was dead,
And the cities said to me: "Why are you dying?
We are satisfied, if you are; but why did I die?"

A Lullaby

For wars his life and half a world away
The soldier sells his family and days.
He learns to fight for freedom and the State;
He sleeps with seven men within six feet.

He picks up matches and he cleans out plates;
Is lied to like a child, cursed like a beast.
They crop his head, his dog tags ring like sheep
As his stiff limbs shift wearily to sleep.

Recalled in dreams or letters, else forgot,
His life is smothered like a grave, with dirt;
And his dull torment mottles like a fly's
The lying amber of the histories.

The Woman at the Washington Zoo

The saris go by me from the embassies.

Cloth from the moon. Cloth from another planet.
They look back at the leopard like the leopard.

And I. . . .
              this print of mine, that has kept its color
Alive through so many cleanings; this dull null
Navy I wear to work, and wear from work, and so
To my bed, so to my grave, with no
Complaints, no comment: neither from my chief,
The Deputy Chief Assistant, nor his chief—
Only I complain. . . . this serviceable
Body that no sunlight dyes, no hand suffuses
But, dome-shadowed, withering among columns,
Wavy beneath fountains—small, far-off, shining
In the eyes of animals, these beings trapped
As I am trapped but not, themselves, the trap,
Aging, but without knowledge of their age,
Kept safe here, knowing not of death, for death—
Oh, bars of my own body, open, open!

The world goes by my cage and never sees me.
And there come not to me, as come to these,
The wild beasts, sparrows pecking the llamas' grain,
Pigeons settling on the bears' bread, buzzards
Tearing the meat the flies have clouded. . . .
                         Vulture,
When you come for the white rat that the foxes left,
Take off the red helmet of your head, the black
Wings that have shadowed me, and step to me as man:
The wild brother at whose feet the white wolves fawn,
To whose hand of power the great lioness
Stalks, purring. . . .
                 You know what I was,
You see what I am: change me, change me!

Next Day

Moving from Cheer to Joy, from Joy to All,
I take a box
And add it to my wild rice, my Cornish game hens.
The slacked or shorted, basketed, identical
Food-gathering flocks
Are selves I overlook. Wisdom, said William James,

Is learning what to overlook. And I am wise
If that is wisdom.
Yet somehow, as I buy All from these shelves
And the boy takes it to my station wagon,
What I've become
Troubles me even if I shut my eyes.

When I was young and miserable and pretty
And poor, I'd wish
What all girls wish: to have a husband,
A house and children. Now that I'm old, my wish
Is womanish:
That the boy putting groceries in my car

See me. It bewilders me he doesn't see me.
For so many years
I was good enough to eat: the world looked at me

And its mouth watered. How often they have undressed me,
The eyes of strangers!
And, holding their flesh within my flesh, their vile

Imaginings within my imagining,
I too have taken
The chance of life. Now the boy pats my dog
And we start home. Now I am good.
The last mistaken,
Ecstatic, accidental bliss, the blind

Happiness that, bursting, leaves upon the palm
Some soap and water—
It was so long ago, back in some Gay
Twenties, Nineties, I don't know . . . Today I miss
My lovely daughter
Away at school, my sons away at school,

My husband away at work—I wish for them.
The dog, the maid,
And I go through the sure unvarying days
At home in them. As I look at my life,
I am afraid
Only that it will change, as I am changing:

I am afraid, this morning, of my face.
It looks at me
From the rear-view mirror, with the eyes I hate,
The smile I hate. Its plain, lined look
Of gray discovery
Repeats to me: "You're old." That's all, I'm old.

And yet I'm afraid, as I was at the funeral
I went to yesterday.
My friend's cold made-up face, granite among its flowers,
Her undressed, operated-on, dressed body
Were my face and body.
As I think of her I hear her telling me

How young I seem; I *am* exceptional;
I think of all I have.
But really no one is exceptional,
No one has anything, I'm anybody,
I stand beside my grave
Confused with my life, that is commonplace and solitary.

JOHN BERRYMAN

(1914 – 1972)

from *The Dream Songs*

1

Huffy Henry hid   the day,
unappeasable Henry sulked.
I see his point, — a trying to put things over.
It was the thought that they thought
they could *do* it made Henry wicked & away.
But he should have come out and talked.

All the world like a woolen lover
once did seem on Henry's side.
Then came a departure.
Thereafter nothing fell out as it might or ought.
I don't see how Henry, pried
open for all the world to see, survived.

What he has now to say is a long
wonder the world can bear & be.
Once in a sycamore I was glad
all at the top, and I sang.
Hard on the land wears the strong sea
and empty grows every bed.

4

Filling her compact & delicious body
with chicken páprika, she glanced at me
twice.
Fainting with interest, I hungered back
and only the fact of her husband & four other people
kept me from springing on her

or falling at her little feet and crying
'You are the hottest one for years of night
Henry's dazed eyes
have enjoyed, Brilliance.' I advanced upon
(despairing) my spumoni. —Sir Bones: is stuffed,
de world, wif feeding girls.

—Black hair, complexion Latin, jewelled eyes
downcast . . . The slob beside her   feasts . . . What
    wonders is
she sitting on, over there?
The restaurant buzzes. She might as well be on Mars.
Where did it all go wrong? There ought to be a law against
    Henry.
—Mr Bones: there is.

5
Henry sats in de bar & was odd,
off in the glass from the glass,
at odds wif de world & its god,
his wife is a complete nothing,
St Stephen
getting even.

Henry sats in de plane & was gay.
Careful Henry nothing said aloud
but where a Virgin out of cloud
to her Mountain dropt in light,
his thought made pockets & the plane buckt.
'Parm me, lady.' 'Orright.'

Henry lay in de netting, wild,
while the brainfever bird did scales;
Mr Heartbreak, the New Man,
come to farm a crazy land;
an image of the dead on the fingernail
of a newborn child.

14

Life, friends, is boring. We must not say so.
After all, the sky flashes, the great sea yearns,
we ourselves flash and yearn,
and moreover my mother told me as a boy
(repeatingly) 'Ever to confess you're bored
means you have no

Inner Resources.' I conclude now I have no
inner resources, because I am heavy bored.
Peoples bore me,
literature bores me, especially great literature,
Henry bores me, with his plights & gripes
as bad as achilles,

who loves people and valiant art, which bores me.
And the tranquil hills, & gin, look like a drag
and somehow a dog
has taken itself & its tail considerably away
into mountains or sea or sky, leaving
behind: me, wag.

21

Some good people, daring & subtle voices
and their tense faces, as I think of it
I see sank underground.
I see. My radar digs. I do not dig.
Cool their flushing blood, them eyes is shut —
eyes?

Appalled: by all the dead: Henry brooded.
Without exception! All.
ALL.
The senior population   waits. Come down! come down!
A ghastly & flashing pause, clothed,
life called; us do.

In a madhouse heard I an ancient man
tube-fed who had not said for fifteen years
(they said) one canny word,
senile forever, who a heart might pierce,
mutter 'O come on down. O come on down.'
Clear whom *he* meant.

26

The glories of the world struck me, made me aria, once.
—What happen then, Mr Bones?
if be you cares to say.
—Henry. Henry became interested in women's bodies,
his loins were & were the   scene of stupendous achievement.
Stupor. Knees, dear. Pray.

All the knobs & softnesses of, my God,
the ducking & trouble it swarm on Henry,
at one time.
—What happen then, Mr Bones?
you seems excited-like.
—Fell Henry back into   the original crime: art, rime

besides a sense of others, my God, my God,
and a jealousy for the honour (alive) of his country,
what can get more odd?
and discontent with the thriving gangs & pride.
—What happen then, Mr Bones?
—I had a most marvellous   piece of luck. I died.

29

There sat down, once, a thing on Henry's heart
só heavy, if he had a hundred years
& more, & weeping, sleepless, in all them time
Henry could not make good.
Starts again always in Henry's ears
the little cough somewhere, an odour, a chime.

And there is another thing he has in mind
like a grave Sienese face a thousand years
would fail to blur the still profiled reproach of. Ghastly,
with open eyes, he attends, blind.
All the bells say: too late. This is not for tears;
thinking.

But never did Henry, as he thought he did,
end anyone and hacks her body up
and hide the pieces, where they may be found.
He knows: he went over everyone, & nobody's missing.
Often he reckons, in the dawn, them up.
Nobody is ever missing.

45

He stared at ruin. Ruin stared straight back.
He thought they was old friends. He felt on the stair
where her papa found them bare
they became familiar. When the papers were lost
rich with pals' secrets, he thought he had the knack
of ruin. Their paths crossed

and once they crossed in jail; they crossed in bed;
and over an unsigned letter their eyes met,
and in an Asian city
directionless & lurchy at two & three,
or trembling to a telephone's fresh threat,
and when some wired his head

to reach a wrong opinion, 'Epileptic'.
But he noted now that: they were not old friends.
He did not know this one.
This one was a stranger, come to make amends
for all the imposters, and to make it stick.
Henry nodded, un-.

53

He lay in the middle of the world, and twitcht.
More Sparine for Pelides,
human (half) & down here as he is,
with probably insulting mail to open
and certainly unworthy words to hear
and his unforgivable memory.

—I seldom *go* to *films*. They are too exciting,
said the Honourable Possum.
—It takes me so long to read the 'paper,
said to me one day a novelist hot as a firecracker,
because I have to identify myself with everyone in it,
including the corpses, pal.

Kierkegaard wanted a society, to refuse to read 'papers,
and that was not, friends, his worst idea.
Tiny Hardy, toward the end, refused to say *anything*,
a programme adopted early on by long Housman,

and Gottfried Benn
said: — We are using our own skins for wallpaper and we
　　cannot win.

77

Seedy Henry rose up shy in de world
& shaved & swung his barbells, duded Henry up
and p.a.'d poor thousands of persons on topics of grand
moment to Henry, ah to those less & none.
Wif a book of his in either hand
he is stript down to move on.

—Come away, Mr Bones.

—Henry is tired of the winter,
& haircuts, & a squeamish comfy　ruin-prone proud national
　　mind,　& Spring (in the city so called).
Henry likes Fall.
Hé would be prepared to líve in a world of Fáll
for ever, impenitent Henry.
But the snows and summers grieve & dream;

thése fierce & airy occupations, and love,
raved away so many of Henry's years
it is a wonder that, with in each hand
one of his own mad books and all,
ancient fires for eyes, his head full
& his heart full, he's making ready to move on.

164

Three limbs, three seasons smashed; well, one to go.
Henry fell smiling through the air below
and through the air above,
the middle air as well did he not neglect
but carefully in all these airs was wrecked
which he got truly tired of.

His friends alas went all about their ways
intact. Couldn't William break at least a collar-bone?
O world so ill arranged!

Henry holds in addition pharmacies
for all his other ills, pills of his own
which frequently get changed

as his despairing doctors change their minds
about what must be best for wilful Henry.
There seems to firm no answer
save from the sexton in the place that blinds
& stones and does not hurt: Henry springs youthfully
in his six-by-two like a dancer.

219

So Long? Stevens

He lifted up, among the actuaries,
a grandee crow. Ah ha & he crowed good.
That funny money-man.
Mutter we all must as well as we can.
He mutter spiffy. He make wonder Henry's
wits, though, with a odd

. . . something . . . something . . . not there in his
    flourishing art.
O veteran of death, you will not mind
a counter-mutter.
What was it missing, then, at the man's heart
so that he does not wound? It is our kind
to wound, as well as utter

a fact of happy world. That metaphysics
he hefted up until we could not breathe
the physics. *On our side,*
monotonous (or ever-fresh) — it sticks
in Henry's throat to judge — brilliant, he seethe;
better than us; less wide.

384

The marker slants, flowerless, day's almost done,
I stand above my father's grave with rage,
often, often before
I've made this awful pilgrimage to one
who cannot visit me, who tore his page
out: I come back for more,

I spit upon this dreadful banker's grave
who shot his heart out in a Florida dawn
O ho alas alas
When will indifference come, I moan & rave
I'd like to scrabble till I got right down
away down under the grass

and ax the casket open ha to see
just how he's taking it, which he sought so hard
we'll tear apart
the mouldering grave clothes ha & then Henry
will heft the ax once more, his final card,
and fell it on the start.

ROBERT LOWELL

(1917–1977)

Where the Rainbow Ends

I saw the sky descending, black and white,
Not blue, on Boston where the winters wore
The skulls to jack-o'-lanterns on the slates,
And Hunger's skin-and-bone retrievers tore
The chickadee and shrike. The thorn tree waits
Its victim and tonight
The worms will eat the deadwood to the foot
Of Ararat: the scythers, Time and Death,
Helmed locusts, move upon the tree of breath;
The wild ingrafted olive and the root

Are withered, and a winter drifts to where
The Pepperpot, ironic rainbow, spans
Charles River and its scales of scorched-earth miles.
I saw my city in the Scales, the pans
Of judgment rising and descending. Piles
Of dead leaves char the air—
And I am a red arrow on this graph
Of Revelations. Every dove is sold.
The Chapel's sharp-shinned eagle shifts its hold
On serpent-Time, the rainbow's epitaph.

In Boston serpents whistle at the cold.
The victim climbs the altar steps and sings:
"Hosannah to the lion, lamb, and beast
Who fans the furnace-face of IS with wings:
I breathe the ether of my marriage feast."
At the high altar, gold
And a fair cloth. I kneel and the wings beat
My cheek. What can the dove of Jesus give
You now but wisdom, exile? Stand and live,
The dove has brought an olive branch to eat.

Sailing Home from Rapallo
(February 1954)

Your nurse could only speak Italian,
but after twenty minutes I could imagine your final week,
and tears ran down my cheeks. . . .

When I embarked from Italy with my Mother's body,
the whole shoreline of the *Golfo di Genova*
was breaking into fiery flower.
The crazy yellow and azure sea-sleds
blasting like jack-hammers across
the *spumante*-bubbling wake of our liner,
recalled the clashing colors of my Ford.
Mother travelled first-class in the hold;
her *Risorgimento* black and gold casket
was like Napoleon's at the *Invalides*. . . .

While the passengers were tanning
on the Mediterranean in deck-chairs,
our family cemetery in Dunbarton
lay under the White Mountains
in the sub-zero weather.
The graveyard's soil was changing to stone —
so many of its deaths had been midwinter.
Dour and dark against the blinding snowdrifts,
its black brook and fir trunks were as smooth as masts.
A fence of iron spear-hafts
black-bordered its mostly Colonial grave-slates.

The only "unhistoric" soul to come here
was Father, now buried beneath his recent
unweathered pink-veined slice of marble.
Even the Latin of his Lowell motto:
Occasionem cognosce,
seemed too businesslike and pushing here,
where the burning cold illuminated
the hewn inscriptions of Mother's relatives:
twenty or thirty Winslows and Starks.
Frost had given their names a diamond edge. . . .

In the grandiloquent lettering on Mother's coffin,
Lowell had been misspelled *LOVEL*.
The corpse
was wrapped like *panetone* in Italian tinfoil.

Waking in the Blue

The night attendant, a B.U. sophomore,
rouses from the mare's-nest of his drowsy head
propped on *The Meaning of Meaning*.
He catwalks down our corridor.
Azure day
makes my agonized blue window bleaker.
Crows maunder on the petrified fairway.
Absence! My heart grows tense
as though a harpoon were sparring for the kill.
(This is the house for the "mentally ill.")

What use is my sense of humor?
I grin at Stanley, now sunk in his sixties,
once a Harvard all-American fullback,
(if such were possible!)
still hoarding the build of a boy in his twenties,
as he soaks, a ramrod
with the muscle of a seal
in his long tub,
vaguely urinous from the Victorian plumbing.
A kingly granite profile in a crimson golf-cap,
worn all day, all night,
he thinks only of his figure,
of slimming on sherbet and ginger ale—
more cut off from words than a seal.

This is the way day breaks in Bowditch Hall at McLean's;
the hooded night lights bring out "Bobbie,"
Porcellian '29,
a replica of Louis XVI
without the wig—

redolent and roly-poly as a sperm whale,
as he swashbuckles about in his birthday suit
and horses at chairs.

These victorious figures of bravado ossified young.

In between the limits of day,
hours and hours go by under the crew haircuts
and slightly too little nonsensical bachelor twinkle
of the Roman Catholic attendants.
(There are no Mayflower
screwballs in the Catholic Church.)

After a hearty New England breakfast,
I weigh two hundred pounds
this morning. Cock of the walk,
I strut in my turtle-necked French sailor's jersey
before the metal shaving mirrors,
and see the shaky future grow familiar
in the pinched, indigenous faces
of these thoroughbred mental cases,
twice my age and half my weight.
We are all old-timers,
each of us holds a locked razor.

Home after Three Months Away

Gone now the baby's nurse,
a lioness who ruled the roost
and made the Mother cry.
She used to tie
gobbets of porkrind in bowknots of gauze —
three months they hung like soggy toast
on our eight foot magnolia tree,
and helped the English sparrows
weather a Boston winter.

Three months, three months!
Is Richard now himself again?
Dimpled with exaltation,
my daughter holds her levee in the tub.

Our noses rub,
each of us pats a stringy lock of hair —
they tell me nothing's gone.
Though I am forty-one,
not forty now, the time I put away
was child's-play. After thirteen weeks
my child still dabs her cheeks
to start me shaving. When
we dress her in her sky-blue corduroy,
she changes to a boy,
and floats my shaving brush
and washcloth in the flush. . . .
Dearest, I cannot loiter here
in lather like a polar bear.

Recuperating, I neither spin nor toil.
Three stories down below,
a choreman tends our coffin's length of soil,
and seven horizontal tulips blow.
Just twelve months ago,
these flowers were pedigreed
imported Dutchmen; now no one need
distinguish them from weed.
Bushed by the late spring snow,
they cannot meet
another year's snowballing enervation.

I keep no rank nor station.
Cured, I am frizzled, stale and small.

Skunk Hour
For Elizabeth Bishop

Nautilus Island's hermit
heiress still lives through winter in her Spartan cottage;
her sheep still graze above the sea.
Her son's a bishop. Her farmer
is first selectman in our village;
she's in her dotage.

Thirsting for
the hierarchic privacy
of Queen Victoria's century,
she buys up all
the eyesores facing her shore,
and lets them fall.

The season's ill —
we've lost our summer millionaire,
who seemed to leap from an L. L. Bean
catalogue. His nine-knot yawl
was auctioned off to lobstermen.
A red fox stain covers Blue Hill.

And now our fairy
decorator brightens his shop for fall;
his fishnet's filled with orange cork,
orange, his cobbler's bench and awl;
there is no money in his work,
he'd rather marry.

One dark night,
my Tudor Ford climbed the hill's skull;
I watched for love-cars. Lights turned down,
they lay together, hull to hull,
where the graveyard shelves on the town. . . .
My mind's not right.

A car radio bleats,
"Love, O careless Love. . . ." I hear
my ill-spirit sob in each blood cell,
as if my hand were at its throat. . . .
I myself am hell;
nobody's here —

only skunks, that search
in the moonlight for a bite to eat.
They march on their soles up Main Street:
white stripes, moonstruck eyes' red fire
under the chalk-dry and spar spire
of the Trinitarian Church.

I stand on top
of our back steps and breathe the rich air —

a mother skunk with her column of kittens swills the garbage
   pail.
She jabs her wedge-head in a cup
of sour cream, drops her ostrich tail,
and will not scare.

For the Union Dead
"Relinquunt Omnia Servare Rem Publicam."

The old South Boston Aquarium stands
in a Sahara of snow now. Its broken windows are boarded.
The bronze weathervane cod has lost half its scales.
The airy tanks are dry.

Once my nose crawled like a snail on the glass;
my hand tingled
to burst the bubbles
drifting from the noses of the cowed, compliant fish.

My hand draws back. I often sigh still
for the dark downward and vegetating kingdom
of the fish and reptile. One morning last March,
I pressed against the new barbed and galvanized

fence on the Boston Common. Behind their cage,
yellow dinosaur steamshovels were grunting
as they cropped up tons of mush and grass
to gouge their underworld garage.

Parking spaces luxuriate like civic
sandpiles in the heart of Boston.
A girdle of orange, Puritan-pumpkin colored girders
braces the tingling Statehouse,

shaking over the excavations, as it faces Colonel Shaw
and his bell-cheeked Negro infantry
on St. Gaudens' shaking Civil War relief,
propped by a plank splint against the garage's earthquake.

Two months after marching through Boston,
half the regiment was dead;
at the dedication,
William James could almost hear the bronze Negroes breathe.

Their monument sticks like a fishbone
in the city's throat.
Its Colonel is as lean
as a compass-needle.

He has an angry wrenlike vigilance,
a greyhound's gentle tautness;
he seems to wince at pleasure,
and suffocate for privacy.

He is out of bounds now. He rejoices in man's lovely,
peculiar power to choose life and die—
when he leads his black soldiers to death,
he cannot bend his back.

On a thousand small town New England greens,
the old white churches hold their air
of sparse, sincere rebellion; frayed flags
quilt the graveyards of the Grand Army of the Republic.

The stone statues of the abstract Union Soldier
grow slimmer and younger each year—
wasp-waisted, they doze over muskets
and muse through their sideburns . . .

Shaw's father wanted no monument
except the ditch,
where his son's body was thrown
and lost with his "niggers."

The ditch is nearer.
There are no statues for the last war here;
on Boylston Street, a commercial photograph
shows Hiroshima boiling

over a Mosler Safe, the "Rock of Ages"
that survived the blast. Space is nearer.
When I crouch to my television set,
the drained faces of Negro school-children rise like balloons.

Colonel Shaw
is riding on his bubble,
he waits
for the blessèd break.

The Aquarium is gone. Everywhere,
giant finned cars nose forward like fish;
a savage servility
slides by on grease.

Waking Early Sunday Morning

O to break loose, like the chinook
salmon jumping and falling back,
nosing up to the impossible
stone and bone-crushing waterfall —
raw-jawed, weak-fleshed there, stopped by ten
steps of the roaring ladder, and then
to clear the top on the last try,
alive enough to spawn and die.

Stop, back off. The salmon breaks
water, and now my body wakes
to feel the unpolluted joy
and criminal leisure of a boy —
no rainbow smashing a dry fly
in the white run is free as I,
here squatting like a dragon on
time's hoard before the day's begun!

Vermin run for their unstopped holes;
in some dark nook a fieldmouse rolls
a marble, hours on end, then stops;
the termite in the woodwork sleeps —
listen, the creatures of the night
obsessive, casual, sure of foot,
go on grinding, while the sun's
daily remorseful blackout dawns.

Fierce, fireless mind, running downhill.
Look up and see the harbor fill:
business as usual in eclipse
goes down to the sea in ships —
wake of refuse, dacron rope,
bound for Bermuda or Good Hope,

all bright before the morning watch
the wine-dark hulls of yawl and ketch.

I watch a glass of water wet
with a fine fuzz of icy sweat,
silvery colors touched with sky,
serene in their neutrality —
yet if I shift, or change my mood,
I see some object made of wood,
background behind it of brown grain,
to darken it, but not to stain.

O that the spirit could remain
tinged but untarnished by its strain!
Better dressed and stacking birch,
or lost with the Faithful at Church —
anywhere, but somewhere else!
And now the new electric bells,
clearly chiming, "Faith of our fathers,"
and now the congregation gathers.

O Bible chopped and crucified
in hymns we hear but do not read,
none of the milder subtleties
of grace or art will sweeten these
stiff quatrains shovelled out four-square —
they sing of peace, and preach despair;
yet they gave darkness some control,
and left a loophole for the soul.

No, put old clothes on, and explore
the corners of the woodshed for
its dregs and dreck: tools with no handle,
ten candle-ends not worth a candle,
old lumber banished from the Temple,
damned by Paul's precept and example,
cast from the kingdom, banned in Israel,
the wordless sign, the tinkling cymbal.

When will we see Him face to face?
Each day, He shines through darker glass.
In this small town where everything
is known, I see His vanishing

emblems, His white spire and flag-
pole sticking out above the fog,
like old white china doorknobs, sad,
slight, useless things to calm the mad.

Hammering military splendor,
top-heavy Goliath in full armor—
little redemption in the mass
liquidations of their brass,
elephant and phalanx moving
with the times and still improving,
when that kingdom hit the crash:
a million foreskins stacked like trash . . .

Sing softer! But what if a new
diminuendo brings no true
tenderness, only restlessness,
excess, the hunger for success,
sanity of self-deception
fixed and kicked by reckless caution,
while we listen to the bells—
anywhere, but somewhere else!

O to break loose. All life's grandeur
is something with a girl in summer . . .
elated as the President
girdled by his establishment
this Sunday morning, free to chaff
his own thoughts with his bear-cuffed staff,
swimming nude, unbuttoned, sick
of his ghost-written rhetoric!

No weekends for the gods now. Wars
flicker, earth licks its open sores,
fresh breakage, fresh promotions, chance
assassinations, no advance.
Only man thinning out his kind
sounds through the Sabbath noon, the blind
swipe of the pruner and his knife
busy about the tree of life . . .

Pity the planet, all joy gone
from this sweet volcanic cone;

peace to our children when they fall
in small war on the heels of small
war—until the end of time
to police the earth, a ghost
orbiting forever lost
in our monotonous sublime.

The March I
For Dwight Macdonald

Under the too white marmoreal Lincoln Memorial,
the too tall marmoreal Washington Obelisk,
gazing into the too long reflecting pool,
the reddish trees, the withering autumn sky,
the remorseless, amplified harangues for peace—
lovely to lock arms, to march absurdly locked
(unlocking to keep my wet glasses from slipping)
to see the cigarette match quaking in my fingers,
then to step off like green Union Army recruits
for the first Bull Run, sped by photographers,
the notables, the girls . . . fear, glory, chaos, rout . . .
our green army staggered out on the miles-long green fields,
met by the other army, the Martian, the ape, the hero,
his new-fangled rifle, his green new steel helmet.

Death and the Bridge
From a Landscape by Frank Parker

Death gallops up the bridge of red railtie girders,
some onetime view of Boston humps the saltmarsh;
it is handpainted: this the eternal, provincial
city Dante saw as Florence and hell. . . .
On weekends too, the local TV station's
garbage disposal starts to grind at daybreak:
keep Sunday clean. We owe the Lord that much;
from the first, God heeded His socialistic conscience,
gave universal capital punishment.

In daylight, the relaxed red scaffolding is almost
breathing: *no man is ever too good to die.* . . .
We will follow our skeletons on the girder,
out of life and Boston, singing with Freud:
'God's ways are dark and very seldom pleasant.'

Harriet

Spring moved to summer — the rude cold rain
hurries the ambitious, flowers and youth;
our flash-tones crackle for an hour, and then
we too follow nature, imperceptibly
change our mouse-brown to white lion's mane,
thin white fading to a freckled, knuckled skull,
bronzed by decay, by many, many suns. . . .
Child of ten, three quarters animal,
three years from Juliet, half Juliet,
already ripened for the night on stage —
beautiful petals, what shall we hope for,
knowing one choice not two is all you're given,
health beyond the measure, dangerous
to yourself, more dangerous to others?

from *Mexico*

1

The difficulties, the impossibilities . . .
I, fifty, humbled with the years' gold garbage,
dead laurel grizzling my back like spines of hay;
you, some sweet, uncertain age, say twenty-seven,
untempted, unseared by honors or deception.
What help then? Not the sun, the scarlet blossom,
and the high fever of this seventh day,
the predestined diarrhea of the pilgrim,
the multiple mosquito spots, round as pesos.
Hope not for God here, or even for the gods;

the Aztecs knew the sun, the source of life,
will die, unless we feed it human blood—
we two are clocks, and only count in time . . .
the hand a knife-edge pressed against the future.

4

South of Boston, south of Washington,
south of any bearing . . . I walk the glazed moonlight:
dew on the grass and nobody about,
drawn on by my unlimited desire,
like a bull with a ring in his nose, a chain in the ring. . . .
We moved far, bull and cow, could one imagine
cattle obliviously pairing six long days:
up road and down, then up again passing the same
brick garden wall, stiff spines of hay stuck in my hide;
and always in full sight of everyone,
from the full sun to silhouetting sunset,
pinned by undimming lights of hurried cars. . . .
You're gone; I am learning to live in history.
What is history? What you cannot touch.

Obit

Our love will not come back on fortune's wheel—

in the end it gets us, though a man know what he'd have:
old cars, old money, old undebased pre-Lyndon
silver, no copper rubbing through . . . old wives;
I could live such a too long time with mine.
In the end, every hypochondriac is his own prophet.
Before the final coming to rest, comes the rest
of all transcendence in a mode of being, hushing
all becoming. I'm for and with myself in my otherness,
in the eternal return of earth's fairer children,
the lily, the rose, the sun on brick at dusk,
the loved, the lover, and their fear of life,
their unconquered flux, insensate oneness, painful "It was. . . ."
After loving you so much, can I forget
you for eternity, and have no other choice?

History

History has to live with what was here,
clutching and close to fumbling all we had —
it is so dull and gruesome how we die,
unlike writing, life never finishes.
Abel was finished; death is not remote,
a flash-in-the-pan electrifies the skeptic,
his cows crowding like skulls against high-voltage wire,
his baby crying all night like a new machine.
As in our Bibles, white-faced, predatory,
the beautiful, mist-drunken hunter's moon ascends —
a child could give it a face: two holes, two holes,
my eyes, my mouth, between them a skull's no-nose —
O there's a terrifying innocence in my face
drenched with the silver salvage of the mornfrost.

Down the Nile

Two in the afternoon. The restlessness.
Greek Islands. Maine. I have counted the catalogue
of ships down half its length, the beaks of the bowsprits. . . .
Yet sometimes the Nile is wet, and life's as painted:
those couples, one in love and marriage, swaying
their children and their slaves the height of children,
supple and gentle as giraffes or newts;
the waist still willowy, the paint still fresh;
decorum without conforming, no harness on
the woman, and no armor on her husband,
the red clay master with his feet of clay
catwalking lightly to his conquests, leaving
one model and dynasties of faithless copies —
we aging downstream faster than a scepter can check.

Watchmaker God

Say life is the one-way trip, the one-way flight,
say this without hysterical undertones —
then you could say you stood in the cold light of science,
seeing as you are seen, espoused to fact.
Strange, life is both the fire and fuel; and we,
the animals and objects, must be here
without striking a spark of evidence
that anything that ever stopped living
ever falls back to living when life stops.
There's a pale romance to the watchmaker God
of Descartes and Paley; He drafted and installed
us in the Apparatus. He loved to tinker;
but having perfected what He had to do,
stood off shrouded in his loneliness.

Stalin

Winds on the stems make them creak like manmade things;
a hedge of vines and bushes — three or four
kinds, grape-leaf, elephant-ear and alder,
an arabesque, imperfect and alive,
a hundred hues of green, the darkest shades
fall short of black, the whitest leaf-back short of white.
The state, if we could see behind the wall,
is woven of perishable vegetation.
Stalin? What shot him clawing up the tree of power —
millions plowed under with the crops they grew,
his intimates dying like the spider-bridegroom?
The large stomach could only chew success. What raised him
was an unusual lust to break the icon,
joke cruelly, seriously, and be himself.

Reading Myself

Like thousands, I took just pride and more than just,
struck matches that brought my blood to a boil;
I memorized the tricks to set the river on fire —
somehow never wrote something to go back to.
Can I suppose I am finished with wax flowers
and have earned my grass on the minor slopes of Parnassus. . . .
No honeycomb is built without a bee
adding circle to circle, cell to cell,
the wax and honey of a mausoleum —
this round dome proves its maker is alive;
the corpse of the insect lives embalmed in honey,
prays that its perishable work live long
enough for the sweet-tooth bear to desecrate —
this open book . . . my open coffin.

End of a Year

These conquered kings pass furiously away;
gods die in flesh and spirit and live in print,
each library a misquoted tyrant's home.
A year runs out in the movies, must be written
in bad, straightforward, unscanning sentences —
stamped, trampled, branded on backs of carbons,
lines, words, letters nailed to letters, words, lines —
the typescript looks like a Rosetta Stone. . . .
One more annus mirabilis, its hero *hero demens,*
ill-starred of men and crossed by his fixed stars,
running his ship past sound-spar on the rocks. . . .
The slush-ice on the east bank of the Hudson
is rose-heather in the New Year sunset;
bright sky, bright sky, carbon scarred with ciphers.

Fishnet

Any clear thing that blinds us with surprise,
your wandering silences and bright trouvailles,
dolphin let loose to catch the flashing fish. . . .
Poets die adolescents, their beat embalms them,
the archetypal voices sing off key;
the old actor cannot read his friends,
and nevertheless he reads himself aloud,
genius hums the auditorium dead.
The line must terminate.
Yet my heart rises, I know I've gladdened a lifetime
knotting, undoing a fishnet of tarred rope;
the net will hang on the wall when the fish are eaten,
nailed like illegible bronze on the futureless future.

For Sheridan

We only live between
before we are and what we were.

In the lost negative
you exist,
a smile, a cypher,
an old-fashioned face
in an old-fashioned hat.

Three ages in a flash:
the same child in the same picture,
he, I, you,
chockablock, one stamp
like mother's wedding silver—

gnome, fish, brute cherubic force.

We could see clearly
and all the same things
before the glass was hurt.

Past fifty, we learn with surprise and a sense
of suicidal absolution

that what we intended and failed
could never have happened —
and must be done better.

Shifting Colors

I fish until the clouds turn blue,
weary of self-torture, ready to paint
lilacs or confuse a thousand leaves,
as landscapists must.

My eye returns to my double,
an ageless big white horse,
slightly discolored by dirt
cropping the green shelf diagonal
to the artificial troutpond —
unmoving, it shifts as I move,
and works the whole field in the course of the day.

Poor measured, neurotic man —
animals are more instinctive virtuosi.

Ducks splash deceptively like fish;
fish break water with the wings of a bird to escape.

A hissing goose sways in stationary anger;
purple bluebells rise in ledges on the lake.

A single cuckoo gifted with a pregnant word
shifts like the sun from wood to wood.

All day my miscast troutfly buzzes about my ears
and empty mind.

But nature is sundrunk with sex —
how could a man fail to notice, man
the one pornographer among the animals?
I seek leave unimpassioned by my body,
I am too weak to strain to remember, or give
recollection the eye of a microscope. I see
horse and meadow, duck and pond,

universal consolatory
description without significance,
transcribed verbatim by my eye.

This is not the directness that catches
everything on the run and then expires —
I would write only in response to the gods,
like Mallarmé who had the good fortune
to find a style that made writing impossible.

Epilogue

Those blessèd structures, plot and rhyme —
why are they no help to me now
I want to make
something imagined, not recalled?
I hear the noise of my own voice:
The painter's vision is not a lens,
it trembles to caress the light.
But sometimes everything I write
with the threadbare art of my eye
seems a snapshot,
lurid, rapid, garish, grouped,
heightened from life,
yet paralyzed by fact.
All's misalliance.
Yet why not say what happened?
Pray for the grace of accuracy
Vermeer gave to the sun's illumination
stealing like the tide across a map
to his girl solid with yearning.
We are poor passing facts,
warned by that to give
each figure in the photograph
his living name.

HOWARD NEMEROV
(1920 –)

On Certain Wits

who amused themselves over the simplicity of
Barnett Newman's paintings shown at Bennington
College in May of 1958

When Moses in Horeb struck the rock,
And water came forth out of the rock,
Some of the people were annoyed with Moses
And said he should have used a fancier stick.

And when Elijah on Mount Carmel brought the rain,
Where the prophets of Baal could not bring rain,
Some of the people said that the rituals of the prophets of Baal
Were aesthetically significant, while Elijah's were very plain.

To David, about His Education

The world is full of mostly invisible things,
And there is no way but putting the mind's eye,
Or its nose, in a book, to find them out,
Things like the square root of Everest
Or how many times Byron goes into Texas,
Or whether the law of the excluded middle
Applies west of the Rockies. For these
And the like reasons, you have to go to school
And study books and listen to what you are told,
And sometimes try to remember. Though I don't know
What you will do with the mean annual rainfall
On Plato's Republic, or the calorie content
Of the Diet of Worms, such things are said to be
Good for you, and you will have to learn them
In order to become one of the grown-ups

Who sees invisible things neither steadily nor whole,
But keeps gravely the grand confusion of the world
Under his hat, which is where it belongs,
And teaches small children to do this in their turn.

Metamorphoses
according to Steinberg

These people, with their illegible diplomas,
Their passports to a landscape full of languages,
Carry their images on banners, or become
Porters of pedestals bearing their own
Statues, or hold up, with and against gravity,
The unbalanced scrollwork of their signatures.
Thumbprints somehow get to be sanderlings,
And the cats keep on appearing, with an air
Of looking at kings even as they claw
Their way up the latticed cage of a graph,
Balance with fish, confront photographers
In family groups, or prowl music paper
Behind the staves.
                    These in themselves, Master,
Are a great teaching. But more than for these
I am grateful for the lesson of the line,
That wandering divider of the world,
So casually able to do anything:
The extended clothesline that will carry trains,
For instance, or the lines of letters whose
Interstices vary the planes between
The far horizon and a very near nose.

The enchanted line, defying gravity and death,
Brings into being and destroys its world
Of marvelous exceptions that prove rules,
Where a hand is taken drawing its own hand,
A man with a pen laboriously sketches
Himself into existence; world of the lost
Characters amazed in their own images:
The woman elided with her rocking chair,
The person trapped behind his signature,
The man who has just crossed himself out.

The Sweeper of Ways

All day, a small mild Negro man with a broom
Sweeps up the leaves that fall along the paths.
He carries his head to one side, looking down
At his leaves, at his broom like a windy beard
Curled with the sweeping habit. Over him
High haughty trees, the hickory and ash,
Dispense their more leaves easily, or else
The district wind, hunting hypocrisy,
Tears at the summer's wall and throws down leaves
To witness of a truth naked and cold.

Hopeless it looks, on these harsh, hastening days
Before the end, to finish all those leaves
Against time. But the broom goes back and forth
With a tree's patience, as though naturally
Erasers would speak the language of pencils.
A thousand thoughts fall on the same blank page,
Though the wind blows them back, they go where he
Directs them, to the archives where disorder
Blazes and a pale smoke becomes the sky.
The ways I walk are splendidly free of leaves.

We meet, we smile good morning, say the weather
Whatever. On a rainy day there'll be
A few leaves stuck like emblems on the walk;
These too he brooms at till they come unstuck.
Masters, we carry our white faces by
In silent prayer, Don't hate me, on a wave-
length which his broom's antennae perfectly
Pick up, we know ourselves so many thoughts
Considered by a careful, kindly mind
Which can do nothing, and is doing that.

Thirtieth Anniversary Report of the Class of '41

We who survived the war and took to wife
And sired the kids and made the decent living,
And piecemeal furnished forth the finished life
Not by grand theft so much as petty thieving—

Who had the routine middle-aged affair
And made our beds and had to lie in them
This way or that because the beds were there,
And turned our bile and choler in for phlegm —

Who saw grandparents, parents, to the vault
And wives and selves grow wrinkled, grey and fat
And children through their acne and revolt
And told the analyst about all that —

Are done with it. What is there to discuss?
There's nothing left for us to say of us.

Snowflakes

Not slowly wrought, nor treasured for their form
In heaven, but by the blind self of the storm
Spun off, each driven individual
Perfected in the moment of his fall.

The Western Approaches

As long as we look forward, all seems free,
Uncertain, subject to the Laws of Chance,
Though strange that chance should lie subject to laws,
But looking back on life it is as if
Our Book of Changes never let us change.

Stories already told a time ago
Were waiting for us down the road, our lives
But filled them out; and dreams about the past
Show us the world is post meridian
With little future left to dream about.

Old stories none but scholars seem to tell
Among us any more, they hide the ways,
Old tales less comprehensible than life
Whence nonetheless we know the things we do
And do the things they say the fathers did.

When I was young I flew past Skerryvore
Where the Nine Maidens still grind Hamlet's meal,
The salt and granite grain of bitter earth,
But knew it not for twenty years and more.
My chances past their changes now, I know

How a long life grows ghostly towards the close
As any man dissolves in Everyman
Of whom the story, as it always did, begins
In a far country, once upon a time,
There lived a certain man and he had three sons . . .

Ginkgoes in Fall

They are the oldest living captive race,
Primitive gymnosperms that in the wild
Are rarely found or never, temple trees
Brought down in line unbroken from the deep
Past where the Yellow Emperor lies tombed.

Their fallen yellow fruit mimics the scent
Of human vomit, the definite statement of
An attitude, and their translucency of leaf,
Filtering a urinary yellow light,
Remarks a delicate wasting of the world,

An innuendo to be clarified
In winter when they defecate their leaves
And bear the burden of their branches up
Alone and bare, dynastic diagrams
Of their distinguished genealogies.

AMY CLAMPITT

(1920 –)

A Procession at Candlemas

1

Moving on or going back to where you came from,
bad news is what you mainly travel with:
a breakup or a breakdown, someone running off

or walking out, called up or called home:
death in the family. Nudged from their stanchions
outside the terminal, anonymous of purpose

as a flock of birds, the bison of the highway
funnel westward onto Route 80, mirroring
an entity that cannot look into itself and know

what makes it what it is. Sooner or later
every trek becomes a funeral procession.
The mother curtained in Intensive Care —

a scene the mind leaves blank, fleeing instead
toward scenes of transhumance, the belled sheep
moving up the Pyrenees, red-tasseled pack llamas

footing velvet-green precipices, the Kurdish
women, jingling with bangles, gorgeous
on their rug-piled mounts — already lying dead,

bereavement altering the moving lights
to a processional, a feast of Candlemas.
Change as child-bearing, birth as a kind

of shucking off: out of what began
as a Mosaic insult — such a loathing
of the common origin, even a virgin,

having given birth, needs purifying —
to carry fire as though it were a flower,
the terror and the loveliness entrusted

into naked hands, supposing God might have,
might actually need a mother: people have
at times found this a way of being happy.

A Candlemas of moving lights along Route 80;
lighted candles in a corridor from Arlington
over the Potomac, for every carried flame

the name of a dead soldier: an element
fragile as ego, frightening as parturition,
necessary and intractable as dreaming.

The lapped, wheelborne integument, layer
within layer, at the core a dream of
something precious, ripped: Where are we?

The sleepers groan, stir, rewrap themselves
about the self's imponderable substance,
or clamber down, numb-footed, half in a drowse

of freezing dark, through a Stonehenge
of fuel pumps, the bison hulks slantwise
beside them, drinking. What is real except

what's fabricated? The jellies glitter
cream-capped in the cafeteria showcase:
gumball globes, Life Savers cinctured

in parcel gilt, plop from their housings
perfect, like miracles. Comb, nail clipper,
lip rouge, mirrors and emollients embody,

niched into the washroom wall case,
the pristine seductiveness of money.
Absently, without inhabitants, this

nowhere oasis wears the place name
of Indian Meadows. The westward-trekking
transhumance, once only, of a people who,

in losing everything they had, lost even
the names they went by, stumbling past
like caribou, perhaps camped here. Who

can assign a trade-in value to that sorrow?
The monk in sheepskin over tucked-up saffron
intoning to a drum becomes the metronome

of one more straggle up Pennsylvania Avenue
in falling snow, a whirl of tenderly
remorseless corpuscles, street gangs

amok among magnolias' pregnant wands,
a stillness at the heart of so much whirling:
beyond the torn integument of childbirth,

sometimes, wrapped like a papoose into a grief
not merely of the ego, you rediscover almost
the rest-in-peace of the placental coracle.

2

Of what the dead were, living, one knows
so little as barely to recognize
the fabric of the backward-ramifying

antecedents, half-noted presences
in darkened rooms: the old, the feared,
the hallowed. Never the same river

drowns the unalterable doorsill. An effigy
in olive wood or pear wood, dank
with the sweat of age, walled in the dark

at Brauron, Argos, Samos: even the unwed
Athene, who had no mother, born — it's declared —
of some man's brain like every other pure idea,

had her own wizened cult object, kept
out of sight like the incontinent whimperer
in the backstairs bedroom, where no child

ever goes — to whom, year after year,
the fair linen of the sacred peplos
was brought in ceremonial procession —

flutes and stringed instruments, wildflower-
hung cattle, nubile Athenian girls, young men
praised for the beauty of their bodies. Who

can unpeel the layers of that seasonal
returning to the dark where memory fails,
as birds re-enter the ancestral flyway?

Daylight, snow falling, knotting of gears:
Chicago. Soot, the rotting backsides
of tenements, grimed trollshapes of ice

underneath the bridges, the tunnel heaving
like a birth canal. Disgorged, the infant
howling in the restroom; steam-table cereal,

pale coffee; wall-eyed TV receivers, armchairs
of molded plastic: the squalor of the day
resumed, the orphaned litter taken up again

unloved, the spawn of botched intentions,
grief a mere hardening of the gut,
a set piece of what can't be avoided:

parents by the tens of thousands living
unthanked, unpaid but in the sour coin
of resentment. Midmorning gray as zinc

along Route 80, corn-stubble quilting
the underside of snowdrifts, the cadaverous
belvedere of windmills, the sullen stare

of feedlot cattle; black creeks puncturing
white terrain, the frozen bottomland
a mush of willow tops; dragnetted in ice,

the Mississippi. Westward toward the dark,
the undertow of scenes come back to, fright
riddling the structures of interior history:

Where is it? Where, in the shucked-off
bundle, the hampered obscurity that has been
for centuries the mumbling lot of women,

did the thread of fire, too frail
ever to discover what it meant, to risk
even the taking of a shape, relinquish

the seed of possibility, unguessed-at
as a dream of something precious? Memory,
that exquisite blunderer, stumbling

like a migrant bird that finds the flyway
it hardly knew it knew except by instinct,
down the long-unentered nave of childhood,

late on a midwinter afternoon, alone
among the snow-hung hollows of the windbreak
on the far side of the orchard, encounters

sheltering among the evergreens, a small
stilled bird, its cap of clear yellow
slit by a thread of scarlet — the untouched

nucleus of fire, the lost connection
hallowing the wizened effigy, the mother
curtained in Intensive Care: a Candlemas

of moving lights along Route 80, at nightfall,
in falling snow, the stillness and the sorrow
of things moving back to where they came from.

The Kingfisher

In a year the nightingales were said to be so loud
they drowned out slumber, and peafowl strolled screaming
beside the ruined nunnery, through the long evening
of a dazzled pub crawl, the halcyon color, portholed
by those eye-spots' stunning tapestry, unsettled
the pastoral nightfall with amazements opening.

Months later, intermission in a pub on Fifty-fifth Street
found one of them still breathless, the other quizzical,
acting the philistine, puncturing Stravinsky — "Tell
me, what *was* that racket in the orchestra about?" —
hauling down the Firebird, harum-scarum, like a kite,
a burnished, breathing wreck that didn't hurt at all.

Among the Bronx Zoo's exiled jungle fowl, they heard
through headphones of a separating panic the bellbird
reiterate its single *chong,* a scream nobody answered.
When he mourned, "The poetry is gone," she quailed,
seeing how his hands shook, sobered into feeling old.
By midnight, yet another fifth would have been killed.

A Sunday morning, the November of their cataclysm
(Dylan Thomas brought in *in extremis* to St. Vincent's
that same week, a symptomatic datum) found them

wandering a downtown churchyard. Among its headstones,
while from unruined choirs the noise of Christendom
poured over Wall Street, a benison in vestments,

a late thrush paused, in transit from some grizzled
spruce bog to the humid equatorial fireside: berry-
eyed, bark-brown above, with dark hints of trauma
in the stigmata of its underparts — or so, too bruised
just then to have invented anything so fancy,
later, reëmbroidering a retrospect, she had supposed.

In gray England, years of muted recrimination (then
dead silence) later, she could not have said how many
spoiled takeoffs, how many entanglements gone sodden,
how many gaudy evenings made frantic by just one
insomniac nightingale, how many liaisons gone down
screaming in a stroll beside the ruined nunnery;

a kingfisher's burnished plunge, the color
of felicity afire, came glancing like an arrow
through landscapes of untended memory: ardor
illuminating with its terrifying currency
now no mere glimpse, no porthole vista
but, down on down, the uninhabitable sorrow.

The Woodlot

Clumped murmuring above a sump of loam —
grass-rich, wood-poor — that first the plow,
then the inventor (his name plowed under
somewhere in the Patent Office) of barbed wire,
taught, if not fine manners, how at least to follow
the surveyor's rule, the woodlot nodes of willow,
evergreen or silver maple gave the prairie grid
what little personality it had.
                        Who could
have learned fine manners where the air,
that rude nomad, still domineered,
without a shape it chose to keep,
oblivious of section lines, in winter
whisking its wolfish spittle to a froth

that turned whole townships into
one white wallow? Barbed wire
kept in the cattle but would not abrade
the hide or draw the blood
of gales hurled gnashing like seawater over fences'
laddered apertures, rigging the landscape
with the perspective of a shipwreck. Land-chained,
the blizzard paused to caterwaul
at every windbreak, a rage the worse
because it was in no way personal.
                                    Against
the involuted tantrums of spring and summer—
sackfuls of ire, the frightful udder
of the dropped mammocumulus
become all mouth, a lamprey
swigging up whole farmsteads, suction
dislodging treetrunks like a rotten tooth—
luck and a cellarhole were all
a prairie dweller had to count on.
                                    Whether
the inventor of barbed wire was lucky
finally in what he found himself
remembering, who knows? Did he
ever, even once, envision
the spread of what he'd done
across a continent: whale-song's
taut dulcimer still thrumming as it strung together
orchard, barnyard, bullpen, feedlot,
windbreak: wire to be clambered over,
crawled through or slid under, shepherded—
the heifers staring—to an enclosure
whose ceiling's silver-maple tops
stir overhead, uneasy, in the interminably
murmuring air? Deep in it, under
appletrees like figures in a ritual, violets
are thick, a blue cellarhole
of pure astonishment.
                        It is
the earliest memory. Before it,
I/you, whatever that conundrum may yet
prove to be, amounts to nothing.

RICHARD WILBUR

(1921–)

The Beautiful Changes

One wading a Fall meadow finds on all sides
The Queen Anne's Lace lying like lilies
On water; it glides
So from the walker, it turns
Dry grass to a lake, as the slightest shade of you
Valleys my mind in fabulous blue Lucernes.

The beautiful changes as a forest is changed
By a chameleon's tuning his skin to it;
As a mantis, arranged
On a green leaf, grows
Into it, makes the leaf leafier, and proves
Any greenness is deeper than anyone knows.

Your hands hold roses always in a way that says
They are not only yours; the beautiful changes
In such kind ways,
Wishing ever to sunder
Things and things' selves for a second finding, to lose
For a moment all that it touches back to wonder.

To an American Poet Just Dead

In the *Boston Sunday Herald* just three lines
Of no-point type for you who used to sing
The praises of imaginary wines,
And died, or so I'm told, of the real thing.

Also gone, but a lot less forgotten,
Are an eminent cut-rate druggist, a lover of Giving,
A lender, and various brokers: gone from this rotten
Taxable world to a higher standard of living.

It is out in the comfy suburbs I read you are dead,
And the soupy summer is settling, full of the yawns
Of Sunday fathers loitering late in bed,
And the ssshh of sprays on all the little lawns.

Will the sprays weep wide for you their chaplet tears?
For you will the deep-freeze units melt and mourn?
For you will Studebakers shred their gears
And sound from each garage a muted horn?

They won't. In summer sunk and stupefied
The suburbs deepen in their sleep of death.
And though they sleep the sounder since you died
It's just as well that now you save your breath.

Mind

Mind in its purest play is like some bat
That beats about in caverns all alone,
Contriving by a kind of senseless wit
Not to conclude against a wall of stone.

It has no need to falter or explore;
Darkly it knows what obstacles are there,
And so may weave and flitter, dip and soar
In perfect courses through the blackest air.

And has this simile a like perfection?
The mind is like a bat. Precisely. Save
That in the very happiest intellection
A graceful error may correct the cave.

The Writer

In her room at the prow of the house
Where light breaks, and the windows are tossed with linden,
My daughter is writing a story.

I pause in the stairwell, hearing
From her shut door a commotion of typewriter-keys
Like a chain hauled over a gunwale.

Young as she is, the stuff
Of her life is a great cargo, and some of it heavy:
I wish her a lucky passage.

But now it is she who pauses,
As if to reject my thought and its easy figure.
A stillness greatens, in which

The whole house seems to be thinking,
And then she is at it again with a bunched clamor
Of strokes, and again is silent.

I remember the dazed starling
Which was trapped in that very room, two years ago;
How we stole in, lifted a sash

And retreated, not to affright it;
And how for a helpless hour, through the crack of the door,
We watched the sleek, wild, dark

And iridescent creature
Batter against the brilliance, drop like a glove
To the hard floor, or the desk-top,

And wait then, humped and bloody,
For the wits to try it again; and how our spirits
Rose when, suddenly sure,

It lifted off from a chair-back,
Beating a smooth course for the right window
And clearing the sill of the world.

It is always a matter, my darling,
Of life or death, as I had forgotten. I wish
What I wished you before, but harder.

Cottage Street, 1953

Framed in her phoenix fire-screen, Edna Ward
Bends to the tray of Canton, pouring tea
For frightened Mrs. Plath; then, turning toward
The pale, slumped daughter, and my wife, and me,

Asks if we would prefer it weak or strong.
Will we have milk or lemon, she enquires?
The visit seems already strained and long.
Each in his turn, we tell her our desires.

It is my office to exemplify
The published poet in his happiness,
Thus cheering Sylvia, who has wished to die;
But half-ashamed, and impotent to bless,

I am a stupid life-guard who has found,
Swept to his shallows by the tide, a girl
Who, far from shore, has been immensely drowned,
And stares through water now with eyes of pearl.

How large is her refusal; and how slight
The genteel chat whereby we recommend
Life, of a summer afternoon, despite
The brewing dusk which hints that it may end.

And Edna Ward shall die in fifteen years,
After her eight-and-eighty summers of
Such grace and courage as permit no tears,
The thin hand reaching out, the last word *love,*

Outliving Sylvia who, condemned to live,
Shall study for a decade, as she must,
To state at last her brilliant negative
In poems free and helpless and unjust.

April 5, 1974

The air was soft, the ground still cold.
In the dull pasture where I strolled
Was something I could not believe.
Dead grass appeared to slide and heave,
Though still too frozen-flat to stir,
And rocks to twitch, and all to blur.
What was this rippling of the land?
Was matter getting out of hand
And making free with natural law?
I stopped and blinked, and then I saw
A fact as eerie as a dream.
There was a subtle flood of steam
Moving upon the face of things.
It came from standing pools and springs
And what of snow was still around;
It came of winter's giving ground
So that the freeze was coming out,
As when a set mind, blessed by doubt,
Relaxes into mother-wit.
Flowers, I said, will come of it.

Lying

To claim, at a dead party, to have spotted a grackle,
When in fact you haven't of late, can do no harm.
Your reputation for saying things of interest
Will not be marred if you hasten to other topics,
Nor will the delicate web of human trust
Be ruptured by that airy fabrication.
Later, however, talking with toxic zest
Of golf, or taxes, or the rest of it
Where the beaked ladle plies the chuckling ice,
You may enjoy a chill of severance, hearing
Above your head the shrug of unreal wings.
Not that the world is tiresome in itself:
We know what boredom is — it is a dull
Impatience or a fierce velleity,

A champing wish, stalled by our lassitude,
To make or do. In the strict sense, of course,
We invent nothing, merely bearing witness
To what each morning brings again to light:
Gold crosses, cornices, astonishment
Of panes, the turbine vent which natural law
Spins on the grill end of the diner's roof,
Then grass and grackles or, at the end of town
In sheen-swept pastureland, the horse's neck
Clothed with its usual thunder, and the stones
Beginning now to tug their shadows in
And track the air with glitter. All these things
Are there before us; there before we look
Or fail to look; there to be seen or not
By us, as by the bee's twelve thousand eyes,
According to our means and purposes.
So, too, with strangeness not to be ignored —
Total eclipse or snow upon the rose —
And so with that most rare conception, nothing.
What is it, after all, but something missed?
It is the water of a dried-up well
Gone to assail the cliffs of Labrador.
There is what galled the arch-negator, sprung
From Hell to probe with intellectual sight
The cells and heavens of a given world
Which he could take but as another prison.
Small wonder that, pretending not to be,
He drifted through the barlike boles of Eden
In a "black mist low creeping," dragging down
And darkening with moody self-absorption
What, when he left it, lifted and, if seen
From the sun's vantage, seethed with vaulting hues.
Closer to making than the deftest fraud
Is seeing how the catbird's tail was made
To counterpoise, on the mock-orange spray,
Its light, up-tilted spine; or, lighter still,
How the shucked tunic of an onion, brushed
To one side on a backlit chopping board
And rocked by trifling currents, prints and prints
Its bright, ribbed shadow like a flapping sail.

Odd that a thing is most itself when likened:
The eye mists over, basil hints of clove,
The river glazes toward the dam and spills
To the drubbed rocks below its crashing cullet,
And in the barnyard near the sawdust pile
Some great thing is tormented. Either it is
A tarp torn loose and in the groaning wind
Now puffed, now flattened, or a hip-shot beast
Which tries again, and once again, to rise.
What, though for pain there is no other word,
Finds pleasure in the cruellest simile?
It is something in us like the catbird's song
From neighbor bushes in the gray of morning
That, harsh or sweet, and of its own accord,
Proclaims its many kin. It is a chant
Of the first springs, and it is tributary
To the great lies told with the eyes half-shut
That have the truth in view: the tale of Chiron,
Who with sage head, wild heart, and planted hoof
Instructed brute Achilles in the lyre,
Or of the garden where we first mislaid
Simplicity of wish and will, forgetting
Out of what cognate splendor all things came
To take their scattering names; and nonetheless
That matter of a baggage train surprised
By a few Gascons in the Pyrenees —
Which, having worked three centuries and more
In the dark caves of France, poured out at last
The blood of Roland, who to Charles his king
And to the dove that hatched the dovetailed world
Was faithful unto death, and shamed the Devil.

JAMES DICKEY
(1923 –)

The Hospital Window

I have just come down from my father.
Higher and higher he lies
Above me in a blùe light
Shed by a tinted window.
I drop through six white floors
And then step out onto pavement.

Still feeling my father ascend,
I start to cross the firm street,
My shoulder blades shining with all
The glass the huge building can raise.
Now I must turn round and face it,
And know his one pane from the others.

Each window possesses the sun
As though it burned there on a wick.
I wave, like a man catching fire.
All the deep-dyed windowpanes flash,
And, behind them, all the white rooms
They turn to the color of Heaven.

Ceremoniously, gravely, and weakly,
Dozens of pale hands are waving
Back, from inside their flames.
Yet one pure pane among these
Is the bright, erased blankness of nothing.
I know that my father is there,

In the shape of his death still living.
The traffic increases around me
Like a madness called down on my head.
The horns blast at me like shotguns,
And drivers lean out, driven crazy—
But now my propped-up father

Lifts his arm out of stillness at last.
The light from the window strikes me
And I turn as blue as a soul,
As the moment when I was born.
I am not afraid for my father —
Look! He is grinning; he is not

Afraid for my life, either,
As the wild engines stand at my knees
Shredding their gears and roaring,
And I hold each car in its place
For miles, inciting its horn
To blow down the walls of the world

That the dying may float without fear
In the bold blue gaze of my father.
Slowly I move to the sidewalk
With my pin-tingling hand half dead
At the end of my bloodless arm.
I carry it off in amazement,

High, still higher, still waving,
My recognized face fully mortal,
Yet not; not at all, in the pale,
Drained, otherworldly, stricken,
Created hue of stained glass.
I have just come down from my father.

Cherrylog Road

Off Highway 106
At Cherrylog Road I entered
The '34 Ford without wheels,
Smothered in kudzu,
With a seat pulled out to run
Corn whiskey down from the hills,

And then from the other side
Crept into an Essex
With a rumble seat of red leather

And then out again, aboard
A blue Chevrolet, releasing
The rust from its other color,

Reared up on three building blocks.
None had the same body heat;
I changed with them inward, toward
The weedy heart of the junkyard,
For I knew that Doris Holbrook
Would escape from her father at noon

And would come from the farm
To seek parts owned by the sun
Among the abandoned chassis,
Sitting in each in turn
As I did, leaning forward
As in a wild stock-car race

In the parking lot of the dead.
Time after time, I climbed in
And out the other side, like
An envoy or movie star
Met at the station by crickets.
A radiator cap raised its head,

Become a real toad or a kingsnake
As I neared the hub of the yard,
Passing through many states,
Many lives, to reach
Some grandmother's long Pierce-Arrow
Sending platters of blindness forth

From its nickel hubcaps
And spilling its tender upholstery
On sleepy roaches,
The glass panel in between
Lady and colored driver
Not all the way broken out,

The back-seat phone
Still on its hook.
I got in as though to exclaim,
"Let us go to the orphan asylum,
John; I have some old toys
For children who say their prayers."

I popped with sweat as I thought
I heard Doris Holbrook scrape
Like a mouse in the southern-state sun
That was eating the paint in blisters
From a hundred car tops and hoods.
She was tapping like code,

Loosening the screws,
Carrying off headlights,
Sparkplugs, bumpers,
Cracked mirrors and gear-knobs,
Getting ready, already,
To go back with something to show

Other than her lips' new trembling
I would hold to me soon, soon,
Where I sat in the ripped back seat
Talking over the interphone,
Praying for Doris Holbrook
To come from her father's farm

And to get back there
With no trace of me on her face
To be seen by her red-haired father
Who would change, in the squalling barn,
Her back's pale skin with a strop,
Then lay for me

In a bootlegger's roasting car
With a string-triggered 12-gauge shotgun
To blast the breath from the air.
Not cut by the jagged windshields,
Through the acres of wrecks she came
With a wrench in her hand,

Through dust where the blacksnake dies
Of boredom, and the beetle knows
The compost has no more life.
Someone outside would have seen
The oldest car's door inexplicably
Close from within:

I held her and held her and held her,
Convoyed at terrific speed
By the stalled, dreaming traffic around us,

So the blacksnake, stiff
With inaction, curved back
Into life, and hunted the mouse

With deadly overexcitement,
The beetles reclaimed their field
As we clung, glued together,
With the hooks of the seat springs
Working through to catch us red-handed
Amidst the gray breathless batting

That burst from the seat at our backs.
We left by separate doors
Into the changed, other bodies
Of cars, she down Cherrylog Road
And I to my motorcycle
Parked like the soul of the junkyard

Restored, a bicycle fleshed
With power, and tore off
Up Highway 106, continually
Drunk on the wind in my mouth,
Wringing the handlebar for speed,
Wild to be wreckage forever.

The Sheep Child

Farm boys wild to couple
With anything   with soft-wooded trees
With mounds of earth   mounds
Of pinestraw   will keep themselves off
Animals by legends of their own:
In the hay-tunnel dark
And dung of barns, they will
Say   I have heard tell

That in a museum in Atlanta
Way back in a corner somewhere
There's this thing that's only half
Sheep   like a woolly baby

Pickled in alcohol   because
Those things can't live   his eyes
Are open   but you can't stand to look
I heard from somebody who . . .

But this is now almost all
Gone. The boys have taken
Their own true wives in the city,
The sheep are safe in the west hill
Pasture   but we who were born there
Still are not sure. Are we,
Because we remember, remembered
In the terrible dust of museums?

Merely with his eyes, the sheep child may

Be saying   saying

> *I am here, in my father's house.*
> *I who am half of your world, came deeply*
> *To my mother in the long grass*
> *Of the west pasture, where she stood like moonlight*
> *Listening for foxes. It was something like love*
> *From another world that seized her*
> *From behind, and she gave, not lifting her head*
> *Out of dew, without ever looking, her best*
> *Self to that great need. Turned loose, she dipped her face*
> *Farther into the chill of the earth, and in a sound*
> *Of sobbing   of something stumbling*
> *Away, began, as she must do,*
> *To carry me. I woke, dying,*
>
> *In the summer sun of the hillside, with my eyes*
> *Far more than human. I saw for a blazing moment*
> *The great grassy world from both sides,*
> *Man and beast in the round of their need,*
> *And the hill wind stirred in my wool,*
> *My hoof and my hand clasped each other,*
> *I ate my one meal*
> *Of milk, and died*
> *Staring. From dark grass I came straight*
>
> *To my father's house, whose dust*
> *Whirls up in the halls for no reason*

When no one comes   piling deep in a hellish mild corner,
And, through my immortal waters,
I meet the sun's grains eye
To eye, and they fail at my closet of glass.
Dead, I am most surely living
In the minds of farm boys: I am he who drives
Them like wolves from the hound bitch and calf
And from the chaste ewe in the wind.
They go into woods   into bean fields   they go
Deep into their known right hands. Dreaming of me,
They groan   they wait . they suffer
Themselves, they marry, they raise their kind.

A. R. AMMONS
(1926 –)

Hardweed Path Going

       Every evening, down into the hardweed
going,
the slop bucket heavy, held-out, wire handle
freezing in the hand, put it down a minute, the jerky
smooth unspilling levelness of the knees,
       meditation of a bucket rim,
lest the wheat meal,
floating on clear greasewater, spill,
down the grown-up path:

       don't forget to slop the hogs,
       feed the chickens,
       water the mule,
       cut the kindling,
       build the fire,
       call up the cow:

       supper is over, it's starting to get
dark early,
better get the scraps together, mix a little meal in,
nothing but swill.

       The dead-purple woods hover on the west.
I know those woods.
Under the tall, ceiling-solid pines, beyond the edge of
field and brush, where the wild myrtle grows,
       I let my jo-reet loose.
A jo-reet is a bird. Nine weeks of summer he
sat on the well bench in a screened box,
a stick inside to walk on,
       "jo-reet," he said, "jo-reet."
       and I
would come up to the well and draw the bucket down

deep into the cold place where red and white marbled
clay oozed the purest water, water celebrated
throughout the county:
   "Grits all gone?"
   "jo-reet."
Throw a dipper of cold water on him. Reddish-black
flutter.
   "reet, reet, reet!"

   Better turn him loose before
cold weather comes on.
   Doom caving in
   inside
   any pleasure, pure
   attachment
   of love.

Beyond the wild myrtle away from cats I turned him loose
and his eye asked me what to do, where to go;
he hopped around, scratched a little, but looked up at me.
Don't look at me. Winter is coming.
Disappear in the bushes. I'm tired of you and will
be alone hereafter. I will go dry in my well.
   I will turn still.
Go south. Grits is not available in any natural form.
Look under leaves, try mushy logs, the floors of pinywoods.
South into the dominion of bugs.

   They're good woods.
But lay me out if a mourning dove far off in the dusky pines
   starts.

   Down the hardweed path going,
leaning, balancing, away from the bucket, to
Sparkle, my favorite hog, sparse, fine black hair,
grunted while feeding if rubbed,
scratched against the hair, or if talked to gently:
got the bottom of the slop bucket:
   "Sparkle . . .
   You hungry?
   Hungry, girly?"
blowing, bubbling in the trough.

Waiting for the first freeze:
"Think it's going to freeze tonight?" say the neighbors,
the neighbors, going by.

Hog-killing.

Oh, Sparkle, when the axe tomorrow morning falls
and the rush is made to open your throat,
I will sing, watching dry-eyed as a man, sing my
love for you in the tender feedings.

She's nothing but a hog, boy.

Bleed out, Sparkle, the moon-chilled bleaches
of your body hanging upside-down
hardening through the mind and night of the first freeze.

Reflective

I found a
weed
that had a

mirror in it
and that
mirror

looked in at
a mirror
in

me that
had a
weed in it

Apologia pro Vita Sua

I started picking up the stones
throwing them into one place
and by sunrise I was going far away

for the large ones
always turning to see never lost
the cairn's height
lengthening my radial reach:

the sun watched with deep concentration
and the heap through the hours grew
and became by nightfall
distinguishable from all the miles around
of slate and sand:

during the night the wind falling
turned earthward its lofty freedom and speed
and the sharp blistering sound muffled
toward dawn and the blanket was
drawn up over a breathless face:

even so you can see in full dawn
the ground there lifts
a foreign thing desertless in origin.

Mountain Talk

I was going along a dusty highroad
when the mountain
across the way
turned me to its silence:
oh I said how come
I don't know your
massive symmetry and rest:
nevertheless, said the mountain,
would you want
to be
lodged here with
a changeless prospect, risen
to an unalterable view:
so I went on
counting my numberless fingers.

Clarity

After the event the rockslide
realized,
in a still diversity of completion,
grain and fissure,
declivity
&
force of upheaval,
whether rain slippage,
ice crawl, root
explosion or
stream erosive undercut:

well I said it is a pity:
one swath of sight will never
be the same: nonetheless,
this
shambles has
relieved a bind, a taut of twist,
revealing streaks &
scores of knowledge
now obvious and quiet.

Hope's Okay

The undergrowth's a conveyance of butterflies
(flusters of clustering) so buoyant and delightful,
filling into a floating impression, diversity's
diversion breaking out into under-piny seas
point by point to the mind's nodes and needs:

let's see, though, said the fire through the undergrowth,
what all this makes into, what difference can
survive it: so I waded through the puffy disgust
and could not help feeling despair of
many a gray, smoke-worming twig, scaly as if alive:

much that was here I said is lost and if I stoop
to ask bright thoughts of roots

do not think I ask for better than was here
or that hope with me rises one leaf higher than
the former growth (higher to an ashless fire) or
that despair came any closer than ash to being total.

Transaction

I attended the burial of all my rosy feelings:
I performed the rites, simple and decisive:
the long box took the spilling of gray ground in
with little evidence of note: I traded slow

work for the usual grief: the services were private:
there was little cause for show, though no cause not
to show: it went indifferently, with an appropriate
gravity and lack of noise: the ceremonies of the self

seem always to occur at a distance from the ruins of men
where there is nothing really much to expect, no arms,
no embraces: the day was all right: certain occasions
outweigh the weather: the woods just to the left

were average woods: well, I turned around finally from
the process, the surface smoothed into a kind of seal,
and tried to notice what might be thought to remain:
everything was there, the sun, the breeze, the woods

(as I said), the little mound of troublesome tufts of
grass: but the trees were upright shadows, the breeze
was as against a shade, the woods stirred gray
as deep water: I looked around for what was left,

the tools, and took them up and went away, leaving
all my treasures where they might never again disturb
me, increase or craze: decision quietens:
shadows are bodiless shapes, yet they have a song.

Treaties

My great wars close:
ahead, papers,
signatures, the glimmering
in shade of
leaf and raised wine:
orchards, orchards,
vineyards, fields:
spiralling slow time while
the medlar
smarts and glows and
empty nests
come out in the open:
fall rain then stirs
the black creek and
the small leaf slips in.

The City Limits

When you consider the radiance, that it does not withhold
itself but pours its abundance without selection into every
nook and cranny not overhung or hidden; when you consider

that birds' bones make no awful noise against the light but
lie low in the light as in a high testimony; when you consider
the radiance, that it will look into the guiltiest

swervings of the weaving heart and bear itself upon them,
not flinching into disguise or darkening; when you consider
the abundance of such resource as illuminates the glow-blue

bodies and gold-skeined wings of flies swarming the dumped
guts of a natural slaughter or the coil of shit and in no
way winces from its storms of generosity; when you consider

that air or vacuum, snow or shale, squid or wolf, rose or lichen,
each is accepted into as much light as it will take, then
the heart moves roomier, the man stands and looks about, the

leaf does not increase itself above the grass, and the dark
work of the deepest cells is of a tune with May bushes
and fear lit by the breadth of such calmly turns to praise.

The Eternal City

After the explosion or cataclysm, that big
display that does its work but then fails
out with destructions, one is left with the

pieces: at first, they don't look very valuable,
but nothing sizable remnant around for
gathering the senses on, one begins to take

an interest, to sort out, to consider closely
what will do and won't, matters having become
not only small but critical: bulbs may have been

uprooted: they should be eaten, if edible, or
got back in the ground: what used to be garages,
even the splinters, should be collected for

fires: some unusually deep holes or cleared
woods may be turned to water supplies or
sudden fields: ruinage is hardly ever a

pretty sight but it must when splendor goes
accept into itself piece by piece all the old
perfect human visions, all the old perfect loves.

Grace Abounding
for E. C.

What is the misery in one that turns one with gladness
to the hedge strung lucid with ice: is it that one's
misery, penetrating there as sight, meets neither

welcome nor reprimand but finds nevertheless a picture
of itself sympathetic, held as the ice-blurred stems
increased: ah, what an abundance is in the universe

when one can go for gladness to the indifferent ghastly,
feel alliances where none may ever take: find one's
misery made clear, borne, as if also, by a hedge of ice.

from *Sphere*

I don't know about you,
but I'm sick of good poems, all those little rondures
splendidly brought off, painted gourds on a shelf: give me

the dumb, debilitated, nasty, and massive, if that's the
alternative: touch the universe anywhere you touch it
everywhere: man's a scourge not because he is man but because

139

he's not man enough: how public like a smog publicity is:
in spite of the spectacularity of the universe (even in the
visual reception) it appears to those who have gone above our

atmosphere that the universe is truly a great darkness, light
in the minority, unsurrendered coals sprinkled in the thinnest
scattering, though, of course, light, even when seen from

afar, attracts the attention most: but out on the periphery
the lights are traveling so fast away their light can't get
back to us, darkness, in our dimension, finally victorious

in the separation: I have dreamed of a stroll-through, the
stars in a close-woven, showering bedazzlement, though
diamond- or ruby-cool, in which I contemplated the universe

140

at length: apparently, now, such dreams, foolish anyway,
must be abandoned and the long, empty, freezing gulfs of
darkness must take their place: come to think of it, though,

I'm not unfamiliar with such gulfs, even from childhood, when
the younger brother sickened and then moved no more: and
ahead lies a gulf light even from slow stars can never penetrate,

a dimension so endless not even the universal scale suits it:
the wise advise, don't get beyond yourself into foolish largeness,
when at my step is a largeness the universe lies within:

to be small and assembled! how comforting: but how perishable!
our life the tiny star and the rest, the rest: this extreme
flotation (it and us) this old, inconstant earth daily born

141

new into thousands of newborn eyes — proceeding by a life's
length here and there, an overlapping mesh of links proceeding:
but, for me, turning aside into rust, reality splintering the

seams, currents going glacial and glassy with knowledge, the
feared worst become the worst: meanwhile, once again the world
comes young, the mother follows her toddler around the cafeteria

and can't see him her eyes so keeping in touch with the admiring
eyes of others: (the old mother, thin-white, thicked-jawed, feels
her way, but barefooted, out to the mailbox: nothing: all

the fucking finished, all the sweet, terrifying children grown
up and blown away, just the geraniums in the tire watered
every day, fussed at, plucked:) let me tell you how I get up

142

in the morning: I get up, take a step or two, and morning jars
and pauses me, and I look down into the bottom of my grave:
shaken, I move, though, as if through iron, on when my life,

my real life, wakes up in a tantrum and shakes me like last
year's beanstakes: I lean against the doorjamb until my life
gags into despair, and then I proceed: I proceed, how, into

what: I say, if I can get through this hour, I won't come to
another one but to life: with a front left, I erect a smile
on it, and right away everybody starts laying his troubles on me:

I say in myself, don't lay any more trouble on me: when here
comes another youth anxious for fame and sorry he doesn't
have it: what can I do, he says: well, I say, why not try

143

whatever you can: by the time you amount to something,
the people you meant it to mean something to are dead and you
are left standing there, your honors in your hands: the

ribbons wilted: the cheese melted: the sausage running:
there at the end (which may be anywhere) after dullish
afternoons and vacant mornings, after settlement from the

disturbance of sex, when you were coward, clown, fool, and
sometimes lord, there saved for the end, a novelty, death,
infinite and nonrepeating, an experience to enter with

both eyes wide open, the long play that ends without boredom:
its unexpectedness such you don't have the materials for
a rehearsal, more surprising than with girls where one

144

approach run through can profit a later one: you go in,
your mouth stretches so wide it turns you inside out,
a shed skin, and you gulp nothingness, your biggest bite,

your greatest appetite, stuffed with vacancy: who knows
whether in the middle years, after the flashing passions
seem less like fountains and more like pools of spent flood

metal, one may not keep on partly because of that black sucker
at the end, mysterious and shiny: my skull, my own skull
(and yours) is to be enclosed — earpits, eye sockets, dangled-open

mouth — with soil, is to lie alone without comfort through
centuries and centuries, face (if any) up, as if anticipating
the return of the dream that will be only the arrival of

145

the nova:

·   ·   ·   ·   ·

Bonus

The hemlocks slumped
already as if bewailing
the branch-loading

shales of ice, the rain
changes and a snow
sifty as fog

begins to fall, brightening
the ice's bruise-glimmer
with white holdings:

the hemlocks, muffled,
deepen to the grim
taking of a further beauty on.

Easter Morning

I have a life that did not become,
that turned aside and stopped,
astonished:
I hold it in me like a pregnancy or
as on my lap a child
not to grow or grow old but dwell on

it is to his grave I most
frequently return and return
to ask what is wrong, what was
wrong, to see it all by
the light of a different necessity
but the grave will not heal
and the child,
stirring, must share my grave
with me, an old man having
gotten by on what was left

when I go back to my home country in these
fresh far-away days, it's convenient to visit
everybody, aunts and uncles, those who used to say,
look how he's shooting up, and the
trinket aunts who always had a little
something in their pocketbooks, cinnamon bark
or a penny or nickel, and uncles who
were the rumored fathers of cousins
who whispered of them as of great, if
troubled, presences, and school
teachers, just about everybody older
(and some younger) collected in one place

waiting, particularly, but not for
me, mother and father there, too, and others
close, close as burrowing
under skin, all in the graveyard
assembled, done for, the world they
used to wield, have trouble and joy
in, gone

the child in me that could not become
was not ready for others to go,
to go on into change, blessings and
horrors, but stands there by the road
where the mishap occurred, crying out for
help, come and fix this or we
can't get by, but the great ones who
were to return, they could not or did
not hear and went on in a flurry and
now, I say in the graveyard, here
lies the flurry, now it can't come
back with help or helpful asides, now
we all buy the bitter
incompletions, pick up the knots of
horror, silently raving, and go on
crashing into empty ends not
completions, not rondures the fullness
has come into and spent itself from

I stand on the stump
of a child, whether myself
or my little brother who died, and
yell as far as I can, I cannot leave this place, for
for me it is the dearest and the worst,
it is life nearest to life which is
life lost: it is my place where
I must stand and fail,
calling attention with tears
to the branches not lofting
boughs into space, to the barren
air that holds the world that was my world

though the incompletions
(& completions) burn out
standing in the flash high-burn

momentary structure of ash, still it
is a picture-book, letter-perfect
Easter morning: I have been for a
walk: the wind is tranquil: the brook
works without flashing in an abundant
tranquility: the birds are lively with
voice: I saw something I had
never seen before: two great birds,
maybe eagles, blackwinged, whitenecked
and -headed, came from the south oaring
the great wings steadily; they went
directly over me, high up, and kept on
due north: but then one bird,
the one behind, veered a little to the
left and the other bird kept on seeming
not to notice for a minute: the first
began to circle as if looking for
something, coasting, resting its wings
on the down side of some of the circles:
the other bird came back and they both
circled, looking perhaps for a draft;
they turned a few more times, possibly
rising — at least, clearly resting —
then flew on falling into distance till
they broke across the local bush and
trees: it was a sight of bountiful
majesty and integrity: the having
patterns and routes, breaking
from them to explore other patterns or
better ways to routes, and then the
return: a dance sacred as the sap in
the trees, permanent in its descriptions
as the ripples round the brook's
ripplestone: fresh as this particular
flood of burn breaking across us now
from the sun.

ALLEN GINSBERG
(1926 –)

.

A Supermarket in California

What thoughts I have of you tonight, Walt Whitman, for I walked down the sidestreets under the trees with a headache self-conscious looking at the full moon.

In my hungry fatigue, and shopping for images, I went into the neon fruit supermarket, dreaming of your enumerations!

What peaches and what penumbras! Whole families shopping at night! Aisles full of husbands! Wives in the avocados, babies in the tomatoes! — and you, García Lorca, what were you doing down by the watermelons?

I saw you, Walt Whitman, childless, lonely old grubber, poking among the meats in the refrigerator and eyeing the grocery boys.

I heard you asking questions of each: Who killed the pork chops? What price bananas? Are you my Angel?

I wandered in and out of the brilliant stacks of cans following you, and followed in my imagination by the store detective.

We strode down the open corridors together in our solitary fancy tasting artichokes, possessing every frozen delicacy, and never passing the cashier.

Where are we going, Walt Whitman? The doors close in an hour. Which way does your beard point tonight?

(I touch your book and dream of our odyssey in the supermarket and feel absurd.)

Will we walk all night through solitary streets? The trees add shade to shade, lights out in the houses, we'll both be lonely.

Will we stroll dreaming of the lost America of love past blue automobiles in driveways, home to our silent cottage?

Ah, dear father, graybeard, lonely old courage-teacher, what America did you have when Charon quit poling his ferry and you got out on a smoking bank and stood watching the boat disappear on the black waters of Lethe?

Sunflower Sutra

I walked on the banks of the tincan banana dock and sat down
    under the huge shade of a Southern Pacific locomotive to
    look at the sunset over the box house hills and cry.
Jack Kerouac sat beside me on a busted rusty iron pole, compan-
    ion, we thought the same thoughts of the soul, bleak and
    blue and sad-eyed, surrounded by the gnarled steel roots
    of trees of machinery.
The oily water on the river mirrored the red sky, sun sank on top
    of final Frisco peaks, no fish in that stream, no hermit in
    those mounts, just ourselves rheumy-eyed and hung-over
    like old bums on the riverbank, tired and wily.
Look at the Sunflower, he said, there was a dead gray shadow
    against the sky, big as a man, sitting dry on top of a pile of
    ancient sawdust—
—I rushed up enchanted—it was my first sunflower, memories
    of Blake—my visions—Harlem
and Hells of the Eastern rivers, bridges clanking Joes Greasy
    Sandwiches, dead baby carriages, black treadless tires for-
    gotten and unretreaded, the poem of the riverbank, con-
    doms & pots, steel knives, nothing stainless, only the
    dank muck and the razor-sharp artifacts passing into the
    past—
and the gray Sunflower poised against the sunset, crackly bleak
    and dusty with the smut and smog and smoke of olden
    locomotives in its eye—
corolla of bleary spikes pushed down and broken like a battered
    crown, seeds fallen out of its face, soon-to-be-toothless
    mouth of sunny air, sunrays obliterated on its hairy head
    like a dried wire spiderweb,
leaves stuck out like arms out of the stem, gestures from the
    sawdust root, broke pieces of plaster fallen out of the black
    twigs, a dead fly in its ear,

Unholy battered old thing you were, my sunflower O my soul, I
    loved you then!

The grime was no man's grime but death and human locomo-
    tives,

all that dress of dust, that veil of darkened railroad skin, that
    smog of cheek, that eyelid of black mis'ry, that sooty hand
    or phallus or protuberance of artificial worse-than-dirt
    —industrial—modern—all that civilization spotting
    your crazy golden crown—

and those blear thoughts of death and dusty loveless eyes and
    ends and withered roots below, in the home-pile of sand
    and sawdust, rubber dollar bills, skin of machinery, the
    guts and innards of the weeping coughing car, the empty
    lonely tincans with their rusty tongues alack, what more
    could I name, the smoked ashes of some cock cigar, the
    cunts of wheelbarrows and the milky breasts of cars,
    wornout asses out of chairs & sphincters of dynamos—
    all these

entangled in your mummied roots—and you there standing
    before me in the sunset, all your glory in your form!

A perfect beauty of a sunflower! a perfect excellent lovely sun-
    flower existence! a sweet natural eye to the new hip moon,
    woke up alive and excited grasping in the sunset shadow
    sunrise golden monthly breeze!

How many flies buzzed round you innocent of your grime, while
    you cursed the heavens of the railroad and your flower
    soul?

Poor dead flower? when did you forget you were a flower? when
    did you look at your skin and decide you were an impotent
    dirty old locomotive? the ghost of a locomotive? the
    specter and shade of a once powerful mad American loco-
    motive?

You were never no locomotive, Sunflower, you were a sunflower!

And you Locomotive, you are a locomotive, forget me not!

So I grabbed up the skeleton thick sunflower and stuck it at my
    side like a scepter,

and deliver my sermon to my soul, and Jack's soul too, and
    anyone who'll listen,

—We're not our skin of grime, we're not our dread bleak dusty
    imageless locomotive, we're all golden sunflowers inside,

blessed by our own seed & hairy naked accomplishment-
bodies growing into mad black formal sunflowers in the
sunset, spied on by our eyes under the shadow of the mad
locomotive riverbank sunset Frisco hilly tincan evening
sitdown vision.

America

America I've given you all and now I'm nothing.
America two dollars and twentyseven cents January 17, 1956.
I can't stand my own mind.
America when will we end the human war?
Go fuck yourself with your atom bomb.
I don't feel good don't bother me.
I won't write my poem till I'm in my right mind.
America when will you be angelic?
When will you take off your clothes?
When will you look at yourself through the grave?
When will you be worthy of your million Trotskyites?
America why are your libraries full of tears?
America when will you send your eggs to India?
I'm sick of your insane demands.
When can I go into the supermarket and buy what I need with my
    good looks?
America after all it is you and I who are perfect not the next
    world.
Your machinery is too much for me.
You made me want to be a saint.
There must be some other way to settle this argument.
Burroughs is in Tangiers I don't think he'll come back it's sinister.
Are you being sinister or is this some form of practical joke?
I'm trying to come to the point.
I refuse to give up my obsession.
America stop pushing I know what I'm doing.
America the plum blossoms are falling.
I haven't read the newspapers for months, everyday somebody
    goes on trial for murder.
America I feel sentimental about the Wobblies.
America I used to be a communist when I was a kid I'm not sorry.

I smoke marijuana every chance I get.

I sit in my house for days on end and stare at the roses in the closet.

When I go to Chinatown I get drunk and never get laid.

My mind is made up there's going to be trouble.

You should have seen me reading Marx.

My psychoanalyst thinks I'm perfectly right.

I won't say the Lord's Prayer.

I have mystical visions and cosmic vibrations.

America I still haven't told you what you did to Uncle Max after he came over from Russia.

I'm addressing you.

Are you going to let your emotional life be run by Time Magazine?

I'm obsessed by Time Magazine.

I read it every week.

Its cover stares at me every time I slink past the corner candystore.

I read it in the basement of the Berkeley Public Library.

It's always telling me about responsibility. Businessmen are serious. Movie producers are serious. Everybody's serious but me.

It occurs to me that I am America.

I am talking to myself again.

Asia is rising against me.

I haven't got a chinaman's chance.

I'd better consider my national resources.

My national resources consist of two joints of marijuana millions of genitals an unpublishable private literature that jetplanes 1400 miles an hour and twentyfive-thousand mental institutions.

I say nothing about my prisons nor the millions of underprivileged who live in my flowerpots under the light of five hundred suns.

I have abolished the whorehouses of France, Tangiers is the next to go.

My ambition is to be President despite the fact that I'm a Catholic.

America how can I write a holy litany in your silly mood?

I will continue like Henry Ford my strophes are as individual as his automobiles more so they're all different sexes.

America I will sell you strophes $2500 apiece $500 down on your
old strophe
America free Tom Mooney
America save the Spanish Loyalists
America Sacco & Vanzetti must not die
America I am the Scottsboro boys.
America when I was seven momma took me to Communist Cell
meetings they sold us garbanzos a handful per ticket a
ticket costs a nickel and the speeches were free everybody
was angelic and sentimental about the workers it was all
so sincere you have no idea what a good thing the party
was in 1835 Scott Nearing was a grand old man a real
mensch Mother Bloor the Silk-strikers' Ewig-Weibliche
made me cry I once saw the Yiddish orator Israel Amter
plain. Everybody must have been a spy.
America you don't really want to go to war.
America it's them bad Russians.
Them Russians them Russians and them Chinamen. And them
Russians.
The Russia wants to eat us alive. The Russia's power mad. She
wants to take our cars from out our garages.
Her wants to grab Chicago. Her needs a Red *Reader's Digest.* Her
wants our auto plants in Siberia. Him big bureaucracy
running our fillingstations.
That no good. Ugh. Him make Indians learn read. Him need big
black niggers. Hah. Her make us all work sixteen hours a
day. Help.
America this is quite serious.
America this is the impression I get from looking in the televi-
sion set.
America is this correct?
I'd better get right down to the job.
It's true I don't want to join the Army or turn lathes in precision
parts factories, I'm nearsighted and psychopathic anyway.
America I'm putting my queer shoulder to the wheel.

Kaddish
For Naomi Ginsberg, 1894 – 1956

I

Strange now to think of you, gone without corsets & eyes, while
    I walk on the sunny pavement of Greenwich Village.
downtown Manhattan, clear winter noon, and I've been up all
    night, talking, talking, reading the Kaddish aloud, listen-
    ing to Ray Charles blues shout blind on the phonograph
the rhythm the rhythm — and your memory in my head three
    years after — And read Adonais' last triumphant stanzas
    aloud — wept, realizing how we suffer —
And how Death is that remedy all singers dream of, sing,
    remember, prophesy as in the Hebrew Anthem, or the
    Buddhist Book of Answers — and my own imagination
    of a withered leaf — at dawn —
Dreaming back thru life, Your time — and mine accelerating
    toward Apocalypse,
the final moment — the flower burning in the Day — and what
    comes after,
looking back on the mind itself that saw an American city
a flash away, and the great dream of Me or China, or you and a
    phantom Russia, or a crumpled bed that never existed —
like a poem in the dark — escaped back to Oblivion —
No more to say, and nothing to weep for but the Beings in the
    Dream, trapped in its disappearance,
sighing, screaming with it, buying and selling pieces of phantom,
    worshipping each other,
worshipping the God included in it all — longing or inevita-
    bility? — while it lasts, a Vision — anything more?
It leaps about me, as I go out and walk the street, look back over
    my shoulder, Seventh Avenue, the battlements of window
    office buildings shouldering each other high, under a
    cloud, tall as the sky an instant — and the sky above — an
    old blue place.
or down the Avenue to the South, to — as I walk toward the
    Lower East Side — where you walked 50 years ago, little
    girl — from Russia, eating the first poisonous tomatoes
    of America — frightened on the dock —

then struggling in the crowds of Orchard Street toward what? —
toward Newark —

toward candy store, first home-made sodas of the century, hand-
churned ice cream in backroom on musty brownfloor
boards —

Toward education marriage nervous breakdown, operation,
teaching school, and learning to be mad, in a dream —
what is this life?

Toward the Key in the window — and the great Key lays its head
of light on top of Manhattan, and over the floor, and lays
down on the sidewalk — in a single vast beam, moving, as
I walk down First toward the Yiddish Theater — and the
place of poverty

you knew, and I know, but without caring now — Strange to
have moved thru Paterson, and the West, and Europe and
here again,

with the cries of Spaniards now in the doorstoops doors and dark
boys on the street, fire escapes old as you

—Tho you're not old now, that's left here with me —

Myself, anyhow, maybe as old as the universe — and I guess that
dies with us — enough to cancel all that comes — What
came is gone forever every time —

That's good! That leaves it open for no regret — no fear radiators,
lacklove, torture even toothache in the end —

Though while it comes it is a lion that eats the soul — and the
lamb, the soul, in us, alas, offering itself in sacrifice to
change's fierce hunger — hair and teeth — and the roar of
bonepain, skull bare, break rib, rot-skin, braintricked Im-
placability.

Ai! ai! we do worse! We are in a fix! And you're out, Death let you
out, Death had the Mercy, you're done with your century,
done with God, done with the path thru it — Done with
yourself at last — Pure — Back to the Babe dark before
your Father, before us all — before the world —

There, rest. No more suffering for you. I know where you've
gone, it's good.

No more flowers in the summer field of New York, no joy now,
no more fear of Louis,

and no more of his sweetness and glasses, his high school de-
cades, debts, loves, frightened telephone calls, conception
beds, relatives, hands —

No more of sister Elanor, — she gone before you — we kept it
   secret — you killed her — or she killed herself to bear with
   you — an arthritic heart — But Death's killed you both
   — No matter —
Nor your memory of your mother, 1915 tears in silent movies
   weeks and weeks — forgetting, agrieve watching Marie
   Dressler address humanity, Chaplin dance in youth,
or Boris Godunov, Chaliapin's at the Met, halling his voice of a
   weeping Czar — by standing room with Elanor & Max —
   watching also the Capitalists take seats in Orchestra,
   white furs, diamonds,
with the YPSL's hitch-hiking thru Pennsylvania, in black baggy
   gym skirts pants, photograph of 4 girls holding each other
   round the waist, and laughing eye, too coy, virginal soli-
   tude of 1920
all girls grown old, or dead, now, and that long hair in the
   grave — lucky to have husbands later —
You made it — I came too — Eugene my brother before (still
   grieving now and will gream on to his last stiff hand, as
   he goes thru his cancer — or kill — later perhaps — soon
   he will think —)
And it's the last moment I remember, which I see them all, thru
   myself, now — tho not you
I didn't foresee what you felt — what more hideous gape of bad
   mouth came first — to you — and were you prepared?
To go where? In that Dark — that — in that God? a radiance? A
   Lord in the Void? Like an eye in the black cloud in a
   dream? Adonoi at last, with you?
Beyond my remembrance! Incapable to guess! Not merely the
   yellow skull in the grave, or a box of worm dust, and a
   stained ribbon — Deathshead with Halo? can you believe
   it?
Is it only the sun that shines once for the mind, only the flash of
   existence, than none ever was?
Nothing beyond what we have — what you had — that so pitiful
   — yet Triumph,
to have been here, and changed, like a tree, broken, or flower —
   fed to the ground — but mad, with its petals, colored,
   thinking Great Universe, shaken, cut in the head, leaf
   stript, hid in an egg crate hospital, cloth wrapped, sore —
   freaked in the moon brain, Naughtless.

No flower like that flower, which knew itself in the garden, and
    fought the knife — lost
Cut down by an idiot Snowman's icy — even in the Spring —
    strange ghost thought — some Death — Sharp icicle in
    his hand — crowned with old roses — a dog for his eyes
    — cock of a sweatshop — heart of electric irons.
All the accumulations of life, that wear us out — clocks, bodies,
    consciousness, shoe, breasts — begotten sons — your
    Communism — 'Paranoia' into hospitals.
You once kicked Elanor in the leg, she died of heart failure later.
    You of stroke. Asleep? within a year, the two of you, sisters
    in death. Is Elanor happy?
Max grieves alive in an office on Lower Broadway, lone large
    mustache over midnight Accountings, not sure. His life
    passes — as he sees — and what does he doubt now? Still
    dream of making money, or that might have made money,
    hired nurse, had children, found even your Immortality,
    Naomi?
I'll see him soon. Now I've got to cut through — to talk to
    you — as I didn't when you had a mouth.
Forever. And we're bound for that, Forever — like Emily Dickin-
    son's horses — headed to the End.
They know the way — These Steeds — run faster than we think
    — it's our own life they cross — and take with them.

Magnificent, mourned no more, marred of heart, mind
behind, married dreamed, mortal changed — Ass and face done
with murder.
    In the world, given, flower maddened, made no Utopia,
shut under pine, almed in Earth, balmed in Lone, Jehovah, ac-
cept.
    Nameless, One Faced, Forever beyond me, beginningless,
endless, Father in death. Tho I am not there for this Prophecy, I
am unmarried, I'm hymnless, I'm Heavenless, headless in bliss-
hood I would still adore
    Thee, Heaven, after Death, only One blessed in Nothing-
ness, not light or darkness, Dayless Eternity —
    Take this, this Psalm, from me, burst from my hand in a
day, some of my Time, now given to Nothing — to praise Thee
— But Death

This is the end, the redemption from Wilderness, way for the Wonderer, House sought for All, black handkerchief washed clean by weeping — page beyond Psalm — Last change of mine and Naomi — to God's perfect Darkness — Death, stay thy phantoms!

II

Over and over — refrain — of the Hospitals — still haven't written your history — leave it abstract — a few images

run thru the mind — like the saxophone chorus of houses and years — remembrance of electrical shocks.

By long nites as a child in Paterson apartment, watching over your nervousness — you were fat — your next move —

By that afternoon I stayed home from school to take care of you — once and for all — when I vowed forever that once man disagreed with my opinion of the cosmos, I was lost —

By my later burden — vow to illuminate mankind — this is release of particulars — (mad as you) — (sanity a trick of agreement) —

But you stared out the window on the Broadway Church corner, and spied a mystical assassin from Newark,

So phoned the Doctor — 'OK go way for a rest' — so I put on my coat and walked you downstreet — On the way a grammarschool boy screamed, unaccountably — 'Where you goin Lady to Death?' I shuddered —

and you covered your nose with motheaten fur collar, gas mask against poison sneaked into downtown atmosphere, sprayed by Grandma —

And was the driver of the cheesebox Public Service bus a member of the gang? You shuddered at his face, I could hardly get you on — to New York, very Times Square, to grab another Greyhound —

where we hung around 2 hours fighting invisible bugs and jewish sickness — breeze poisoned by Roosevelt —

out to get you — and me tagging along, hoping it would end in a quiet room in a Victorian house by a lake.

Ride 3 hours thru tunnels past all American industry, Bayonne preparing for World War II, tanks, gas fields, soda factories, diners, locomotive roundhouse fortress — into piney woods New Jersey Indians — calm towns — long roads thru sandy tree fields —

Bridges by deerless creeks, old wampum loading the streambed — down there a tomahawk or Pocahantas bone — and a million old ladies voting for Roosevelt in brown small houses, roads off the Madness highway —

perhaps a hawk in a tree, or a hermit looking for an owl-filled branch —

All the time arguing — afraid of strangers in the forward double seat, snoring regardless — what busride they snore on now?

'Allen, you don't understand — it's — ever since those 3 big sticks up my back — they did something to me in Hospital, they poisoned me, they want to see me dead — 3 big sticks, 3 big sticks —

'The Bitch! Old Grandma! Last week I saw her, dressed in pants like an old man, with a sack on her back, climbing up the brick side of the apartment

'On the fire escape, with poison germs, to throw on me — at night — maybe Louis is helping her — he's under her power —

'I'm your mother, take me to Lakewood' (near where Graf Zeppelin had crashed before, all Hitler in Explosion) 'where I can hide.'

We got there — Dr. Whatzis rest home — she hid behind a closet — demanded a blood transfusion.

We were kicked out — tramping with valise to unknown shady lawn houses — dusk, pine trees after dark — long dead street filled with crickets and poison ivy —

I shut her up by now — big house REST HOME ROOMS — gave the landlady her money for the week — carried up the iron valise — sat on bed waiting to escape —

Neat room in attic with friendly bedcover — lace curtains — spinning wheel rug — Stained wallpaper old as Naomi. We were home.

I left on the next bus to New York — lay my head back in the last seat, depressed — the worst yet to come? — abandoning her, rode in torpor — I was only 12.

Would she hide in her room and come out cheerful for breakfast? Or lock her door and stare thru the window for side-street spies? Listen at keyholes for Hitlerian invisible gas? Dream in a chair — or mock me, by — in front of a mirror, alone?

12 riding the bus at nite thru New Jersey, have left Naomi to Parcae in Lakewood's haunted house — left to my own fate bus — sunk in a seat — all violins broken — my heart sore in my ribs — mind was empty — Would she were safe in her coffin —

Or back at Normal School in Newark, studying up on America in a black skirt — winter on the street without lunch—a penny a pickle — home at night to take care of Elanor in the bedroom —

First nervous breakdown was 1919 — she stayed home from school and lay in a dark room for three weeks — something bad — never said what — every noise hurt — dreams of the creaks of Wall Street —

Before the grey Depression — went upstate New York — recovered — Lou took photo of her sitting crossleg on the grass — her long hair wound with flowers — smiling — playing lullabies on mandoline — poison ivy smoke in left-wing summer camps and me in infancy saw trees —

or back teaching school, laughing with idiots, the backward classes — her Russian speciality — morons with dreamy lips, great eyes, thin feet & sicky fingers, swaybacked, rachitic

great heads pendulous over Alice in Wonderland, a blackboard full of C A T.

Naomi reading patiently, story out of a Communist fairy book — Tale of the Sudden Sweetness of The Dictator — Forgiveness of Warlocks — Armies Kissing —

Deathsheads Around the Green Table — The King & the Workers — Paterson Press printed them up in the 30's till she went mad, or they folded, both.

O Paterson! I got home late that nite. Louis was worried. How could I be so — didn't I think? I shouldn't have left her. Mad in Lakewood. Call the Doctor. Phone the home in the pines. Too late.

Went to bed exhausted, wanting to leave the world (probably that year newly in love with R— my high school mind hero, jewish boy who came a doctor later — then silent neat kid —

I later laying down life for him, moved to Manhattan — followed him to college — Prayed on ferry to help mankind if admitted — vowed, the day I journeyed to Entrance Exam —

by being honest revolutionary labor lawyer — would train for that — inspired by Sacco Vanzetti, Norman Thomas, Debs, Altgeld, Sandburg, Poe — Little Blue Books. I wanted to be President, or Senator.

ignorant woe — later dreams of kneeling by R's shocked knees declaring my love of 1941 — What sweetness he'd have shown me, tho, that I'd wished him & despaired — first love — a crush —

Later a mortal avalanche, whole mountains of homosexuality, Matterhorns of cock, Grand Canyons of asshole — weight on my melancholy head —

meanwhile I walked on Broadway imagining Infinity like a rubber ball without space beyond — what's outside? — coming home to Graham Avenue still melancholy passing the lone green hedges across the street, dreaming after the movies —)

The telephone rang at 2 A.M. — Emergency — she'd gone mad — Naomi hiding under the bed screaming bugs of Mussolini — Help! Louis! Buba! Fascists! Death! — the landlady frightened — old fag attendant screaming back at her —

Terror, that woke the neighbors — old ladies on the second floor recovering from menopause — all those rags between thighs, clean sheets, sorry over lost babies — husbands ashen — children sneering at Yale, or putting oil in hair at CCNY — or trembling in Montclair State Teachers College like Eugene —

Her big leg crouched to her breast, hand outstretched Keep Away, wool dress on her thighs, fur coat dragged under the bed — she barricaded herself under bedspring with suitcases.

Louis in pyjamas listening to phone, frightened — do now? — Who could know? — my fault, delivering her to solitude? — sitting in the dark room on the sofa, trembling, to figure out —

He took the morning train to Lakewood, Naomi still under bed — thought he brought poison Cops — Naomi screaming — Louis what happened to your heart then? Have you been killed by Naomi's ecstasy?

Dragged her out, around the corner, a cab, forced her in with valise, but the driver left them off at drugstore. Bus stop, two hours' wait.

I lay in bed nervous in the 4-room apartment, the big bed in living room, next to Louis' desk — shaking — he came home that nite, late, told me what happened.

Naomi at the prescription counter defending herself from the enemy — racks of children's books, douche bags, aspirins, pots, blood — 'Don't come near me — murderers! Keep away! Promise not to kill me!'

Louis in horror at the soda fountain — with Lakewood girlscouts — coke addicts — nurses — busmen hung on schedule — Police from country precinct, dumbed — and a priest dreaming of pigs on an ancient cliff?

Smelling the air — Louis pointing to emptiness? — Customers vomiting their cokes — or staring — Louis humiliated — Naomi triumphant — The Announcement of the Plot. Bus arrives, the drivers won't have them on trip to New York.

Phonecalls to Dr. Whatzis, 'She needs a rest,' The mental hospital — State Greystone Doctors — 'Bring her here, Mr. Ginsberg.'

Naomi, Naomi — sweating, bulge-eyed, fat, the dress unbuttoned at one side — hair over brow, her stocking hanging evilly on her legs — screaming for a blood transfusion — one righteous hand upraised — a shoe in it — barefoot in the Pharmacy —

The enemies approach — what poisons? Tape recorders? FBI? Zhdanov hiding behind the counter? Trotsky mixing rat bacteria in the back of the store? Uncle Sam in Newark, plotting deathly perfumes in the Negro district? Uncle Ephraim, drunk with murder in the politician's bar, scheming of Hague? Aunt Rose passing water thru the needles of the Spanish Civil War?

till the hired $35 ambulance came from Red Bank—— Grabbed her arms — strapped her on the stretcher — moaning, poisoned by imaginaries, vomiting chemicals thru Jersey, begging mercy from Essex County to Morristown —

And back to Greystone where she lay three years — that was the last breakthrough, delivered her to Madhouse again —

On what wards — I walked there later, oft — old catatonic ladies, grey as cloud or ash or walls — sit crooning over floorspace — Chairs — and the wrinkled hags acreep, accusing — begging my 13-year-old mercy —

'Take me home' — I went alone sometimes looking for the lost Naomi, taking Shock — and I'd say, 'No, you're crazy Mama, — Trust the Drs.' —

And Eugene, my brother, her elder son, away studying Law in a furnished room in Newark —

came Paterson-ward next day — and he sat on the brokendown couch in the living room — 'We had to send her back to Greystone' —

—his face perplexed, so young, then eyes with tears—
then crept weeping all over his face—'What for?' wail vibrating
in his cheekbones, eyes closed up, high voice—Eugene's face of
pain.

Him faraway, escaped to an Elevator in the Newark Li-
brary, his bottle daily milk on windowsill of $5 week furn room
downtown at trolley tracks—

He worked 8 hrs. a day for $20/wk—thru Law School
years—stayed by himself innocent near negro whorehouses.

Unlaid, poor virgin—writing poems about Ideals and
politics letters to the editor Pat Eve News—(we both wrote,
denouncing Senator Borah and Isolationists—and felt mysteri-
ous toward Paterson City Hall—

I sneaked inside it once—local Moloch tower with
phallus spire & cap o' ornament, strange gothic Poetry that stood
on Market Street—replica Lyons' Hotel de Ville—

wings, balcony & scrollwork portals, gateway to the giant
city clock, secret map room full of Hawthorne—dark Debs in
the Board of Tax—Rembrandt smoking in the gloom—

Silent polished desks in the great committee room—
Aldermen? Bd of Finance? Mosca the hairdresser aplot—Crapp
the gangster issuing orders from the john—The madmen strug-
gling over Zone, Fire, Cops & Backroom Metaphysics—we're
all dead—outside by the bus-stop Eugene stared thru child-
hood—

where the Evangelist preached madly for 3 decades, hard-
haired, cracked & true to his mean Bible—chalked Prepare to
Meet Thy God on civic pave—

or God is Love on the railroad overpass concrete—he
raved like I would rave, the lone Evangelist—Death on City
Hall—)

But Gene, young,—been Montclair Teachers College 4
years—taught half year & quit to go ahead in life—afraid of
Discipline Problems—dark sex Italian students, raw girls getting
laid, no English, sonnets disregarded—and he did not know
much—just that he lost—

so broke his life in two and paid for Law—read huge blue
books and rode the ancient elevator 13 miles away in Newark &
studied up hard for the future

just found the Scream of Naomi on his failure doorstep,
for the final time, Naomi gone, us lonely—home—him sitting
there—

Then have some chicken soup, Eugene. The Man of Evangel wails in front of City Hall. And this year Lou has poetic loves of suburb middle-age — in secret — music from his 1937 book — Sincere — he longs for beauty —

No love since Naomi screamed — since 1923? — now lost in Greystone ward — new shock for her — Electricity, following the 40 Insulin.

And Metrasol had made her fat.

So that a few years later she came home again — we'd much advanced and planned — I waited for that day — my Mother again to cook & — play the piano — sing at mandoline — Lung Stew, & Stenka Razin, & the communist line on the war with Finland — and Louis in debt — suspected to be poisoned money — mysterious capitalisms

— & walked down the long front hall & looked at the furniture. She never remembered it all. Some amnesia. Examined the doilies — and the dining room set was sold —

the Mahogany table — 20 years love — gone to the junk man — we still had the piano — and the book of Poe — and the Mandolin, tho needed some string, dusty —

She went to the backroom to lie down in bed and ruminate, or nap, hide — I went in with her, not leave her by herself — lay in bed next to her — shades pulled, dusky, late afternoon — Louis in front room at desk, waiting — perhaps boiling chicken for supper —

'Don't be afraid of me because I'm just coming back home from the mental hospital — I'm your mother —'

Poor love, lost — a fear — I lay there — Said, 'I love you Naomi,' — stiff, next to her arm. I would have cried, was this the comfortless lone union? — Nervous, and she got up soon.

Was she ever satisfied? And — by herself sat on the new couch by the front windows, uneasy — cheek leaning on her hand — narrowing eye — at what fate that day —

Picking her tooth with her nail, lips formed an O, suspicion — thought's old worn vagina — absent sideglance of eye — some evil debt written in the wall, unpaid — & the aged breasts of Newark come near —

May have heard radio gossip thru the wires in her head, controlled by 3 big sticks left in her back by gangsters in amnesia, thru the hospital — caused pain between her shoulders —

Into her head — Roosevelt should know her case, she told me — Afraid to kill her, now, that the government knew their names — traced back to Hitler — wanted to leave Louis' house forever.

One night, sudden attack — her noise in the bathroom — like croaking up her soul — convulsions and red vomit coming out of her mouth — diarrhea water exploding from her behind — on all fours in front of the toilet — urine running between her legs — left retching on the tile floor smeared with her black feces — unfainted —

At forty, varicosed, nude, fat, doomed, hiding outside the apartment door near the elevator calling Police, yelling for her girl-friend Rose to help —

Once locked herself in with razor or iodine — could hear her cough in tears at sink — Lou broke through glass green-painted door, we pulled her out to the bedroom.

Then quiet for months that winter — walks, alone, nearby on Broadway, read Daily Worker — Broke her arm, fell on icy street —

Began to scheme escape from cosmic financial murder plots — later she ran away to the Bronx to her sister Elanor. And there's another saga of late Naomi in New York.

Or thru Elanor or the Workman's Circle, where she worked, addressing envelopes, she made out — went shopping for Campbell's tomato soup — saved money Louis mailed her —

Later she found a boyfriend, and he was a doctor — Dr. Isaac worked for National Maritime Union — now Italian bald and pudgy old doll — who was himself an orphan — but they kicked him out — Old cruelties —

Sloppier, sat around on bed or chair, in corset dreaming to herself — 'I'm hot — I'm getting fat — I used to have such a beautiful figure before I went to the hospital — You should have seen me in Woodbine — ' This in a furnished room around the NMU hall, 1943.

Looking at naked baby pictures in the magazine — baby powder advertisements, strained lamb carrots — 'I will think nothing but beautiful thoughts.'

Revolving her head round and round on her neck at window light in summertime, in hypnotize, in doven-dream recall —

'I touch his cheek, I touch his cheek, he touches my lips with his hand, I think beautiful thoughts, the baby has a beautiful hand.' —

Or a No-shake of her body, disgust — some thought of Buchenwald — some insulin passes thru her head — a grimace nerve shudder at Involuntary (as shudder when I piss) — bad chemical in her cortex — 'No don't think of that. He's a rat.'

Naomi: 'And when we die we become an onion, a cabbage, a carrot, or a squash, a vegetable.' I come downtown from Columbia and agree. She reads the Bible, thinks beautiful thoughts all day.

'Yesterday I saw God. What did he look like? Well, in the afternoon I climbed up a ladder — he has a cheap cabin in the country, like Monroe, NY the chicken farms in the wood. He was a lonely old man with a white beard.

'I cooked supper for him. I made him a nice supper — lentil soup, vegetables, bread & butter — miltz — he sat down at the table and ate, he was sad.

'I told him, Look at all those fightings and killings down there, What's the matter? Why don't you put a stop to it?

'I try, he said — That's all he could do, he looked tired. He's a bachelor so long, and he likes lentil soup.'

Serving me meanwhile, a plate of cold fish — chopped raw cabbage dript with tapwater — smelly tomatoes — week-old health food — grated beets & carrots with leaky juice, warm — more and more disconsolate food — I can't eat it for nausea sometimes — the Charity of her hands stinking with Manhattan, madness, desire to please me, cold undercooked fish — pale red near the bones. Her smells — and oft naked in the room, so that I stare ahead, or turn a book ignoring her.

One time I thought she was trying to make me come lay her — flirting to herself at sink — lay back on huge bed that filled most of the room, dress up round her hips, big slash of hair, scars of operations, pancreas, belly wounds, abortions, appendix, stitching of incisions pulling down in the fat like hideous thick zippers — ragged long lips between her legs — What, even, smell of asshole? I was cold — later revolted a little, not much — seemed perhaps a good idea to try — know the Monster of the Beginning Womb — Perhaps — that way. Would she care? She needs a lover.

Yisborach, v'yistabach, v'yispoar, v'yisroman, v'yisnaseh, v'yishador, v'yishalleh, v'yishallol, sh'meh d'kudsho, b'rich hu.

And Louis reestablishing himself in Paterson grimy apartment in negro district — living in dark rooms — but found himself a girl he later married, falling in love again — tho sere & shy — hurt with 20 years Naomi's mad idealism.

Once I came home, after longtime in N.Y., he's lonely — sitting in the bedroom, he at desk chair turned round to face me — weeps, tears in red eyes under his glasses —

That we'd left him — Gene gone strangely into army — she out on her own in NY, almost childish in her furnished room. So Louis walked downtown to postoffice to get mail, taught in highschool — stayed at poetry desk, forlorn — ate grief at Bickford's all these years — are gone.

Eugene got out of the Army, came home changed and lone — cut off his nose in jewish operation — for years stopped girls on Broadway for cups of coffee to get laid — Went to NYU, serious there, to finish Law. —

And Gene lived with her, ate naked fishcakes, cheap, while she got crazier — He got thin, or felt helpless, Naomi striking 1920 poses at the moon, half-naked in the next bed.

bit his nails and studied — was the weird nurse-son — Next year he moved to a room near Columbia — though she wanted to live with her children —

'Listen to your mother's plea, I beg you' — Louis still sending her checks — I was in bughouse that year 8 months — my own visions unmentioned in this here Lament —

But then went half mad — Hitler in her room, she saw his mustache in the sink — afraid of Dr. Isaac now, suspecting that he was in on the Newark plot — went up to Bronx to live near Elanor's Rheumatic Heart —

And Uncle Max never got up before noon, tho Naomi at 6 A.M. was listening to the radio for spies — or searching the windowsill,

for in the empty lot downstairs, an old man creeps with his bag stuffing packages of garbage in his hanging black overcoat.

Max's sister Edie works — 17 years bookkeeper at Gimbels — lived downstairs in apartment house, divorced — so Edie took in Naomi on Rochambeau Ave —

Woodlawn Cemetery across the street, vast dale of graves where Poe once — Last stop on Bronx subway — lots of communists in that area.

Who enrolled for painting classes at night in Bronx Adult High School — walked alone under Van Cortlandt Elevated line to class — paints Naomiisms —

Humans sitting on the grass in some Camp No-Worry summers yore — saints with droopy faces and long-ill-fitting pants, from hospital —

Brides in front of Lower East Side with short grooms — lost El trains running over the Babylonian apartment rooftops in the Bronx —

Sad paintings — but she expressed herself. Her mandolin gone, all strings broke in her head, she tried. Toward Beauty? or some old life Message?

But started kicking Elanor, and Elanor had heart trouble — came upstairs and asked her about Spydom for hours, — Elanor frazzled. Max away at office, accounting for cigar stores till at night.

'I am a great woman — am truly a beautiful soul — and because of that they (Hitler, Grandma, Hearst, the Capitalists, Franco, Daily News, the 20's, Mussolini, the living dead) want to shut me up — Buba's the head of a spider network — '

Kicking the girls, Edie & Elanor — Woke Edie at midnite to tell her she was a spy and Elanor a rat. Edie worked all day and couldn't take it — She was organizing the union. — And Elanor began dying, upstairs in bed.

The relatives call me up, she's getting worse — I was the only one left — Went on the subway with Eugene to see her, ate stale fish —

'My sister whispers in the radio — Louis must be in the apartment — his mother tells him what to say — LIARS! — I cooked for my two children — I played the mandolin — '

Last night the nightingale woke me/ Last night when all was still/ it sang in the golden moonlight/ from on the wintry hill. She did.

I pushed her against the door and shouted 'DON'T KICK ELANOR!' — she stared at me — Contempt — die — disbelief her sons are so naive, so dumb — 'Elanor is the worst spy! She's taking orders!'

'—No wires in the room!'—I'm yelling at her—last ditch, Eugene listening on the bed—what can he do to escape that fatal Mama—'You've been away from Louis years already —Grandma's too old to walk—'

We're all alive at once then—even me & Gene & Naomi in one mythological Cousinesque room—screaming at each other in the Forever—I in Columbia jacket, she half undressed.

I banging against her head which saw Radios, Sticks, Hitlers—the gamut of Hallucinations—for real—her own universe—no road that goes elsewhere—to my own—No America, not even a world—

That you go as all men, as Van Gogh, as mad Hannah, all the same—to the last doom—Thunder, Spirits, Lightning!

I've seen your grave! O strange Naomi! My own—cracked grave! Shema Y'Israel—I am Svul Avrum—you—in death?

Your last night in the darkness of the Bronx—I phonecalled—thru hospital to secret police.

That came, when you and I were alone, shrieking at Elanor in my ear—who breathed hard in her own bed, got thin—

Nor will forget, the doorknock, at your fright of spies,— Law advancing, on my honor—Eternity entering the room— you running to the bathroom undressed, hiding in protest from the last heroic fate—

staring at my eyes, betrayed—the final cops of madness rescuing me—from your foot against the broken heart of Elanor,

your voice at Edie weary of Gimbels coming home to broken radio—and Louis needing a poor divorce, he wants to get married soon—Eugene dreaming, hiding at 125 St., suing negros for money on crud furniture, defending black girls—

Protests from the bathroom—Said you were sane— dressing in a cotton robe, your shoes, then new, your purse and newspaper clippings—no—your honesty—

as you vainly made your lips more real with lipstick, look- ing in the mirror to see if the Insanity was Me or a carful of police.

or Grandma spying at 78—Your vision—Her climbing over the walls of the cemetery with political kidnapper's bag— or what you saw on the walls of the Bronx, in pink nightgown at midnight, staring out the window on the empty lot—

Ah Rochambeau Ave — Playground of Phantoms — last apartment in the Bronx for spies — last home for Elanor or Naomi, here these communist sisters lost their revolution —

'All right — put on your coat Mrs. — let's go — We have the wagon downstairs — you want to come with her to the station?'

The ride then — held Naomi's hand, and held her head to my breast, I'm taller — kissed her and said I did it for the best — Elanor sick — and Max with heart condition — Needs —

To me — 'Why did you do this?' — 'Yes Mrs., your son will have to leave you in an hour' — The Ambulance

came in a few hours — drove off at 4 A.M. to some Bellevue in the night downtown — gone to the hospital forever. I saw her led away — she waved, tears in her eyes.

Two years, after a trip to Mexico — bleak in the flat plain near Brentwood, scrub brush and grass around the unused RR train track to the crazyhouse —

new brick 20 story central building — lost on the vast lawns of madtown on Long Island — huge cities of the moon.

Asylum spreads out giant wings above the path to a minute black hole — the door — entrance thru crotch —

I went in — smelt funny — the halls again — up elevator — to a glass door on a Woman's Ward — to Naomi — Two nurses buxom white — They led her out, Naomi stared — and I gaspt — She'd had a stroke —

Too thin, shrunk on her bones — age come to Naomi — now broken into white hair — loose dress on her skeleton — face sunk, old! withered — cheek of crone —

One hand stiff — heaviness of forties & menopause reduced by one heart stroke, lame now — wrinkles — a scar on her head, the lobotomy — ruin, the hand dipping downwards to death —

O Russian faced, woman on the grass, your long black hair is crowned with flowers, the mandolin is on your knees —

Communist beauty, sit here married in the summer among daisies, promised happiness at hand —

holy mother, now you smile on your love, your world is born anew, children run naked in the field spotted with dandelions, they eat in the plum tree grove at the end of the meadow and find a cabin where a white-haired negro teaches the mystery of his rainbarrel —

blessed daughter come to America, I long to hear your voice again, remembering your mother's music, in the Song of the Natural Front —

O glorious muse that bore me from the womb, gave suck first mystic life & taught me talk and music, from whose pained head I first took Vision —

Tortured and beaten in the skull — What mad hallucinations of the damned that drive me out of my own skull to seek Eternity till I find Peace for Thee, O Poetry — and for all humankind call on the Origin

Death which is the mother of the universe! — Now wear your nakedness forever, white flowers in your hair, your marriage sealed behind the sky — no revolution might destroy that maidenhood —

O beautiful Garbo of my Karma — all photographs from 1920 in Camp Nicht-Gedeiget here unchanged — with all the teachers from Newark — Nor Elanor be gone, nor Max await his specter — nor Louis retire from this High School —

Back! You! Naomi! Skull on you! Gaunt immortality and revolution come — small broken woman — the ashen indoor eyes of hospitals, ward grayness on skin —

'Are you a spy?' I sat at the sour table, eyes filling with tears — 'Who are you? Did Louis send you? — The wires — '

in her hair, as she beat on her head — 'I'm not a bad girl — don't murder me! — I hear the ceiling — I raised two children — '

Two years since I'd been there — I started to cry — She stared — nurse broke up the meeting a moment — I went into the bathroom to hide, against the toilet white walls

'The Horror' I weeping — to see her again — 'The Horror' — as if she were dead thru funeral rot in — 'The Horror!'

I came back she yelled more — they led her away — 'You're not Allen — ' I watched her face — but she passed by me, not looking —

Opened the door to the ward, — she went thru without a glance back, quiet suddenly — I stared out — she looked old — the verge of the grave — 'All the Horror!'

Another year, I left N.Y. — on West Coast in Berkeley cottage dreamed of her soul — that, thru life, in what form it stood in that body, ashen or manic, gone beyond joy —

near its death — with eyes — was my own love in its form, the Naomi, my mother on earth still — sent her long letter — & wrote hymns to the mad — Work of the merciful Lord of Poetry.

that causes the broken grass to be green, or the rock to break in grass — or the Sun to be constant to earth — Sun of all sunflowers and days on bright iron bridges — what shines on old hospitals — as on my yard —

Returning from San Francisco one night, Orlovsky in my room — Whalen in his peaceful chair — a telegram from Gene, Naomi dead —

Outside I bent my head to the ground under the bushes near the garage — knew she was better —

at last — not left to look on Earth alone — 2 years of solitude — no one, at age nearing 60 — old woman of skulls — once long-tressed Naomi of Bible —

or Ruth who wept in America — Rebecca aged in Newark — David remembering his Harp, now lawyer at Yale

or Svul Avrum — Israel Abraham — myself — to sing in the wilderness toward God — O Elohim! — so to the end — 2 days after her death I got her letter —

Strange Prophecies anew! She wrote — 'The key is in the window, the key is in the sunlight at the window — I have the key — Get married Allen don't take drugs — the key is in the bars, in the sunlight in the window.

Love,

your mother'

which is Naomi —

Hymmnn

In the world which He has created according to his will Blessed
    Praised
Magnified Lauded Exalted the Name of the Holy One Blessed is
    He!
In the house in Newark Blessed is He! In the madhouse Blessed is
    He! In the house of Death Blessed is He!

Blessed be He in homosexuality! Blessed be He in Paranoia!
Blessed be He in the city! Blessed be He in the Book!
Blessed be He who dwells in the shadow! Blessed be He! Blessed
be He!
Blessed be you Naomi in tears! Blessed be you Naomi in fears!
Blessed Blessed Blessed in sickness!
Blessed be you Naomi in Hospitals! Blessed be you Naomi in
solitude! Blest be your triumph! Blest be your bars! Blest
be your last years' loneliness!
Blest be your failure! Blest be your stroke! Blest be the close of
your eye! Blest be the gaunt of your cheek! Blest be your
withered thighs!
Blessed be Thee Naomi in Death! Blessed be Death! Blessed be
Death!
Blessed be He Who leads all sorrow to Heaven! Blessed be He in
the end!
Blessed be He who builds Heaven in Darkness! Blessed Blessed
Blessed be He! Blessed be He! Blessed be Death on us All!

III

Only to have not forgotten the beginning in which she drank
cheap sodas in the morgues of Newark,
only to have seen her weeping on grey tables in long wards of her
universe
only to have known the weird ideas of Hitler at the door, the
wires in her head, the three big sticks
rammed down her back, the voices in the ceiling shrieking out
her ugly early lays for 30 years,
only to have seen the time-jumps, memory lapse, the crash of
wars, the roar and silence of a vast electric shock,
only to have seen her painting crude pictures of Elevateds run-
ning over the rooftops of the Bronx
her brothers dead in Riverside or Russia, her lone in Long Island
writing a last letter — and her image in the sunlight at the
window
'The key is in the sunlight at the window in the bars the key is in
the sunlight,'
only to have come to that dark night on iron bed by stroke when
the sun gone down on Long Island
and the vast Atlantic roars outside the great call of Being to its
own

to come back out of the Nightmare — divided creation — with
    her head lain on a pillow of the hospital to die
— in one last glimpse — all Earth one everlasting Light in the
    familiar blackout — no tears for this vision —
But that the key should be left behind — at the window — the
    key in the sunlight — to the living — that can take
that slice of light in hand — and turn the door — and look back
    see
Creation glistening backwards to the same grave, size of uni-
    verse,
size of the tick of the hospital's clock on the archway over the
    white door —

IV

O mother
what have I left out
O mother
what have I forgotten
O mother
farewell
with a long black shoe
farewell
with Communist Party and a broken stocking
farewell
with six dark hairs on the wen of your breast
farewell
with your old dress and a long black beard around the vagina
farewell
with your sagging belly
with your fear of Hitler
with your mouth of bad short stories
with your fingers of rotten mandolines
with your arms of fat Paterson porches
with your belly of strikes and smokestacks
with your chin of Trotsky and the Spanish War
with your voice singing for the decaying overbroken workers
with your nose of bad lay with your nose of the smell of the
    pickles of Newark
with your eyes
with your eyes of Russia

with your eyes of no money
with your eyes of false China
with your eyes of Aunt Elanor
with your eyes of starving India
with your eyes pissing in the park
with your eyes of America taking a fall
with your eyes of your failure at the piano
with your eyes of your relatives in California
with your eyes of Ma Rainey dying in an ambulance
with your eyes of Czechoslovakia attacked by robots
with your eyes going to painting class at night in the Bronx
with your eyes of the killer Grandma you see on the horizon from
    the Fire-Escape
with your eyes running naked out of the apartment screaming
    into the hall
with your eyes being led away by policemen to an ambulance
with your eyes strapped down on the operating table
with your eyes with the pancreas removed
with your eyes of appendix operation
with your eyes of abortion
with your eyes of ovaries removed
with your eyes of shock
with your eyes of lobotomy
with your eyes of divorce
with your eyes of stroke
with your eyes alone
with your eyes
with your eyes
with your Death full of Flowers

V

Caw caw caw crows shriek in the white sun over grave stones in
    Long Island
Lord Lord Lord Naomi underneath this grass my halflife and my
    own as hers
caw caw my eye be buried in the same Ground where I stand in
    Angel
Lord Lord great Eye that stares on All and moves in a black cloud
caw caw strange cry of Beings flung up into sky over the waving
    trees

Lord Lord O Grinder of giant Beyonds my voice in a boundless
    field in Sheol
Caw caw the call of Time rent out of foot and wing an instant in
    the universe
Lord Lord an echo in the sky the wind through ragged leaves the
    roar of memory
caw caw all years my birth a dream caw caw New York the bus the
    broken shoe the vast highschool caw caw all Visions of the
    Lord
Lord Lord Lord caw caw caw Lord Lord Lord caw caw caw Lord

The Lion for Real

"Soyez muette pour moi, Idole contemplative . . . "

I came home and found a lion in my living room
Rushed out on the fire-escape screaming Lion! Lion!
Two stenographers pulled their brunette hair and banged the
    window shut
I hurried home to Paterson and stayed two days.

Called up my old Reichian analyst
who'd kicked me out of therapy for smoking marijuana
'It's happened' I panted 'There's a Lion in my room'
'I'm afraid any discussion would have no value' he hung up.

I went to my old boyfriend we got drunk with his girlfriend
I kissed him and announced I had a lion with a mad gleam in my
    eye
We wound up fighting on the floor I bit his eyebrow & he kicked
    me out
I ended masturbating in his jeep parked in the street moaning
    'Lion.'

Found Joey my novelist friend and roared at him 'Lion!'
He looked at me interested and read me his spontaneous ignu
    high poetries
I listened for lions all I heard was Elephant Tiglon Hippogriff
    Unicorn Ants
But figured he really understood me when we made it in Ignaz
    Wisdom's bathroom.

But next day he sent me a leaf from his Smoky Mountain retreat
'I love you little Bo-Bo with your delicate golden lions
But there being no Self and No Bars therefore the Zoo of your
    dear Father hath no Lion
You said your mother was mad don't expect me to produce the
    Monster for your Bridegroom.'

Confused dazed and exalted bethought me of real lion starved in
    his stink in Harlem
Opened the door the room was filled with the bomb blast of his
    anger
He roaring hungrily at the plaster walls but nobody could hear
    him outside thru the window
My eye caught the edge of the red neighbor apartment building
    standing in deafening stillness

We gazed at each other his implacable yellow eye in the red halo of
    fur
Waxed rheumy on my own but he stopped roaring and bared a
    fang greeting.
I turned my back and cooked broccoli for supper on an iron gas
    stove
boilt water and took a hot bath in the old tub under the sink
    board.

He didn't eat me, tho I regretted him starving in my presence.
Next week he wasted away a sick rug full of bones wheaten hair
    falling out
enraged and reddening eye as he lay aching huge hairy head on his
    paws
by the egg-crate bookcase filled up with thin volumes of Plato,
    & Buddha.

Sat by his side every night averting my eyes from his hungry
    motheaten face
stopped eating myself he got weaker and roared at night while I
    had nightmares
Eaten by lion in bookstore on Cosmic Campus, a lion myself
    starved by Professor Kandisky, dying in a lion's flophouse
    circus,
I woke up mornings the lion still added dying on the floor—
    'Terrible Presence!' I cried 'Eat me or die!'

It got up that afternoon — walked to the door with its paw on the
    wall to steady its trembling body
Let out a soul-rending creak from the bottomless roof of his
    mouth
thundering from my floor to heaven heavier than a volcano at
    night in Mexico
Pushed the door open and said in a gravelly voice 'Not this time
    Baby — but I will be back again.'

Lion that eats my mind now for a decade knowing only your
    hunger
Not the bliss of your satisfaction O roar of the Universe how am
    I chosen
In this life I have heard your promise I am ready to die I have
    served
Your starved and ancient Presence O Lord I wait in my room at
    your Mercy.

American Change

    The first I looked on, after a long time far from home in
mid Atlantic on a summer day
    Dolphins breaking the glassy water under the blue sky,
    a gleam of silver in my cabin, fished up out of my jangling
new pocket of coins and green dollars
    — held in my palm, the head of the feathered indian, old
Buck-Rogers eagle eyed face, a gash of hunger in the cheek
    gritted jaw of the vanished man begone like a Hebrew
with hairlock combed down the side — O Rabbi Indian
    what visionary gleam 100 years ago on Buffalo prairie
under the molten cloud shot sky, 'the same clear light 10000
miles in all directions'
    but now with all the violin music of Vienna, gone into
the great slot machine of Kansas City, Reno —
    The coin seemed so small after vast European coppers
thick francs leaden pesetas, lira endless and heavy,
    a miniature primeval memorialized in 5¢ nickel candy-
store nostalgia of the redskin, dead on silver coin,
    with shaggy buffalo on reverse, hump-backed little tail

incurved, head butting against the rondure of Eternity,

cock forelock below, bearded shoulder muscle folded below muscle, head of prophet, bowed,

vanishing beast of Time, hoar body rubbed clean of wrinkles and shining like polished stone, bright metal in my forefinger, ridiculous buffalo — Go to New York.

Dime next I found, Minerva, sexless cold & chill, ascending goddess of money — and was it the wife of Wallace Stevens, truly?

and now from the locks flowing the miniature wings of speedy thought,

executive dyke, Minerva, goddess of Madison Avenue, forgotten useless dime that can't buy hot dog, dead dime —

Then we've George Washington, less primitive, the snub-nosed quarter, smug eyes and mouth, some idiot's design of the sexless Father,

naked down to his neck, a ribbon in his wig, high forehead, Roman line down the nose, fat cheeked, still showing his falsetooth ideas — O Eisenhower & Washington — O Fathers — No movie star dark beauty — O thou Bignoses —

Quarter, remembered quarter, 40¢ in all — What'll you buy me when I land — one icecream soda? —

poor pile of coins, original reminders of the sadness, forgotten money of America —

nostalgia of the first touch of those coins, American change,

the memory in my aging hand, the same old silver reflective there,

the thin dime hidden between my thumb and forefinger

All the struggles for those coins, the sadness of their reappearance

my reappearance on those fabled shores

and the failure of that Dream, that Vision of Money reduced to this haunting recollection

of the gas lot in Paterson where I found half a dollar gleaming in the grass —

I have a $5 bill in my pocket — it's Lincoln's sour black head moled wrinkled, forelocked too, big eared, flags of announcement flying over the bill, stamps in green and spiderweb black,

long numbers in racetrack green, immense promise, a girl, a hotel, a busride to Albany, a night of brilliant drunk in some faraway corner of Manhattan

a stick of several teas, or paper or cap of Heroin, or a $5 strange present to the blind.

Money money, reminder, I might as well write poems to you — dear American money — O statue of Liberty I ride enfolded in money in my mind to you — and last

Ahhh! Washington again, on the Dollar, same poetic black print, dark words, The United States of America, innumerable numbers

R956422481 One Dollar This Certificate is Legal Tender (tender!) for all debts public and private

My God My God why have you forsaken me

Ivy Baker Priest Series 1953 F

and over, the Eagle, wild wings outspread, halo of the Stars encircled by puffs of smoke & flame —

a circle the Masonic Pyramid, the sacred Swedenborgian Dollar America, bricked up to the top, & floating surreal above

the triangle of holy outstaring Eye sectioned out of the aire, shining

light emitted from the eyebrowless triangle — and a desert of cactus, scattered all around, clouds afar,

this being the Great Seal of our Passion, Annuit Coeptis, Novus Ordo Seculorum,

the whole surrounded by green spiderwebs designed by T-Men to prevent foul counterfeit —

ONE

Chances "R"

Nymph and shepherd raise electric tridents
     glowing red against the plaster wall,
The jukebox beating out magic syllables,
A line of painted boys snapping fingers
       & shaking thin Italian trouserlegs
          or rough dungarees on big asses
            bumping and dipping
ritually, with no religion but the
        old one of cocksuckers
naturally, in Kansas center of America
      the farmboys in Diabolic bar light
    alone stiff necked or lined up
     dancing row on row like Afric husbands
& the music's sad here, whereas Sunset Trip or
Jukebox Corner it's ecstatic pinball machines —
Religiously, with concentration and free
        prayer; fairy boys of the plains
        and their gay sisters of the city
step together to the center of the floor
      illumined by machine eyes, screaming drumbeats,
        passionate voices of Oklahoma City
          chanting No Satisfaction
Suspended from Heaven the Chances R
    Club floats rayed by stars
      along a Wichita tree avenue
    traversed with streetlights on the plain.

from *Mugging*

Tonite I walked out of my red apartment door on East tenth
    street's dusk —
Walked out of my home ten years, walked out in my honking
    neighborhood
Tonite at seven walked out past garbage cans chained to concrete
    anchors
Walked under black painted fire escapes, giant castiron plate
    covering a hole in ground

—Crossed the street, traffic lite red, thirteen bus roaring by liquor store,

past corner pharmacy iron grated, past Coca Cola & Mylai posters fading scraped on brick

Past Chinese Laundry wood door'd, & broken cement stoop steps For Rent hall painted green & purple Puerto Rican style

Along E. 10th's glass splattered pavement, kid blacks & Spanish oiled hair adolescents' crowded house fronts —

Ah, tonite I walked out on my block NY City under humid summer sky Halloween,

thinking what happened Timothy Leary joining brain police for a season?

thinking what's all this Weathermen, secrecy & selfrighteousness beyond reason — F.B.I. plots?

Walked past a taxicab controlling the bottle strewn curb —

past young fellows with their umbrella handles & canes leaning against ravaged Buick

—and as I looked at the crowd of kids on the stoop — a boy stepped up, put his arm around my neck

tenderly I thought for a moment, squeezed harder, his umbrella handle against my skull,

and his friends took my arm, a young brown companion tripped his foot 'gainst my ankle —

as I went down shouting Om Ah Hūṃ to gangs of lovers on the stoop watching

slowly appreciating, why this is a raid, these strangers mean strange business

with what — my pockets, bald head, broken-healed-bone leg, my softshoes, my heart —

Have they knives? Om Ah Hūṃ — Have they sharp metal wood to shove in eye ear ass? Om Ah Hūṃ

& slowly reclined on the pavement, struggling to keep my woolen bag of poetry address calendar & Leary-lawyer notes hung from my shoulder

dragged in my neat orlon shirt over the crossbar of a broken metal door

dragged slowly onto the fire-soiled floor an abandoned store, laundry candy counter 1929 —

now a mess of papers & pillows & plastic car seat covers cracked cockroach-corpsed ground —

my wallet back pocket passed over the iron foot step guard
and fell out, stole by God Muggers' lost fingers, Strange —
Couldn't tell — snakeskin wallet actually plastic, 70 dollars my
 bank money for a week,
old broken wallet — and dreary plastic contents — Amex card &
 Manf. Hanover Trust Credit too — business card from
 Mr. Spears British Home Minister Drug Squad — my
 draft card — membership ACLU & Naropa Institute In-
 structor's identification
Om Ah Hūm I continued chanting Om Ah Hūm
Putting my palm on the neck of an 18 year old boy fingering my
 back pocket crying "Where's the money"
"Om Ah Hūm there isn't any"
My card Chief Boo-Hoo Neo American Church New Jersey &
 Lower East Side
Om Ah Hūm — what not forgotten crowded wallet — Mobil
 Credit, Shell? old lovers addresses on cardboard pieces,
 booksellers calling cards —
— "Shut up or we'll murder you" — "Om Ah Hūm take it easy"
Lying on the floor shall I shout more loud? — the metal door
 closed on blackness
one boy felt my broken healed ankle, looking for hundred dollar
 bills behind my stocking weren't even there — a third boy
 untied my Seiko Hong Kong watch rough from right wrist
 leaving a clasp-prick skin tiny bruise
"Shut up and we'll get out of here" — and so they left,
as I rose from the cardboard mattress thinking Om Ah Hūm
 didn't stop em enough,
the tone of voice too loud — my shoulder bag with 10,000 dollars
 full of poetry left on the broken floor —

JAMES MERRILL
(1926 –)

The Broken Home

Crossing the street,
I saw the parents and the child
At their window, gleaming like fruit
With evening's mild gold leaf.

In a room on the floor below,
Sunless, cooler — a brimming
Saucer of wax, marbly and dim —
I have lit what's left of my life.

I have thrown out yesterday's milk
And opened a book of maxims.
The flame quickens. The word stirs.

Tell me, tongue of fire,
That you and I are as real
At least as the people upstairs.

My father, who had flown in World War I,
Might have continued to invest his life
In cloud banks well above Wall Street and wife.
But the race was run below, and the point was to win.

Too late now, I make out in his blue gaze
(Through the smoked glass of being thirty-six)
The soul eclipsed by twin black pupils, sex
And business; time was money in those days.

Each thirteenth year he married. When he died
There were already several chilled wives
In sable orbit — rings, cars, permanent waves.
We'd felt him warming up for a green bride.

He could afford it. He was "in his prime"
At three score ten. But money was not time.

When my parents were younger this was a popular act:
A veiled woman would leap from an electric, wine-dark car
To the steps of no matter what — the Senate or the Ritz Bar —
And bodily, at newsreel speed, attack

No matter whom — Al Smith or José Maria Sert
Or Clemenceau — veins standing out on her throat
As she yelled *War mongerer! Pig! Give us the vote!*,
And would have to be hauled away in her hobble skirt.

What had the man done? Oh, made history.
Her business (he had implied) was giving birth,
Tending the house, mending the socks.

Always that same old story —
Father Time and Mother Earth,
A marriage on the rocks.

One afternoon, red, satyr-thighed
Michael, the Irish setter, head
Passionately lowered, led
The child I was to a shut door. Inside,

Blinds beat sun from the bed.
The green-gold room throbbed like a bruise.
Under a sheet, clad in taboos
Lay whom we sought, her hair undone, outspread,

And of a blackness found, if ever now, in old
Engravings where the acid bit.
I must have needed to touch it
Or the whiteness — was she dead?
Her eyes flew open, startled strange and cold.
The dog slumped to the floor. She reached for me. I fled.

Tonight they have stepped out onto the gravel.
The party is over. It's the fall
Of 1931. They love each other still.

She: Charlie, I can't stand the pace.
He: Come on, honey — why, you'll bury us all!

A lead soldier guards my windowsill:
Khaki rifle, uniform, and face.
Something in me grows heavy, silvery, pliable.

How intensely people used to feel!
Like metal poured at the close of a proletarian novel,
Refined and glowing from the crucible,
I see those two hearts, I'm afraid,
Still. Cool here in the graveyard of good and evil,
They are even so to be honored and obeyed.

. . . Obeyed, at least, inversely. Thus
I rarely buy a newspaper, or vote.
To do so, I have learned, is to invite
The tread of a stone guest within my house.

Shooting this rusted bolt, though, against him,
I trust I am no less time's child than some
Who on the heath impersonate Poor Tom
Or on the barricades risk life and limb.

Nor do I try to keep a garden, only
An avocado in a glass of water —
Roots pallid, gemmed with air. And later,

When the small gilt leaves have grown
Fleshy and green, I let them die, yes, yes,
And start another. I am earth's no less.

A child, a red dog roam the corridors,
Still, of the broken home. No sound. The brilliant
Rag runners halt before wide-open doors.
My old room! Its wallpaper — cream, medallioned
With pink and brown — brings back the first nightmares,
Long summer colds, and Emma, sepia-faced,
Perspiring over broth carried upstairs
Aswim with golden fats I could not taste.

The real house became a boarding-school.
Under the ballroom ceiling's allegory
Someone at last may actually be allowed
To learn something; or, from my window, cool
With the unstiflement of the entire story,
Watch a red setter stretch and sink in cloud.

Days of 1964

Houses, an embassy, the hospital,
Our neighborhood sun-cured if trembling still
In pools of the night's rain . . .
Across the street that led to the center of town
A steep hill kept one company part way
Or could be climbed in twenty minutes
For some literally breathtaking views,
Framed by umbrella pines, of city and sea.
Underfoot, cyclamen, autumn crocus grew
Spangled as with fine sweat among the relics
Of good times had by all. If not Olympus,
An out-of-earshot, year-round hillside revel.

I brought home flowers from my climbs.
Kyria Kleo who cleans for us
Put them in water, sighing *Virgin, Virgin.*
Her legs hurt. She wore brown, was fat, past fifty,
And looked like a Palmyra matron
Copied in lard and horsehair. How she loved
You, me, loved us all, the bird, the cat!
I think now she *was* love. She sighed and glistened
All day with it, or pain, or both.
(We did not notably communicate.)
She lived nearby with her pious mother
And wastrel son. She called me her real son.

I paid her generously, I dare say.
Love makes one generous. Look at us. We'd known
Each other so briefly that instead of sleeping
We lay whole nights, open, in the lamplight,
And gazed, or traded stories.
One hour comes back—you gasping in my arms
With love, or laughter, or both,
I having just remembered and told you
What I'd looked up to see on my way downtown at noon:
Poor old Kleo, her aching legs,
Trudging into the pines. I called,
Called three times before she turned.
Above a tight, skyblue sweater, her face
Was painted. Yes. Her face was painted

Clown-white, white of the moon by daylight,
Lidded with pearl, mouth a poinsettia leaf,
Eat me, pay me — the erotic mask
Worn the world over by illusion
To weddings of itself and simple need.

Startled mute, we had stared — was love illusion? —
And gone our ways. Next, I was crossing a square
In which a moveable outdoor market's
Vegetables, chickens, pottery kept materializing
Through a dream-press of hagglers each at heart
Leery lest he be taken, plucked,
The bird, the flower of that November mildness,
Self lost up soft clay paths, or found, foothold,
Where the bud throbs awake
The better to be nipped, self on its knees in mud —
Here I stopped cold, for both our sakes;

And calmer on my way home bought us fruit.

Forgive me if you read this. (And may Kyria Kleo,
Should someone ever put it into Greek
And read it aloud to her, forgive me, too.)
I had gone so long without loving,
I hardly knew what I was thinking.

Where I hid my face, your touch, quick, merciful,
Blindfolded me. A god breathed from my lips.
If that was illusion, I wanted it to last long;
To dwell, for its daily pittance, with us there,
Cleaning and watering, sighing with love or pain.
I hoped it would climb when it needed to the heights
Even of degradation, as I for one
Seemed, those days, to be always climbing
Into a world of wild
Flowers, feasting, tears — or was I falling, legs
Buckling, heights, depths,
Into a pool of each night's rain?
But you were everywhere beside me, masked,
As who was not, in laughter, pain, and love.

Matinees

For David Kalstone

A gray maidservant lets me in
To Mrs. Livingston's box. It's already begun!
The box is full of grownups. She sits me down
Beside her. Meanwhile a ravishing din

Swells from below — Scene One
Of *Das Rheingold*. The entire proscenium
Is covered with a rippling azure scrim.
The three sopranos dart hither and yon

On invisible strings. Cold lights
Cling to bare arms, fair tresses. Flat
And natural aglitter like paillettes
Upon the great green sonorous depths float

Until with pulsing wealth the house is filled,
No one believing, everybody thrilled.

Lives of the Great Composers make it sound
Too much like cooking: "Sore beset,
He put his heart's blood into that quintet . . . "
So let us try the figure turned around

As in some Lives of Obscure Listeners:
"The strains of Cimarosa and Mozart
Flowed through his veins, and fed his solitary heart.
Long beyond adolescence [One infers

Your elimination, sweet Champagne
Drunk between acts!] the aria's remote
Control surviving his worst interval,

Tissue of sound and tissue of the brain
Would coalesce, and what the Masters wrote
Itself compose his features sharp and small."

Hilariously Dr Scherer took the guise
Of a bland smoothshaven Alberich whose ageold
Plan had been to fill my tooth with gold.
Another whiff of laughing gas,

And the understanding was implicit
That we must guard each other, this gold and I,
Against amalgamation by
The elemental pit.

Vague as to what dentist and tooth "stood for,"
One patient dreamer gathered something more.
A voice said in the speech of birds,

"My father having tampered with your mouth,
From now on, metal, music, myth
Will seem to taint its words."

We love the good, said Plato? He was wrong.
We love as well the wicked and the weak.
Flesh hugs its shaved plush. Twenty-four-hour-long
Galas fill the hulk of the Comique.

Flesh knows by now what dishes to avoid,
Tries not to brood on bomb or heart attack.
Anatomy is destiny, said Freud.
Soul is the brilliant hypochondriac.

Soul will cough blood and sing, and softer sing,
Drink poison, breathe her joyous last, a waltz
Rubato from his arms who sobs and stays

Behind, death after death, who fairly melts
Watching her turn from him, restored, to fling
Kisses into the furnace roaring praise.

The fallen cake, the risen price of meat,
Staircase run ten times up and down like scales
(Greek proverb: He who has no brain has feet) —
One's household opera never palls or fails.

The pipes' aubade. Recitatives. — Come back!
—I'm out of pills! — We'd love to! — What? — *Nothing,*
Let me be! — No, no, I'll drink it black . . .
The neighbors' chorus. The quick darkening

In which a prostrate figure must inquire
With every earmark of its being meant
Why God in Heaven harries him/her so.

The love scene (often cut). The potion. The tableau:
Sleepers folded in a magic fire,
Tongues flickering up from humdrum incident.

When Jan Kiepura sang His Handsomeness
Of Mantua those high airs light as lust
Attuned one's bare throat to the dagger-thrust.
Living for them would have been death no less.

Or Lehmann's Marschallin! — heartbreak so shrewd,
So ostrich-plumed, one ached to disengage
Oneself from a last love, at center stage,
To the beloved's dazzled gratitude.

What havoc certain Saturday afternoons
Wrought upon a bright young person's morals
I now leave to the public to condemn.

The point thereafter was to arrange for one's
Own chills and fever, passions and betrayals,
Chiefly in order to make song of them.

You and I, caro, seldom
Risk the real thing any more.
It's all too silly or too solemn.
Enough to know the score

From records or transcription
For our four hands. Old beauties, some
In advanced stages of decomposition,

Float up through the sustaining
Pedal's black and fluid medium.
Days like today

Even recur (wind whistling themes
From *Lulu,* and sun shining
On the rough Sound) when it seems
Kinder to remember than to play.

Dear Mrs. Livingston,
I want to say that I am still in a daze
From yesterday afternoon.
I will treasure the experience ́always —

My very first Grand Opera! It was very
Thoughtful of you to invite
Me and am so sorry
That I was late, and for my coughing fit.

I play my record of the Overture
Over and over. I pretend
I am still sitting in the theatre.

I also wrote a poem which my Mother
Says I should copy out and send.
Ever gratefully, Your little friend . . .

from *In Nine Sleep Valley*

Geode, the troll's melon
Rind of crystals velvet smoke meat blue
Formed far away under fantastic
Pressures, then cloven in two
By the taciturn rock shop man, twins now forever

Will they hunger for each other
When one goes north and one goes east?

I expect minerals never do.
Enough for them was a feast
Of flaws, the molten start and glacial sleep,
The parting kiss.

Still face to face in halfmoonlight
Sparkling comes easy to the Gemini.

Centimeters deep yawns the abyss.

Syrinx

Bug, flower, bird on slipware fired and fluted,
The summer day breaks everywhere at once.

Worn is the green of things that have known dawns
Before this, and the darkness before them.

Among the wreckage, bent in Christian weeds,
Illiterate — X my mark — I tremble, still

A thinking reed. Who puts his mouth to me
Draws out the scale of love and dread —

O ramify, sole antidote! Foxglove
Each year, cloud, hornet, fatal growths

Proliferating by metastasis
Rooted their total in the gliding stream.

Some formula not relevant any more
To flower children might express it yet

Like $\sqrt{\left(\dfrac{x}{y}\right)^{n}} = 1$

— Or equals zero, one forgets —

The *y* standing for you, dear friend, at least
Until that hour he reaches for me, then

Leaves me cold, the great god Pain,
Letting me slide back into my scarred case

Whose silvery breath-tarnished tones
No longer rivet bone and star in place

Or keep from shriveling, leather round a stone,
The sunbather's precocious apricot

Or stop the four winds racing overhead

Nought

Waste   Eased

Sought

Lost in Translation

For Richard Howard

Diese Tage, die leer dir scheinen
und wertlos für das All,
haben Wurzeln zwischen den Steinen
und trinken dort überall.

A card table in the library stands ready
To receive the puzzle which keeps never coming.
Daylight shines in or lamplight down
Upon the tense oasis of green felt.
Full of unfulfillment, life goes on,
Mirage arisen from time's trickling sands
Or fallen piecemeal into place:
German lesson, picnic, see-saw, walk
With the collie who "did everything but talk" —
Sour windfalls of the orchard back of us.
A summer without parents in the puzzle,
Or should be. But the boy, day after day,
Writes in his Line-a-Day *No puzzle.*

He's in love, at least. His French Mademoiselle,
In real life a widow since Verdun,
Is stout, plain, carrot-haired, devout.
She prays for him, as does a curé in Alsace,
Sews costumes for his marionettes,
Helps him to keep behind the scene
Whose sidelit goosegirl, speaking with his voice,
Plays Guinevere as well as Gunmoll Jean.
Or else at bedtime in his tight embrace
Tells him her own French hopes, her German fears,
Her — but what more is there to tell?
Having known grief and hardship, Mademoiselle
Knows little more. Her languages. Her place.
Noon coffee. Mail. The watch that also waited
Pinned to her heart, poor gold, throws up its hands —
No puzzle! Steaming bitterness
Her sugars draw pops back into his mouth, translated:
"Patience, chéri. Geduld, mein Schatz."
(Thus, reading Valéry the other evening
And seeming to recall a Rilke version of "Palme,"

That sunlit paradigm whereby the tree
Taps a sweet wellspring of authority,
The hour came back. Patience dans l'azur.
Geduld im . . . Himmelblau? Mademoiselle.)

Out of the blue, as promised, of a New York
Puzzle-rental shop the puzzle comes —
A superior one, containing a thousand hand-sawn,
Sandal-scented pieces. Many take
Shapes known already — the craftsman's repertoire
Nice in its limitation — from other puzzles:
Witch on broomstick, ostrich, hourglass,
Even (surely not just in retrospect)
An inchling, innocently branching palm.
These can be put aside, made stories of
While Mademoiselle spreads out the rest face-up,
Herself excited as a child; or questioned
Like incoherent faces in a crowd,
Each with its scrap of highly colored
Evidence the Law must piece together.
Sky-blue ostrich? Likely story.
Mauve of the witch's cloak white, severed fingers
Pluck? Detain her. The plot thickens
As all at once two pieces interlock.

Mademoiselle does borders — (Not so fast.
A London dusk, December last.
Chatter silenced in the library
This grown man reenters, wearing grey.
A medium. All except him have seen
Panel slid back, recess explored,
An object at once unique and common
Displayed, planted in a plain tole
Casket the subject now considers
Through shut eyes, saying in effect:
"Even as voices reach me vaguely
A dry saw-shriek drowns them out,
Some loud machinery — a lumber mill?
Far uphill in the fir forest
Trees tower, tense with shock,
Groaning and cracking as they crash groundward.

But hidden here is a freak fragment
Of a pattern complex in appearance only.
What it seems to show is superficial
Next to that long-term lamination
Of hazard and craft, the karma that has
Made it matter in the first place.
Plywood, Piece of a puzzle." Applause
Acknowledged by an opening of lids
Upon the thing itself. A sudden dread—
But to go back. All this lay years ahead.)

Mademoiselle does borders. Straight-edge pieces
Align themselves with earth or sky
In twos and threes, naive cosmogonists
Whose views clash. Nomad inlanders meanwhile
Begin to cluster where the totem
Of a certain vibrant egg-yolk yellow
Or pelt of what emerging animal
Acts on the straggler like a trumpet call
To form a more sophisticated unit.
By suppertime two ragged wooden clouds
Have formed. In one, a Sheik with beard
And flashing sword hilt (he is all but finished)
Steps forward on a tiger skin. A piece
Snaps shut, and fangs gnash out at us!
In the second cloud—they gaze from cloud to cloud
With marked if undecipherable feeling—
Most of a dark-eyed woman veiled in mauve
Is being helped down from her camel (kneeling)
By a small backward-looking slave or page-boy
(Her son, thinks Mademoiselle mistakenly)
Whose feet have not been found. But lucky finds
In the last minutes before bed
Anchor both factions to the scene's limits
And, by so doing, orient
Them eye to eye across the green abyss.
The yellow promises, oh bliss,
To be in time a sumptuous tent.

Puzzle begun I write in the day's space,
Then, while she bathes, peek at Mademoiselle's
Page to the curé: " . . . cette innocente mère,

Ce pauvre enfant, que deviendront-ils?"
Her azure script is curlicued like pieces
Of the puzzle she will be telling him about.
(Fearful incuriosity of childhood!
"Tu as l'accent allemand," said Dominique.
Indeed. Mademoiselle was only French by marriage.
Child of an English mother, a remote
Descendant of the great explorer Speke,
And Prussian father. No one knew. I heard it
Long afterwards from her nephew, a UN
Interpreter. His matter-of-fact account
Touched old strings. My poor Mademoiselle,
With 1939 about to shake
This world where "each was the enemy, each the friend"
To its foundations, kept, though signed in blood,
Her peace a shameful secret to the end.)
"Schlaf wohl, chéri." Her kiss. Her thumb
Crossing my brow against the dreams to come.

This World that shifts like sand, its unforeseen
Consolidations and elate routine,
Whose Potentate had lacked a retinue?
Lo! it assembles on the shrinking Green.

Gunmetal-skinned or pale, all plumes and scars,
Of Vassalage the noblest avatars —
The very coffee-bearer in his vair
Vest is a swart Highness, next to ours.

Kef easing Boredom, and iced syrups, thirst,
In guessed-at glooms old wives who know the worst
Outsweat that virile fiction of the New:
"Insh'Allah, he will tire — " " — or kill her first!"

(Hardly a proper subject for the Home,
Work of — dear Richard, I shall let *you* comb
Archives and learned journals for his name —
A minor lion attending on Gérôme.)

While, thick as Thebes whose presently complete
Gates close behind them, Houri and Afreet
Both claim the Page. He wonders whom to serve,
And what his duties are, and where his feet,

And if we'll find, as some before us did,
That piece of Distance deep in which lies hid
Your tiny apex sugary with sun,
Eternal Triangle, Great Pyramid!

Then Sky alone is left, a hundred blue
Fragments in revolution, with no clue
To where a Niche will open. Quite a task,
Putting together Heaven, yet we do.

It's done. Here under the table all along
Were those missing feet. It's done.

The dog's tail thumping. Mademoiselle sketching
Costumes for a coming harem drama
To star the goosegirl. All too soon the swift
Dismantling. Lifted by two corners,
The puzzle hung together—and did not.
Irresistibly a populace
Unstitched of its attachments, rattled down.
Power went to pieces as the witch
Slithered easily from Virtue's gown.
The blue held out for time, but crumbled, too.
The city had long fallen, and the tent,
A separating sauce mousseline,
Been swept away. Remained the green
On which the grown-ups gambled. A green dusk.
First lightning bugs. Last glow of west
Green in the false eyes of (coincidence)
Our mangy tiger safe on his bared hearth.

Before the puzzle was boxed and readdressed
To the puzzle shop in the mid-Sixties,
Something tells me that one piece contrived
To stay in the boy's pocket. How do I know?
I know because so many later puzzles
Had missing pieces—Maggie Teyte's high notes
Gone at the war's end, end of the vogue for collies,
A house torn down; and hadn't Mademoiselle
Kept back her pitiful bit of truth as well?
I've spent the last days, furthermore,
Ransacking Athens for that translation of "Palme."
Neither the Goethehaus nor the National Library

Seems able to unearth it. Yet I can't
Just be imagining. I've seen it. Know
How much of the sun-ripe original
Felicity Rilke made himself forego
(Who loved French words — verger, mûr, parfumer)
In order to render its underlying sense.
Know already in that tongue of his
What Pains, what monolithic Truths
Shadow stanza to stanza's symmetrical
Rhyme-rutted pavement. Know that ground plan left
Sublime and barren, where the warm Romance
Stone by stone faded, cooled; the fluted nouns
Made taller, lonelier than life
By leaf-carved capitals in the afterglow.
The owlet umlaut peeps and hoots
Above the open vowel. And after rain
A deep reverberation fills with stars.

Lost, is it, buried? One more missing piece?

But nothing's lost. Or else: all is translation
And every bit of us is lost in it
(Or found — I wander through the ruin of S
Now and then, wondering at the peacefulness)
And in that loss a self-effacing tree,
Color of context, imperceptibly
Rustling with its angel, turns the waste
To shade and fiber, milk and memory.

from *Divine Comedies*

Life like the periodical not yet
Defunct kept hitting the stands. We seldom failed
To leaf through each new issue — war, election,
Starlet; write, scratch out; eat steak au poivre,
Chat with Ephraim. Above Water Street
Things were advancing in our high retreat.
We patched where snow and rain had come to call,

Renewed the flame upon the mildewed wall.
Unpacked and set in place a bodhisattva
Green with age — its smile, to which clung crumbs
Of gold, like traces of a meal,
Proof against the Eisenhower grin
Elsewhere so disarming. Tediums
Ignited into quarrels, each "a scene
From real life," we concluded as we vowed
Not to repeat it. People still unmet
Had bought the Baptist church for reconversion.
A slight, silverhaired man in a sarong,
Noticing us from his tower window, bowed.
Down at the point, the little beach we'd missed
Crawled with infantry, and wavelets hissed.
Wet sand, as pages turned, covered a skull
Complete with teeth and helmet. Beautiful —
Or were they? — ash-black poppies filled the lens.
Delinquency was rising. Maisie made
Eyes at shadows — time we had her spayed.
Now from California DJ's parents
Descended. The nut-brown old maniac
Strode about town haranguing citizens
While Mary, puckered pale by slack
Tucks the years had taken, reminisced,
Thread snapping at the least attention paid.
They left no wiser our mysterious East.
David and I lived on, limbs thickening
For better and worse in one another's shade.

Remembered, is that summer we came back
Really so unlike the present one?
The friends who stagger clowning through U.S.
Customs in a dozen snapshots old
Enough to vote, so different from us
Here, now? Oh god, these days . . .
Thermometer at 90, July haze
Heavy with infamy from Washington.
Impeachment ripens round the furrowed stone
Face of a story-teller who has given
Fiction a bad name (I at least thank heaven
For my executive privilege vis-à-vis
Transcripts of certain private hours with E).

The whole house needs repairs. Neither can bring
Himself to say so. Hardly lingering,
We've reached the point, where the tired Sound just washes
Up to, then avoids our feet. One wishes —
I mean we've got this ton of magazines
Which *someone* might persuade the girl who cleans
To throw out. Sunset. On the tower a gull
Opens and shuts its beak. Ephemeral
Orange lilies grow beneath like wild.
Our self-effacing neighbor long since willed
His dust to them, the church is up for sale.
This evening's dinner: fried soup, jellied sole.
Three more weeks, and the stiff upper lip
Of luggage shuts on us. We'll overlap
By winter, somewhere. Meanwhile, no escape
From Greece for me, then Venice . . . D must cope
With the old people, who are fading fast . . .
But that's life too. A death's-head to be faced.

No, no! Set in our ways
As in a garden's, glittered
A whole small globe — our life, our life, our life:
Rinsed with mercury
Throughout to this bespattered
Fruit of reflection, rife

With Art Nouveau distortion
(Each other, clouds and trees).
What made a mirror flout its flat convention?
Surfacing as a solid
Among our crudities,
To toss them like a salad?

And what was the sensation
When stars alone like bees
Crawled numbly over it?
And why did all the birds eye it with caution?
It did no harm, just brightly
Kept up appearances.

Not always. On occasion
Fatigue or disbelief
Mottled the silver lining.

Then, as it were, our life saw through that craze
Of its own creation
Into another life.

Lit by a single candle after dining
TRY THINKING OF THE BEDROOM WALLPAPER
And without having to close my eyes come
Gray-blue irises, wine intervals.
A window gasping back of me. The oil-lamp
Twirling white knobs of an unvarnished bureau.
It's sunset next. It's no place that I've been.
Outside, the veldt stops at a red ravine,
The bad pain in my chest grown bearable.
WHO ARE U   A name comes: I'm Rufus . . . Farmer?
FARMETTON DEC 1925
December? YES DECEMBER AND   Deceased!
How much of this is my imagination
Sweating to graduate from private school?
I'm in bed. Younger than myself. I can't . . .
GO ON   I hear them in the vestibule.
WHO   Peter? YES &   Hedwig? PETERS AUNT
And Peter is my . . . YR GREAT HAPPINESS
So, bit by bit, the puzzle's put together
Or else it's disassembled, bit by bit.
Hot pebbles. Noon is striking. U HAVE STUMBLED
Upon an entry in a childish hand.
The whole book quivers. Strikes me like a curse:
These clues, so lightly scattered in reverse
Order, aren't they plain from where I stand?
The journal lies on Peter's desk. HE NOW
NO LONGER LOCKS HIS ROOM not since my illness,
Heart-room where misgivings gnaw, I *know*.
I've woken. And two eyes, blue, stricken, stare
Back at me through a shock of reddish hair
— Can we stop now please? U DID WELL JM
DEATHS ARE TRAUMATIC   FEW REMEMBER THEM.

. . . . .

Zero hour. Waiting yet again
For someone to fix the furnace. Zero week
Of the year's end. Bed that keeps restlessly
Making itself anew from lamé drifts.
Mercury dropping. Cost of living high.
Night has fallen in the glass studio
Upstairs. The fire we huddle with our drinks by
Pops and snaps. Throughout the empty house
(Tenants away until the New Year) taps
Glumly trickling keep the pipes from freezing.
Summers ago this whole room was a garden —
Orange tree, plumbago, fuchsia, palm;
One of us at the piano playing his
Gymnopédie, the other entering
Stunned by hot news from the sundeck. Now
The plants, the sorry few that linger, scatter
Leaflets advocating euthanasia.
Windows and sliding doors are wadded shut.
A blind raised here and there, what walls us in
Trembles with dim slides, transparencies
Of our least motion foisted on a thereby
Realer — falser? — night. Whichever term
Adds its note of tension and relief.
Downstairs, doors are locked against the thief:
Night before last, returning from a dinner,
We found my bedroom ransacked, lights on, loud
Tick of alarm, the mirror off its hook
Looking daggers at the ceiling fixture.
A burglar here in the Enchanted Village —
Unheard of! Not that he took anything.
We had no television, he no taste
For Siamese bronze or Greek embroidery.
Except perhaps some loose change on the bureau
Nothing we can recollect is missing.
"Lucky boys," declared the chief of police
Risking a wise look at our curios.
The threat remains, though, of there still being
A presence in our midst, unknown, unseen,
Unscrupulous to take what he can get.
Next morning in my study — stranger yet —

I found a dusty carton out of place.
Had it been rummaged through? What could he fancy
Lay buried here among these — oh my dear,
Letters scrawled by my own hand unable
To keep pace with the tempest in the cup —
These old love-letters from the other world.
We've set them down at last beside the fire.
Are they for burning, now that the affair
Has ended? (Has it ended?) Any day
It's them or the piano, says DJ.
Who'll ever read them over? Take this one.
Limp, chill, it shivers in the glow, as when
The tenor having braved orchestral fog
First sees Brünnhilde sleeping like a log.
Laid on the fire, it would hesitate,
Trying to think, to feel — then the elate
Burst of satori, plucking final sense
Boldly from inconclusive evidence.
And that (unless it floated, spangled ash,
Outward, upward, one lone carp aflash
Languorously through its habitat
For crumbs that once upon a . . .) would be that.
So, do we burn the — Wait the phone is ringing:
Bad connection; babble of distant talk;
No getting through. We must improve the line
In every sense, for life. Again at nine
Sharp above the village clock, *ring-ring*.
It's Bob the furnace man. He's on his way.
Will find, if not an easy-to-repair
Short circuit, then the failure long foreseen
As total, of our period machine.
Let's be downstairs, leave all this, put the light out.
Fix a screen to the proscenium
Still flickering. Let that carton be. Too much
Already, here below, has met its match.
Yet nothing's gone, or nothing we recall.
And look, the stars have wound in filigree
The ancient, ageless woman of the world.
She's seen us. She is not particular —
Everyone gets her injured, musical
"Why do you no longer come to me?"
To which there's no reply. For here we are.

from *Mirabell: Book 9*

The world was everything that was the case?
Open the case. Lift out the fabulous
Necklace, in form a spiral molecule
Whose sparklings outmaneuver time, space, us.
Here where the table glistens, cleared, one candle
Shines invisibly in the slant light
Beside our nameless houseplant. It's the hour
When Hell (a syllable identified
In childhood as the German word for *bright*
— So that my father's cheerful "Go to Hell",
Long unheard, and Vaughan's unbeatable
"They are all gone into a world of light"
Come, even now at times, to the same thing) —
The hour when Hell shall render what it owes.
Render to whom? how? What at this late date
Can be done with the quaint idiom that slips
From nowhere to my tongue — or from the parchment
Of some old scribe of the apocalypse —
But render *it* as the long rendering to
Light of this very light stored by our cells
These past five million years, these past five minutes
Here by the window, taking in through panes
Still bleary from the hurricane a gull's
Ascending aureole of decibels,
As numberless four-pointed brilliancies
Upon the Sound's mild silver grid come, go?
The message hardly needs decoding, so
Sheer the text, so innocent and fleet
These overlapping pandemonia:
Birdlife, leafplay, rockface, waterglow
Lending us their being, till the given
Moment comes to render what we owe.

Samos

And still, at sea all night, we had a sense
Of sunrise, golden oil poured upon water,
Soothing its heave, letting the sleeper sense
What inborn, amniotic homing sense
Was ferrying him — now through the dream-fire
In which (it has been felt) each human sense
Burns, now through ship's radar's cool sixth sense,
Or mere unerring starlight — to an island.
Here we were. The twins of Sea and Land,
Up and about for hours — hues, cries, scents —
Had placed at eye level a single light
Croissant: the harbor glazed with warm pink light.

Fire-wisps were weaving a string bag of light
For sea stones. Their astounding color sense!
Porphyry, alabaster, chrysolite
Translucences that go dead in daylight
Asked only the quick dip in holy water
For the saint of cell on cell to come alight —
Illuminated crystals thinking light,
Refracting it, the gray prismatic fire
Or yellow-gray of sea's dilute sapphire . . .
Wavelengths daily deeply score the leit-
Motifs of Loom and Wheel upon this land.
To those who listen, it's the Promised Land.

A little spin today? Dirt roads inland
Jounce and revolve in a nerve-jangling light,
Doing the ancient dances of the land
Where, gnarled as olive trees that shag the land
With silver, old men — their two-bladed sense
Of spendthrift poverty, the very land
Being, if not loaf, tomb — superbly land
Upright on the downbeat. We who water
The local wine, which "drinks itself" like water,
Clap for more, cry out to *be* this island
Licked all over by a white, salt fire,
Be noon's pulsing ember raked by fire,

Know nothing, now, but Earth, Air, Water, Fire!
For once out of the frying pan to land
Within their timeless, everlasting fire!
Blood's least red monocle, O magnifier
Of the great Eye that sees by its own light
More pictures in "the world's enchanted fire"
Than come and go in any shrewd crossfire
Upon the page, of syllable and sense,
We want unwilled excursions and ascents,
Crave the upward-rippling rungs of fire,
The outward-rippling rings (enough!) of water . . .
(Now some details — how else will this hold water?)

Our room's three flights above the whitewashed water-
front where Pythagoras was born. A fire
Escape of sky-blue iron leads down to water.
Yachts creak on mirror berths, and over water
Voices from Sweden or Somaliland
Tell how this or that one crossed the water
To Ephesus, came back with toilet water
And a two kilo box of Turkish delight
—Trifles. Yet they shine with such pure light
In memory, even they, that the eyes water.
As with the setting sun, or innocence,
Do things that fade especially make sense?

Samos. We keep trying to make sense
Of what we can. Not souls of the first water —
Although we've put on airs, and taken fire —
We shall be dust of quite another land
Before the seeds here planted come to light.

FRANK O'HARA

(1926 – 1966)

Blocks

1

Yippee! she is shooting in the harbor! he is jumping
up to the maelstrom! she is leaning over the giant's
cart of tears which like a lava cone let fall to fly
from the cross-eyed tantrum-tousled ninth grader's
splayed fist is freezing on the cement! he is throwing
up his arms in heavenly desperation, spacious Y of his
tumultuous love-nerves flailing like a poinsettia in
its own nailish storm against the glass door of the
cumulus which is withholding her from these divine
pastures she has filled with the flesh of men as stones!
O fatal eagerness!

2

O boy, their childhood was like so many oatmeal cookies.
I need you, you need me, yum, yum. Anon it became suddenly

3

like someone always losing something and never knowing what.
Always so. They were so fond of eating bread and butter and
sugar, they were slobs, the mice used to lick the floorboards
after they went to bed, rolling their light tails against
the rattling marbles of granulation. Vivo! the dextrose
those children consumed, lavished, smoked, in their knobby
candy bars. Such pimples! such hardons! such moody loves.
And thus they grew like giggling fir trees.

A Step Away from Them

It's my lunch hour, so I go
for a walk among the hum-colored
cabs. First, down the sidewalk
where laborers feed their dirty
glistening torsos sandwiches
and Coca-Cola, with yellow helmets
on. They protect them from falling
bricks, I guess. Then onto the
avenue where skirts are flipping
above heels and blow up over
grates. The sun is hot, but the
cabs stir up the air. I look
at bargains in wristwatches. There
are cats playing in sawdust.
                      On
to Times Square, where the sign
blows smoke over my head, and higher
the waterfall pours lightly. A
Negro stands in a doorway with a
toothpick, languorously agitating.
A blonde chorus girl clicks: he
smiles and rubs his chin. Everything
suddenly honks: it is 12:40 of
a Thursday.
           Neon in daylight is a
great pleasure, as Edwin Denby would
write, as are light bulbs in daylight.
I stop for a cheeseburger at JULIET's
CORNER. Giulietta Masina, wife of
Federico Fellini, *è bell' attrice.*
And chocolate malted. A lady in
foxes on such a day puts her poodle
in a cab.
          There are several Puerto
Ricans on the avenue today, which
makes it beautiful and warm. First
Bunny died, then John Latouche,
then Jackson Pollock. But is the
earth as full as life was full, of them?

And one has eaten and one walks,
past the magazines with nudes
and the posters for BULLFIGHT and
the Manhattan Storage Warehouse,
which they'll soon tear down. I
used to think they had the Armory
Show there.
        A glass of papaya juice
and back to work. My heart is in my
pocket, it is Poems by Pierre Reverdy.

The Day Lady Died

It is 12:20 in New York a Friday
three days after Bastille day, yes
it is 1959 and I go get a shoeshine
because I will get off the 4:19 in Easthampton
at 7:15 and then go straight to dinner
and I don't know the people who will feed me

I walk up the muggy street beginning to sun
and have a hamburger and a malted and buy
an ugly NEW WORLD WRITING to see what the poets
in Ghana are doing these days
        I go on to the bank
and Miss Stillwagon (first name Linda I once heard)
doesn't even look up my balance for once in her life
and in the GOLDEN GRIFFIN I get a little Verlaine
for Patsy with drawings by Bonnard although I do
think of Hesiod, trans. Richmond Lattimore or
Brendan Behan's new play or *Le Balcon* or *Les Nègres*
of Genet, but I don't, I stick with Verlaine
after practically going to sleep with quandariness

and for Mike I just stroll into the PARK LANE
Liquor Store and ask for a bottle of Strega and
then I go back where I came from to 6th Avenue
and the tobacconist in the Ziegfeld Theatre and
casually ask for a carton of Gauloises and a carton
of Picayunes, and a NEW YORK POST with her face on it

and I am sweating a lot by now and thinking of
leaning on the john door in the 5 SPOT
while she whispered a song along the keyboard
to Mal Waldron and everyone and I stopped breathing

Ave Maria

Mothers of America
      let your kids go to the movies!
get them out of the house so they won't know what you're up to
it's true that fresh air is good for the body
      but what about the soul
that grows in darkness, embossed by silvery images
and when you grow old as grow old you must
      they won't hate you
they won't criticize you they won't know
      they'll be in some glamorous country
they first saw on a Saturday afternoon or playing hookey
they may even be grateful to you
      for their first sexual experience
which only cost you a quarter
      and didn't upset the peaceful home
they will know where candy bars come from
      and gratuitous bags of popcorn
as gratuitous as leaving the movie before it's over
with a pleasant stranger whose apartment is in the Heaven
  on Earth Bldg
near the Williamsburg Bridge
      oh mothers you will have made the little tykes
so happy because if nobody does pick them up in the movies
they won't know the difference
      and if somebody does it'll be sheer gravy
and they'll have been truly entertained either way
instead of hanging around the yard
      or up in their room
         hating you
prematurely since you won't have done anything horribly
  mean yet
except keeping them from the darker joys
      it's unforgivable the latter

so don't blame me if you won't take this advice
     and the family breaks up
and your children grow old and blind in front of a TV set
     seeing
movies you wouldn't let them see when they were young

An Image of Leda

The cinema is cruel
like a miracle. We
sit in the darkened
room asking nothing
of the empty white
space but that it
remain pure. And
suddenly despite us
it blackens. Not by
the hand that holds
the pen. There is
no message. We our-
selves appear naked
on the river bank
spread-eagled while
the machine wings
nearer. We scream
chatter prance and
wash our hair! Is
it our prayer or
wish that this
occur? Oh what is
this light that
holds us fast? Our
limbs quicken even
to disgrace under
this white eye as
if there were real
pleasure in loving
a shadow and caress-
ing a disguise!

Poetry

The only way to be quiet
is to be quick, so I scare
you clumsily, or surprise
you with a stab. A praying
mantis knows time more
intimately than I and is
more casual. Crickets use
time for accompaniment to
innocent fidgeting. A zebra
races counterclockwise.
All this I desire. To
deepen you by my quickness
and delight as if you
were logical and proven,
but still be quiet as if
I were used to you; as if
you would never leave me
and were the inexorable
product of my own time.

Why I Am Not a Painter

I am not a painter, I am a poet.
Why? I think I would rather be
a painter, but I am not. Well,

for instance, Mike Goldberg
is starting a painting. I drop in.
"Sit down and have a drink" he
says. I drink; we drink. I look
up. "You have SARDINES in it."
"Yes, it needed something there."
"Oh." I go and the days go by
and I drop in again. The painting
is going on, and I go, and the days
go by. I drop in. The painting is
finished. "Where's SARDINES?"
All that's left is just
letters, "It was too much," Mike says.

But me? One day I am thinking of
a color: orange. I write a line
about orange. Pretty soon it is a
whole page of words, not lines.
Then another page. There should be
so much more, not of orange, of
words, of how terrible orange is
and life. Days go by. It is even in
prose, I am a real poet. My poem
is finished and I haven't mentioned
orange yet. It's twelve poems, I call
it ORANGES. And one day in a gallery
I see Mike's painting, called SARDINES.

A True Account of Talking to the Sun
at Fire Island

The Sun woke me this morning loud
and clear, saying "Hey! I've been
trying to wake you up for fifteen
minutes. Don't be so rude, you are
only the second poet I've ever chosen
to speak to personally
                        so why
aren't you more attentive? If I could
burn you through the window I would
to wake you up. I can't hang around
here all day."
                "Sorry, Sun, I stayed
up late last night talking to Hal."

"When I woke up Mayakovsky he was
a lot more prompt" the Sun said
petulantly. "Most people are up
already waiting to see if I'm going
to put in an appearance."
                          I tried
to apologize "I missed you yesterday."
"That's better" he said. "I didn't
know you'd come out." "You may be
wondering why I've come so close?"

"Yes" I said beginning to feel hot
wondering if maybe he wasn't burning me
anyway.

      "Frankly I wanted to tell you
I like your poetry. I see a lot
on my rounds and you're okay. You may
not be the greatest thing on earth, but
you're different. Now, I've heard some
say you're crazy, they being excessively
calm themselves to my mind, and other
crazy poets think that you're a boring
reactionary. Not me.

      Just keep on
like I do and pay no attention. You'll
find that people always will complain
about the atmosphere, either too hot
or too cold too bright or too dark, days
too short or too long.

      If you don't appear
at all one day they think you're lazy
or dead. Just keep right on, I like it.

And don't worry about your lineage
poetic or natural. The Sun shines on
the jungle, you know, on the tundra
the sea, the ghetto. Wherever you were
I knew it and saw you moving. I was waiting
for you to get to work.

      And now that you
are making your own days, so to speak,
even if no one reads you but me
you won't be depressed. Not
everyone can look up, even at me. It
hurts their eyes."

      "Oh Sun, I'm so grateful to you!"

"Thanks and remember I'm watching. It's
easier for me to speak to you out
here. I don't have to slide down
between buildings to get your ear.
I know you love Manhattan, but
you ought to look up more often.

And
always embrace things, people earth
sky stars, as I do, freely and with
the appropriate sense of space. That
is your inclination, known in the heavens
and you should follow it to hell, if
necessary, which I doubt.
Maybe we'll
speak again in Africa, of which I too
am specially fond. Go back to sleep now
Frank, and I may leave a tiny poem
in that brain of yours as my farewell."

"Sun, don't go!" I was awake
at last. "No, go I must, they're calling
me."
"Who are they?"
Rising he said "Some
day you'll know. They're calling to you
too." Darkly he rose, and then I slept.

JOHN ASHBERY
(1927–)

Some Trees

These are amazing: each
Joining a neighbor, as though speech
Were a still performance.
Arranging by chance

To meet as far this morning
From the world as agreeing
With it, you and I
Are suddenly what the trees try

To tell us we are:
That their merely being there
Means something; that soon
We may touch, love, explain.

And glad not to have invented
Such comeliness, we are surrounded:
A silence already filled with noises,
A canvas on which emerges

A chorus of smiles, a winter morning.
Placed in a puzzling light, and moving,
Our days put on such reticence
These accents seem their own defense.

The Painter

Sitting between the sea and the buildings
He enjoyed painting the sea's portrait.
But just as children imagine a prayer

Is merely silence, he expected his subject
To rush up the sand, and, seizing a brush,
Plaster its own portrait on the canvas.

So there was never any paint on his canvas
Until the people who lived in the buildings
Put him to work: "Try using the brush
As a means to an end. Select, for a portrait,
Something less angry and large, and more subject
To a painter's moods, or, perhaps, to a prayer."

How could he explain to them his prayer
That nature, not art, might usurp the canvas?
He chose his wife for a new subject,
Making her vast, like ruined buildings,
As if, forgetting itself, the portrait
Had expressed itself without a brush.

Slightly encouraged, he dipped his brush
In the sea, murmuring a heartfelt prayer:
"My soul, when I paint this next portrait
Let it be you who wrecks the canvas."
The news spread like wildfire through the buildings:
He had gone back to the sea for his subject.

Imagine a painter crucified by his subject!
Too exhausted even to lift his brush,
He provoked some artists leaning from the buildings
To malicious mirth: "We haven't a prayer
Now, of putting ourselves on canvas,
Or getting the sea to sit for a portrait!"

Others declared it a self-portrait.
Finally all indications of a subject
Began to fade, leaving the canvas
Perfectly white. He put down the brush.
At once a howl, that was also a prayer,
Arose from the overcrowded buildings.

They tossed him, the portrait, from the tallest of the buildings;
And the sea devoured the canvas and the brush
As though his subject had decided to remain a prayer.

These Lacustrine Cities

These lacustrine cities grew out of loathing
Into something forgetful, although angry with history.
They are the product of an idea: that man is horrible, for instance,
Though this is only one example.

They emerged until a tower
Controlled the sky, and with artifice dipped back
Into the past for swans and tapering branches,
Burning, until all that hate was transformed into useless love.

Then you are left with an idea of yourself
And the feeling of ascending emptiness of the afternoon
Which must be charged to the embarrassment of others
Who fly by you like beacons.

The night is a sentinel.
Much of your time has been occupied by creative games
Until now, but we have all-inclusive plans for you.
We had thought, for instance, of sending you to the middle of
    the desert,

To a violent sea, or of having the closeness of the others be air
To you, pressing you back into a startled dream
As sea-breezes greet a child's face.
But the past is already here, and you are nursing some private
    project.

The worst is not over, yet I know
You will be happy here. Because of the logic
Of your situation, which is something no climate can outsmart.
Tender and insouciant by turns, you see

You have built a mountain of something,
Thoughtfully pouring all your energy into this single monument,
Whose wind is desire starching a petal,
Whose disappointment broke into a rainbow of tears.

Soonest Mended

Barely tolerated, living on the margin
In our technological society, we were always having to be rescued
On the brink of destruction, like heroines in *Orlando Furioso*
Before it was time to start all over again.
There would be thunder in the bushes, a rustling of coils,
And Angelica, in the Ingres painting, was considering
The colorful but small monster near her toe, as though
    wondering whether forgetting
The whole thing might not, in the end, be the only solution.
And then there always came a time when
Happy Hooligan in his rusted green automobile
Came plowing down the course, just to make sure everything
    was O.K.,
Only by that time we were in another chapter and confused
About how to receive this latest piece of information.
Was it information? Weren't we rather acting this out
For someone else's benefit, thoughts in a mind
With room enough and to spare for our little problems (so
    they began to seem),
Our daily quandary about food and the rent and bills to be paid?
To reduce all this to a small variant,
To step free at last, minuscule on the gigantic plateau —
This was our ambition: to be small and clear and free.
Alas, the summer's energy wanes quickly,
A moment and it is gone. And no longer
May we make the necessary arrangements, simple as they are.
Our star was brighter perhaps when it had water in it.
Now there is no question even of that, but only
Of holding on to the hard earth so as not to get thrown off,
With an occasional dream, a vision: a robin flies across
The upper corner of the window, you brush your hair away
And cannot quite see, or a wound will flash
Against the sweet faces of the others, something like:
This is what you wanted to hear, so why
Did you think of listening to something else? We are all talkers
It is true, but underneath the talk lies
The moving and not wanting to be moved, the loose
Meaning, untidy and simple like a threshing floor.

These then were some hazards of the course,
Yet though we knew the course *was* hazards and nothing else
It was still a shock when, almost a quarter of a century later,
The clarity of the rules dawned on you for the first time.
They were the players, and we who had struggled at the game
Were merely spectators, though subject to its vicissitudes
And moving with it out of the tearful stadium, borne on
  shoulders, at last.
Night after night this message returns, repeated
In the flickering bulbs of the sky, raised past us, taken away
  from us,
Yet ours over and over until the end that is past truth,
The being of our sentences, in the climate that fostered them,
Not ours to own, like a book, but to be with, and sometimes
To be without, alone and desperate.
But the fantasy makes it ours, a kind of fence-sitting
Raised to the level of an esthetic ideal. These were moments,
  years,
Solid with reality, faces, namable events, kisses, heroic acts,
But like the friendly beginning of a geometrical progression
Not too reassuring, as though meaning could be cast aside
  some day
When it had been outgrown. Better, you said, to stay cowering
Like this in the early lessons, since the promise of learning
Is a delusion, and I agreed, adding that
Tomorrow would alter the sense of what had already been learned,
That the learning process is extended in this way, so that from
  this standpoint
None of us ever graduates from college,
For time is an emulsion, and probably thinking not to grow up
Is the brightest kind of maturity for us, right now at any rate.
And you see, both of us were right, though nothing
Has somehow come to nothing; the avatars
Of our conforming to the rules and living
Around the home have made — well, in a sense, "good
  citizens" of us.
Brushing the teeth and all that, and learning to accept
The charity of the hard moments as they are doled out,
For this is action, this not being sure, this careless
Preparing, sowing the seeds crooked in the furrow,
Making ready to forget, and always coming back
To the mooring of starting out, that day so long ago.

As One Put Drunk into the Packet-Boat

I tried each thing, only some were immortal and free.
Elsewhere we are as sitting in a place where sunlight
Filters down, a little at a time,
Waiting for someone to come. Harsh words are spoken,
As the sun yellows the green of the maple tree. . . .

So this was all, but obscurely
I felt the stirrings of new breath in the pages
Which all winter long had smelled like an old catalogue.
New sentences were starting up. But the summer
Was well along, not yet past the mid-point
But full and dark with the promise of that fullness,
That time when one can no longer wander away
And even the least attentive fall silent
To watch the thing that is prepared to happen.

A look of glass stops you
And you walk on shaken: was I the perceived?
Did they notice me, this time, as I am,
Or is it postponed again? The children
Still at their games, clouds that arise with a swift
Impatience in the afternoon sky, then dissipate
As limpid, dense twilight comes.
Only in that tooting of a horn
Down there, for a moment, I thought
The great, formal affair was beginning, orchestrated,
Its colors concentrated in a glance, a ballade
That takes in the whole world, now, but lightly,
Still lightly, but with wide authority and tact.

The prevalence of those gray flakes falling?
They are sun motes. You have slept in the sun
Longer than the sphinx, and are none the wiser for it.
Come in. And I thought a shadow fell across the door
But it was only her come to ask once more
If I was coming in, and not to hurry in case I wasn't.

The night sheen takes over. A moon of cistercian pallor
Has climbed to the center of heaven, installed,
Finally involved with the business of darkness.
And a sigh heaves from all the small things on earth,

The books, the papers, the old garters and union-suit buttons
Kept in a white cardboard box somewhere, and all the lower
Versions of cities flattened under the equalizing night.
The summer demands and takes away too much,
But night, the reserved, the reticent, gives more than it takes.

Self-Portrait in a Convex Mirror

As Parmigianino did it, the right hand
Bigger than the head, thrust at the viewer
And swerving easily away, as though to protect
What it advertises. A few leaded panes, old beams,
Fur, pleated muslin, a coral ring run together
In a movement supporting the face, which swims
Toward and away like the hand
Except that it is in repose. It is what is
Sequestered. Vasari says, "Francesco one day set himself
To take his own portrait, looking at himself for that purpose
In a convex mirror, such as is used by barbers . . .
He accordingly caused a ball of wood to be made
By a turner, and having divided it in half and
Brought it to the size of the mirror, he set himself
With great art to copy all that he saw in the glass,"
Chiefly his reflection, of which the portrait
Is the reflection once removed.
The glass chose to reflect only what he saw
Which was enough for his purpose: his image
Glazed, embalmed, projected at a 180-degree angle.
The time of day or the density of the light
Adhering to the face keeps it
Lively and intact in a recurring wave
Of arrival. The soul establishes itself.
But how far can it swim out through the eyes
And still return safely to its nest? The surface
Of the mirror being convex, the distance increases
Significantly; that is, enough to make the point
That the soul is a captive, treated humanely, kept
In suspension, unable to advance much farther
Than your look as it intercepts the picture.

Pope Clement and his court were "stupefied"
By it, according to Vasari, and promised a commission
That never materialized. The soul has to stay where it is,
Even though restless, hearing raindrops at the pane,
The sighing of autumn leaves thrashed by the wind,
Longing to be free, outside, but it must stay
Posing in this place. It must move
As little as possible. This is what the portrait says.
But there is in that gaze a combination
Of tenderness, amusement and regret, so powerful
In its restraint that one cannot look for long.
The secret is too plain. The pity of it smarts,
Makes hot tears spurt: that the soul is not a soul,
Has no secret, is small, and it fits
Its hollow perfectly: its room, our moment of attention.
That is the tune but there are no words.
The words are only speculation
(From the Latin *speculum,* mirror):
They seek and cannot find the meaning of the music.
We see only postures of the dream,
Riders of the motion that swings the face
Into view under evening skies, with no
False disarray as proof of authenticity.
But it is life englobed.
One would like to stick one's hand
Out of the globe, but its dimension,
What carries it, will not allow it.
No doubt it is this, not the reflex
To hide something, which makes the hand loom large
As it retreats slightly. There is no way
To build it flat like a section of wall:
It must join the segment of a circle,
Roving back to the body of which it seems
So unlikely a part, to fence in and shore up the face
On which the effort of this condition reads
Like a pinpoint of a smile, a spark
Or star one is not sure of having seen
As darkness resumes. A perverse light whose
Imperative of subtlety dooms in advance its
Conceit to light up: unimportant but meant.
Francesco, your hand is big enough

To wreck the sphere, and too big,
One would think, to weave delicate meshes
That only argue its further detention.
(Big, but not coarse, merely on another scale,
Like a dozing whale on the sea bottom
In relation to the tiny, self-important ship
On the surface.) But your eyes proclaim
That everything is surface. The surface is what's there
And nothing can exist except what's there.
There are no recesses in the room, only alcoves,
And the window doesn't matter much, or that
Sliver of window or mirror on the right, even
As a gauge of the weather, which in French is
Le temps, the word for time, and which
Follows a course wherein changes are merely
Features of the whole. The whole is stable within
Instability, a globe like ours, resting
On a pedestal of vacuum, a ping-pong ball
Secure on its jet of water.
And just as there are no words for the surface, that is,
No words to say what it really is, that it is not
Superficial but a visible core, then there is
No way out of the problem of pathos vs. experience.
You will stay on, restive, serene in
Your gesture which is neither embrace nor warning
But which holds something of both in pure
Affirmation that doesn't affirm anything.

The balloon pops, the attention
Turns dully away. Clouds
In the puddle stir up into sawtoothed fragments.
I think of the friends
Who came to see me, of what yesterday
Was like. A peculiar slant
Of memory that intrudes on the dreaming model
In the silence of the studio as he considers
Lifting the pencil to the self-portrait.
How many people came and stayed a certain time,
Uttered light or dark speech that became part of you
Like light behind windblown fog and sand,
Filtered and influenced by it, until no part

Remains that is surely you. Those voices in the dusk
Have told you all and still the tale goes on
In the form of memories deposited in irregular
Clumps of crystals. Whose curved hand controls,
Francesco, the turning seasons and the thoughts
That peel off and fly away at breathless speeds
Like the last stubborn leaves ripped
From wet branches? I see in this only the chaos
Of your round mirror which organizes everything
Around the polestar of your eyes which are empty,
Know nothing, dream but reveal nothing.
I feel the carousel starting slowly
And going faster and faster: desk, papers, books,
Photographs of friends, the window and the trees
Merging in one neutral band that surrounds
Me on all sides, everywhere I look.
And I cannot explain the action of leveling,
Why it should all boil down to one
Uniform substance, a magma of interiors.
My guide in these matters is your self,
Firm, oblique, accepting everything with the same
Wraith of a smile, and as time speeds up so that it is soon
Much later, I can know only the straight way out,
The distance between us. Long ago
The strewn evidence meant something,
The small accidents and pleasures
Of the day as it moved gracelessly on,
A housewife doing chores. Impossible now
To restore those properties in the silver blur that is
The record of what you accomplished by sitting down
"With great art to copy all that you saw in the glass"
So as to perfect and rule out the extraneous
Forever. In the circle of your intentions certain spars
Remain that perpetuate the enchantment of self with self:
Eyebeams, muslin, coral. It doesn't matter
Because these are things as they are today
Before one's shadow ever grew
Out of the field into thoughts of tomorrow.

Tomorrow is easy, but today is uncharted,
Desolate, reluctant as any landscape
To yield what are laws of perspective

After all only to the painter's deep
Mistrust, a weak instrument though
Necessary. Of course some things
Are possible, it knows, but it doesn't know
Which ones. Some day we will try
To do as many things as are possible
And perhaps we shall succeed at a handful
Of them, but this will not have anything
To do with what is promised today, our
Landscape sweeping out from us to disappear
On the horizon. Today enough of a cover burnishes
To keep the supposition of promises together
In one piece of surface, letting one ramble
Back home from them so that these
Even stronger possibilities can remain
Whole without being tested. Actually
The skin of the bubble-chamber's as tough as
Reptile eggs; everything gets "programmed" there
In due course: more keeps getting included
Without adding to the sum, and just as one
Gets accustomed to a noise that
Kept one awake but now no longer does,
So the room contains this flow like an hourglass
Without varying in climate or quality
(Except perhaps to brighten bleakly and almost
Invisibly, in a focus sharpening toward death — more
Of this later). What should be the vacuum of a dream
Becomes continually replete as the source of dreams
Is being tapped so that this one dream
May wax, flourish like a cabbage rose,
Defying sumptuary laws, leaving us
To awake and try to begin living in what
Has now become a slum. Sydney Freedberg in his
Parmigianino says of it: "Realism in this portrait
No longer produces an objective truth, but a *bizarria*. . . .
However its distortion does not create
A feeling of disharmony. . . . The forms retain
A strong measure of ideal beauty," because
Fed by our dreams, so inconsequential until one day
We notice the hole they left. Now their importance
If not their meaning is plain. They were to nourish
A dream which includes them all, as they are

Finally reversed in the accumulating mirror.
They seemed strange because we couldn't actually see them.
And we realize this only at a point where they lapse
Like a wave breaking on a rock, giving up
Its shape in a gesture which expresses that shape.
The forms retain a strong measure of ideal beauty
As they forage in secret on our idea of distortion.
Why be unhappy with this arrangement, since
Dreams prolong us as they are absorbed?
Something like living occurs, a movement
Out of the dream into its codification.

As I start to forget it
It presents its stereotype again
But it is an unfamiliar stereotype, the face
Riding at anchor, issued from hazards, soon
To accost others, "rather angel than man" (Vasari).
Perhaps an angel looks like everything
We have forgotten, I mean forgotten
Things that don't seem familiar when
We meet them again, lost beyond telling,
Which were ours once. This would be the point
Of invading the privacy of this man who
"Dabbled in alchemy, but whose wish
Here was not to examine the subtleties of art
In a detached, scientific spirit: he wished through them
To impart the sense of novelty and amazament to the spectator"
(Freedberg). Later portraits such as the Uffizi
"Gentleman," the Borghese "Young Prelate" and
The Naples "Antea" issue from Mannerist
Tensions, but here, as Freedberg points out,
The surprise, the tension are in the concept
Rather than its realization.
The consonance of the High Renaissance
Is present, though distorted by the mirror.
What is novel is the extreme care in rendering
The velleities of the rounded reflecting surface
(It is the first mirror portrait),
So that you could be fooled for a moment
Before you realize the reflection
Isn't yours. You feel then like one of those

Hoffmann characters who have been deprived
Of a reflection, except that the whole of me
Is seen to be supplanted by the strict
Otherness of the painter in his
Other room. We have surprised him
At work, but no, he has surprised us
As he works. The picture is almost finished,
The surprise almost over, as when one looks out,
Startled by a snowfall which even now is
Ending in specks and sparkles of snow.
It happened while you were inside, asleep,
And there is no reason why you should have
Been awake for it, except that the day
Is ending and it will be hard for you
To get to sleep tonight, at least until late.

The shadow of the city injects its own
Urgency: Rome where Francesco
Was at work during the Sack: his inventions
Amazed the soldiers who burst in on him;
They decided to spare his life, but he left soon after;
Vienna where the painting is today, where
I saw it with Pierre in the summer of 1959; New York
Where I am now, which is a logarithm
Of other cities. Our landscape
Is alive with filiations, shuttlings;
Business is carried on by look, gesture,
Hearsay. It is another life to the city,
The backing of the looking glass of the
Unidentified but precisely sketched studio. It wants
To siphon off the life of the studio, deflate
Its mapped space to enactments, island it.
That operation has been temporarily stalled
But something new is on the way, a new preciosity
In the wind. Can you stand it,
Francesco? Are you strong enough for it?
This wind brings what it knows not, is
Self-propelled, blind, has no notion
Of itself. It is inertia that once
Acknowledged saps all activity, secret or public:
Whispers of the word that can't be understood

But can be felt, a chill, a blight
Moving outward along the capes and peninsulas
Of your nervures and so to the archipelagoes
And to the bathed, aired secrecy of the open sea.
This is its negative side. Its positive side is
Making you notice life and the stresses
That only seemed to go away, but now,
As this new mode questions, are seen to be
Hastening out of style. If they are to become classics
They must decide which side they are on.
Their reticence has undermined
The urban scenery, made its ambiguities
Look willful and tired, the games of an old man.
What we need now is this unlikely
Challenger pounding on the gates of an amazed
Castle. Your argument, Francesco,
Had begun to grow stale as no answer
Or answers were forthcoming. If it dissolves now
Into dust, that only means its time had come
Some time ago, but look now, and listen:
It may be that another life is stocked there
In recesses no one knew of; that it,
Not we, are the change; that we are in fact it
If we could get back to it, relive some of the way
It looked, turn our faces to the globe as it sets
And still be coming out all right:
Nerves normal, breath normal. Since it is a metaphor
Made to include us, we are a part of it and
Can live in it as in fact we have done,
Only leaving our minds bare for questioning
We now see will not take place at random
But in an orderly way that means to menace
Nobody—the normal way things are done,
Like the concentric growing up of days
Around a life: correctly, if you think about it.

A breeze like the turning of a page
Brings back your face: the moment
Takes such a big bite out of the haze
Of pleasant intuition it comes after.
The locking into place is "death itself,"

As Berg said of a phrase in Mahler's Ninth;
Or, to quote Imogen in *Cymbeline,* "There cannot
Be a pinch in death more sharp than this," for,
Though only exercise or tactic, it carries
The momentum of a conviction that had been building.
Mere forgetfulness cannot remove it
Nor wishing bring it back, as long as it remains
The white precipitate of its dream
In the climate of sighs flung across our world,
A cloth over a birdcage. But it is certain that
What is beautiful seems so only in relation to a specific
Life, experienced or not, channeled into some form
Steeped in the nostalgia of a collective past.
The light sinks today with an enthusiasm
I have known elsewhere, and known why
It seemed meaningful, that others felt this way
Years ago. I go on consulting
This mirror that is no longer mine
For as much brisk vacancy as is to be
My portion this time. And the vase is always full
Because there is only just so much room
And it accommodates everything. The sample
One sees is not to be taken as
Merely that, but as everything as it
May be imagined outside time — not as a gesture
But as all, in the refined, assimilable state.
But what is this universe the porch of
As it veers in and out, back and forth,
Refusing to surround us and still the only
Thing we can see? Love once
Tipped the scales but now is shadowed, invisible,
Though mysteriously present, around somewhere.
But we know it cannot be sandwiched
Between two adjacent moments, that its windings
Lead nowhere except to further tributaries
And that these empty themselves into a vague
Sense of something that can never be known
Even though it seems likely that each of us
Knows what it is and is capable of
Communicating it to the other. But the look
Some wear as a sign makes one want to

Push forward ignoring the apparent
Naïveté of the attempt, not caring
That no one is listening, since the light
Has been lit once and for all in their eyes
And is present, unimpaired, a permanent anomaly,
Awake and silent. On the surface of it
There seems no special reason why that light
Should be focused by love, or why
The city falling with its beautiful suburbs
Into space always less clear, less defined,
Should read as the support of its progress,
The easel upon which the drama unfolded
To its own satisfaction and to the end
Of our dreaming, as we had never imagined
It would end, in worn daylight with the painted
Promise showing through as a gage, a bond.
This nondescript, never-to-be defined daytime is
The secret of where it takes place
And we can no longer return to the various
Conflicting statements gathered, lapses of memory
Of the principal witnesses. All we know
Is that we are a little early, that
Today has that special, lapidary
Todayness that the sunlight reproduces
Faithfully in casting twig-shadows on blithe
Sidewalks. No previous day would have been like this.
I used to think they were all alike,
That the present always looked the same to everybody
But this confusion drains away as one
Is always cresting into one's present.
Yet the "poetic," straw-colored space
Of the long corridor that leads back to the painting,
Its darkening opposite — is this
Some figment of "art," not to be imagined
As real, let alone special? Hasn't it too its lair
In the present we are always escaping from
And falling back into, as the waterwheel of days
Pursues its uneventful, even serene course?
I think it is trying to say it is today
And we must get out of it even as the public
Is pushing through the museum now so as to

Be out by closing time. You can't live there.
The gray glaze of the past attacks all know-how:
Secrets of wash and finish that took a lifetime
To learn and are reduced to the status of
Black-and-white illustrations in a book where colorplates
Are rare. That is, all time
Reduces to no special time. No one
Alludes to the change; to do so might
Involve calling attention to oneself
Which would augment the dread of not getting out
Before having seen the whole collection
(Except for the sculptures in the basement:
They are where they belong).
Our time gets to be veiled, compromised
By the portrait's will to endure. It hints at
Our own, which we were hoping to keep hidden.
We don't need paintings or
Doggerel written by mature poets when
The explosion is so precise, so fine.
Is there any point even in acknowledging
The existence of all that? Does it
Exist? Certainly the leisure to
Indulge stately pastimes doesn't,
Any more. Today has no margins, the event arrives
Flush with its edges, is of the same substance,
Indistinguishable. "Play" is something else;
It exists, in a society specifically
Organized as a demonstration of itself.
There is no other way, and those assholes
Who would confuse everything with their mirror games
Which seem to multiply stakes and possibilities, or
At least confuse issues by means of an investing
Aura that would corrode the architecture
Of the whole in a haze of suppressed mockery,
Are beside the point. They are out of the game,
Which doesn't exist until they are out of it.
It seems like a very hostile universe
But as the principle of each individual thing is
Hostile to, exists at the expense of all the others
As philosophers have often pointed out, at least
This thing, the mute, undivided present,

Has the justification of logic, which
In this instance isn't a bad thing
Or wouldn't be, if the way of telling
Didn't somehow intrude, twisting the end result
Into a caricature of itself. This always
Happens, as in the game where
A whispered phrase passed around the room
Ends up as something completely different.
It is the principle that makes works of art so unlike
What the artist intended. Often he finds
He has omitted the thing he started out to say
In the first place. Seduced by flowers,
Explicit pleasures, he blames himself (though
Secretly satisfied with the result), imagining
He had a say in the matter and exercised
An option of which he was hardly conscious,
Unaware that necessity circumvents such resolutions
So as to create something new
For itself, that there is no other way,
That the history of creation proceeds according to
Stringent laws, and that things
Do get done in this way, but never the things
We set out to accomplish and wanted so desperately
To see come into being. Parmigianino
Must have realized this as he worked at his
Life-obstructing task. One is forced to read
The perfectly plausible accomplishment of a purpose
Into the smooth, perhaps even bland (but so
Enigmatic) finish. Is there anything
To be serious about beyond this otherness
That gets included in the most ordinary
Forms of daily activity, changing everything
Slightly and profoundly, and tearing the matter
Of creation, any creation, not just artistic creation
Out of our hands, to install it on some monstrous, near
Peak, too close to ignore, too far
For one to intervene? This otherness, this
"Not-being-us" is all there is to look at
In the mirror, though no one can say
How it came to be this way. A ship
Flying unknown colors has entered the harbor.

You are allowing extraneous matters
To break up your day, cloud the focus
Of the crystal ball. Its scene drifts away
Like vapor scattered on the wind. The fertile
Thought-associations that until now came
So easily, appear no more, or rarely. Their
Colorings are less intense, washed out
By autumn rains and winds, spoiled, muddied,
Given back to you because they are worthless.
Yet we are such creatures of habit that their
Implications are still around *en permanence,* confusing
Issues. To be serious only about sex
Is perhaps one way, but the sands are hissing
As they approach the beginning of the big slide
Into what happened. This past
Is now here: the painter's
Reflected face, in which we linger, receiving
Dreams and inspirations on an unassigned
Frequency, but the hues have turned metallic,
The curves and edges are not so rich. Each person
Has one big theory to explain the universe
But it doesn't tell the whole story
And in the end it is what is outside him
That matters, to him and especially to us
Who have been given no help whatever
In decoding our own man-size quotient and must rely
On second-hand knowledge. Yet I know
That no one else's taste is going to be
Any help, and might as well be ignored.
Once it seemed so perfect — gloss on the fine
Freckled skin, lips moistened as though about to part
Releasing speech, and the familiar look
Of clothes and furniture that one forgets.
This could have been our paradise: exotic
Refuge within an exhausted world, but that wasn't
In the cards, because it couldn't have been
The point. Aping naturalness may be the first step
Toward achieving an inner calm
But it is the first step only, and often
Remains a frozen gesture of welcome etched
On the air materializing behind it,

A convention. And we have really
No time for these, except to use them
For kindling. The sooner they are burnt up
The better for the roles we have to play.
Therefore I beseech you, withdraw that hand,
Offer it no longer as shield or greeting,
The shield of a greeting, Francesco:
There is room for one bullet in the chamber:
Our looking through the wrong end
Of the telescope as you fall back at a speed
Faster than that of light to flatten ultimately
Among the features of the room, an invitation
Never mailed, the "it was all a dream"
Syndrome, though the "all" tells tersely
Enough how it wasn't. Its existence
Was real, though troubled, and the ache
Of this waking dream can never drown out
The diagram still sketched on the wind,
Chosen, meant for me and materialized
In the disguising radiance of my room.
We have seen the city; it is the gibbous
Mirrored eye of an insect. All things happen
On its balcony and are resumed within,
But the action is the cold, syrupy flow
Of a pageant. One feels too confined,
Sifting the April sunlight for clues,
In the mere stillness of the ease of its
Parameter. The hand holds no chalk
And each part of the whole falls off
And cannot know it knew, except
Here and there, in cold pockets
Of remembrance, whispers out of time.

Street Musicians

One died, and the soul was wrenched out
Of the other in life, who, walking the streets
Wrapped in an identity like a coat, sees on and on
The same corners, volumetrics, shadows

Under trees. Farther than anyone was ever
Called, through increasingly suburban airs
And ways, with autumn falling over everything:
The plush leaves the chattels in barrels
Of an obscure family being evicted
Into the way it was, and is. The other beached
Glimpses of what the other was up to:
Revelations at last. So they grew to hate and forget each other.

So I cradle this average violin that knows
Only forgotten showtunes, but argues
The possibility of free declamation anchored
To a dull refrain, the year turning over on itself
In November, with the spaces among the days
More literal, the meat more visible on the bone.
Our question of a place of origin hangs
Like smoke: how we picnicked in pine forests,
In coves with the water always seeping up, and left
Our trash, sperm and excrement everywhere, smeared
On the landscape, to make of us what we could.

Syringa

Orpheus liked the glad personal quality
Of the things beneath the sky. Of course, Eurydice was a part
Of this. Then one day, everything changed. He rends
Rocks into fissures with lament. Gullies, hummocks
Can't withstand it. The sky shudders from one horizon
To the other, almost ready to give up wholeness.
Then Apollo quietly told him: "Leave it all on earth.
Your lute, what point? Why pick at a dull pavan few care to
Follow, except a few birds of dusty feather,
Not vivid performances of the past." But why not?
All other things must change too.
The seasons are no longer what they once were,
But it is the nature of things to be seen only once,
As they happen along, bumping into other things, getting along
Somehow. That's where Orpheus made his mistake.
Of course Eurydice vanished into the shade;

She would have even if he hadn't turned around.
No use standing there like a gray stone toga as the whole wheel
Of recorded history flashes past, struck dumb, unable to utter
  an intelligent
Comment on the most thought-provoking element in its train.
Only love stays on the brain, and something these people,
These other ones, call life. Singing accurately
So that the notes mount straight up out of the well of
Dim noon and rival the tiny, sparkling yellow flowers
Growing around the brink of the quarry, encapsulizes
The different weights of the things.
                                 But it isn't enough
To just go on singing. Orpheus realized this
And didn't mind so much about his reward being in heaven
After the Bacchantes had torn him apart, driven
Half out of their minds by his music, what it was doing to them.
Some say it was for his treatment of Eurydice.
But probably the music had more to do with it, and
The way music passes, emblematic
Of life and how you cannot isolate a note of it
And say it is good or bad. You must
Wait till it's over. "The end crowns all,"
Meaning also that the "tableau"
Is wrong. For although memories, of a season, for example,
Melt into a single snapshot, one cannot guard, treasure
That stalled moment. It too is flowing, fleeting;
It is a picture of flowing, scenery, though living, mortal,
Over which an abstract action is laid out in blunt,
Harsh strokes. And to ask more than this
Is to become the tossing reeds of that slow,
Powerful stream, the trailing grasses
Playfully tugged at, but to participate in the action
No more than this. Then in the lowering gentian sky
Electric twitches are faintly apparent first, then burst forth
Into a shower of fixed, cream-colored flares. The horses
Have each seen a share of the truth, though each thinks,
"I'm a maverick. Nothing of this is happening to me,
Though I can understand the language of birds, and
The itinerary of the lights caught in the storm is fully apparent
  to me.

Their jousting ends in music much
As trees move more easily in the wind after a summer storm
And is happening in lacy shadows of shore-trees, now, day
    after day."

But how late to be regretting all this, even
Bearing in mind that regrets are always late, too late!
To which Orpheus, a bluish cloud with white contours,
Replies that these are of course not regrets at all,
Merely a careful, scholarly setting down of
Unquestioned facts, a record of pebbles along the way.
And no matter how all this disappeared,
Or got where it was going, it is no longer
Material for a poem. Its subject
Matters too much, and not enough, standing there helplessly
While the poem streaked by, its tail afire, a bad
Comet screaming hate and disaster, but so turned inward
That the meaning, good or other, can never
Become known. The singer thinks
Constructively, builds up his chant in progressive stages
Like a skyscraper, but at the last minute turns away.
The song is engulfed in an instant in blackness
Which must in turn flood the whole continent
With blackness, for it cannot see. The singer
Must then pass out of sight, not even relieved
Of the evil burthen of the words. Stellification
Is for the few, and comes about much later
When all record of these people and their lives
Has disappeared into libraries, onto microfilm.
A few are still interested in them. "But what about
So-and-so?" is still asked on occasion. But they lie
Frozen and out of touch until an arbitrary chorus
Speaks of a totally different incident with a similar name
In whose tale are hidden syllables
Of what happened so long before that
In some small town, one indifferent summer.

Many Wagons Ago

At first it was as though you had passed,
But then no, I said, he is still here,
Forehead refreshed. A light is kindled. And
Another. But no I said

Nothing in this wide berth of lights like weeds
Stays to listen. Doubled up, fun is inside,
The lair a surface compact with the night.
It needs only one intervention,

A stitch, two, three, and then you see
How it is all false equation planted with
Enchanting blue shrubbery on each terrace
That night produces, and they are backing up.

How easily we could spell if we could follow,
Like thread looped through the eye of a needle,
The grooves of light. It resists. But we stay behind, among them,
The injured, the adored.

A Love Poem

And they have to get it right. We just need
A little happiness, and when the clever things
Are taken up (O has the mouth shaped that letter?
What do we have bearing down on it?) as the last thin curve
("Positively the last," they say) before the dark:
(The sky is pure and faint, the pavement still wet) and

The dripping is in the walls, within sleep
Itself. I mean there is no escape
From me, from it. The night is itself sleep
And what goes on in it, the naming of the wind,
Our notes to each other, always repeated, always the same.

Landscapeople

Long desired, the journey is begun. The suppliants
Climb aboard the damaged carrousel:
Some have been hacked to death, one has learned
Some new thing, and all are touched
With the same blight, like a snowfall
Of moments as they are read back to the monitor
Which only projects.

                 Some can decipher it,
The outline of an eddy that traced itself
Before moving on, yet its place had to be,
Such was the appetite of those times. A ring
Of places existed around the central one,
And of course these died away eventually.
Everything has turned out for the best,
The "eggs of the sun" have been returned anonymously,
And the new ways are as simple as the old ones,
Only more firmly anchored to the spectacle
Of the madness of the seasons as it unfolds
With iron-clad rigidity, filling the sky with light.
We began in an anonymous sensuality
And lived most of it out before the difference
Of time got in the way, filling up the margins of the days
With pictures of fruit, light, colors, music, and vines,
Until it ceases to be a problem.

Drunken Americans

I saw the reflection in the mirror
And it doesn't count, or not enough
To make a difference, fabricating itself
Out of the old, average light of a college town,

And afterwards, when the bus trip
Had depleted my pocket of its few pennies
He was seen arguing behind steamed glass,
With an invisible proprietor. What if you can't own

This one either? For it seems that all
Moments are like this: thin, unsatisfactory
As gruel, worn away more each time you return to them.
Until one day you rip the canvas from its frame

And take it home with you. You think the god-given
Assertiveness in you has triumphed
Over the stingy scenario: these objects are real as meat,
As tears. We are all soiled with this desire, at the last moment,
    the last.

At North Farm

Somewhere someone is traveling furiously toward you,
At incredible speed, traveling day and night,
Through blizzards and desert heat, across torrents, through
    narrow passes.
But will he know where to find you,
Recognize you when he sees you,
Give you the thing he has for you?

Hardly anything grows here,
Yet the granaries are bursting with meal,
The sacks of meal piled to the rafters.
The streams run with sweetness, fattening fish;
Birds darken the sky. Is it enough
That the dish of milk is set out at night,
That we think of him sometimes,
Sometimes and always, with mixed feelings?

The Ongoing Story

I could say it's the happiest period of my life.
It hasn't got much competition! Yesterday
It seemed a flatness, hotness. As though it barely stood out
From the rocks of all the years before. Today it sheds
That old name, without assuming any new one. I think it's
    still there.

It was as though I'd been left with the empty street
A few seconds after the bus pulled out. A dollop of afternoon
    wind.
Others tell you to take your attention off it
For awhile, refocus the picture. Plan to entertain,
To get out. (Do people really talk that way?)

We could pretend that all that isn't there never existed anyway.
The great ideas? What good are they if they're misplaced,
In the wrong order, if you can't remember one
At the moment you're so to speak mounting the guillotine
Like Sydney Carton, and can't think of anything to say?
Or is this precisely material covered in a course
Called Background of the Great Ideas, and therefore it isn't
    necessary
To say anything or even know anything? The breath of the
    moment
Is breathed, we fall and still feel better. The phone rings,

It's a wrong number, and your heart is lighter,
Not having to be faced with the same boring choices again
Which doesn't undermine a feeling for people in general and
Especially in particular: you,
In your deliberate distinctness, whom I love and gladly
Agree to walk blindly into the night with,
Your realness is real to me though I would never take any of it
Just to see how it grows. A knowledge that people live close by is,
I think, enough. And even if only first names are ever exchanged
The people who own them seem rock-true and marvelously
    self-sufficient.

Down by the Station, Early in the Morning

It all wears out. I keep telling myself this, but
I can never believe me, though others do. Even things do.
And the things they do. Like the rasp of silk, or a certain
Glottal stop in your voice as you are telling me how you
Didn't have time to brush your teeth but gargled with Listerine
Instead. Each is a base one might wish to touch once more

Before dying. There's the moment years ago in the station in
    Venice,
The dark rainy afternoon in fourth grade, and the shoes then,
Made of a dull crinkled brown leather that no longer exists.
And nothing does, until you name it, remembering, and even
    then
It may not have existed, or existed only as a result
Of the perceptual dysfunction you've been carrying around
    for years.
The result is magic, then terror, then pity at the emptiness,
Then air gradually bathing and filling the emptiness as it leaks,
Emoting all over something that is probably mere reportage
But nevertheless likes being emoted on. And so each day
Culminates in merriment as well as a deep shock like an electric
    one,

As the wrecking ball bursts through the wall with the
    bookshelves
Scattering the works of famous authors as well as those
Of more obscure ones, and books with no author, letting in
Space, and an extraneous babble from the street
Confirming the new value the hollow core has again, the light
From the lighthouse that protects as it pushes us away.

Never Seek To Tell Thy Love

Many colors will take you to themselves
But now I want someone to tell me how to get home.
The way back there is streaked and stippled,
A shaded place. It belongs where it is going

Not where it is. The flowers don't talk to Ida now.
They speak only the language of flowers,
Saying things like, How hard I tried to get there.
It must mean I'm not here yet. But you,
You seem so formal, so serious. You can't read poetry,
Not the way they taught us back in school.

Returning to the point was always the main thing, then.
Did we ever leave it? I don't think so. It was our North Pole.
We skulked and hungered there for years, and now,

Like dazzled insects skimming the bright airs,
You are back on the road again, the path leading
Vigorously upward, through intelligent and clear spaces.
They don't make rocks like us any more.

And holding on to the thread, fine as a cobweb, but incredibly
    strong,
Each of us advances into his own labyrinth.
The gift of invisibility
Has been granted to all but the gods, so we say such things,
Filling the road up with colors, faces,
Tender speeches, until they feed us to the truth.

W. S. MERWIN
(1927–)

Noah's Raven

Why should I have returned?
My knowledge would not fit into theirs.
I found untouched the desert of the unknown,
Big enough for my feet. It is my home.
It is always beyond them. The future
Splits the present with the echo of my voice.
Hoarse with fulfilment, I never made promises.

Some Last Questions

What is the head
        A. Ash
What are the eyes
        A. The wells have fallen in and have
           Inhabitants
What are the feet
        A. Thumbs left after the auction
No what are the feet
        A. Under them the impossible road is moving
           Down which the broken necked mice push
           Balls of blood with their noses
What is the tongue
        A. The black coat that fell off the wall
           With sleeves trying to say something
What are the hands
        A. Paid
No what are the hands
        A. Climbing back down the museum wall
           To their ancestors the extinct shrews that will
           Have left a message

What is the silence
             A. As though it had a right to more
Who are the compatriots
             A. They make the stars of bone

For the Anniversary of My Death

Every year without knowing it I have passed the day
When the last fires will wave to me
And the silence will set out
Tireless traveller
Like the beam of a lightless star

Then I will no longer
Find myself in life as in a strange garment
Surprised at the earth
And the love of one woman
And then shamelessness of men
As today writing after three days of rain
Hearing the wren sing and the falling cease
And bowing not knowing to what

The Asians Dying

When the forests have been destroyed their darkness remains
The ash the great walker follows the possessors
Forever
Nothing they will come to is real
Nor for long
Over the watercourses
Like ducks in the time of the ducks
The ghosts of the villages trail in the sky
Making a new twilight

Rain falls into the open eyes of the dead
Again again with its pointless sound
When the moon finds them they are the color of everything

The nights disappear like bruises but nothing is healed
The dead go away like bruises
The blood vanishes into the poisoned farmlands
Pain the horizon
Remains
Overhead the seasons rock
They are paper bells
Calling to nothing living

The possessors move everywhere under Death their star
Like columns of smoke they advance into the shadows
Like thin flames with no light
They with no past
And fire their only future

For a Coming Extinction

Gray whale
Now that we are sending you to The End
That great god
Tell him
That we who follow you invented forgiveness
And forgive nothing

I write as though you could understand
And I could say it
One must always pretend something
Among the dying
When you have left the seas nodding on their stalks
Empty of you
Tell him that we were made
On another day

The bewilderment will diminish like an echo
Winding along your inner mountains
Unheard by us
And find its way out
Leaving behind it the future
Dead
And ours

When you will not see again
The whale calves trying the light
Consider what you will find in the black garden
And its court
The sea cows the Great Auks the gorillas
The irreplaceable hosts ranged countless
And fore-ordaining as stars
Our sacrifices

Join your word to theirs
Tell him
That it is we who are important

Elegy

Who would I show it to

The Fields

Saturday on Seventh Street
full-waisted gray-haired women in Sunday sweaters
moving through the tan shades of their booths
bend over cakes they baked at home
they gaze down onto the sleep of stuffed cabbages
they stir with huge spoons sauerkraut and potato dumplings
cooked as those dishes were cooked on deep
misty plains among the sounds of horses
beside fields of black earth on the other side of the globe
that only the oldest think they remember
looking down from their windows into the world
where everybody is now

none of the young has yet wept at the smell
of cabbages
those leaves all face
none of the young after long journeys
weeks in vessels
and staring at strange coasts through fog in first light

has been recognized by the steam of sauerkraut
that is older than anyone living
so on the street they play the music
of what they do not remember
they sing of places they have not known
they dance in new costumes under the windows
in the smell of cabbages from fields
nobody has seen

JAMES WRIGHT
(1927– 1980)

A Note Left in Jimmy Leonard's Shack

Near the dry river's water-mark we found
    Your brother Minnegan,
Flopped like a fish against the muddy ground.
Beany, the kid whose yellow hair turns green,
Told me to find you, even in the rain,
    And tell you he was drowned.

I hid behind the chassis on the bank,
    The wreck of someone's Ford:
I was afraid to come and wake you drunk:
You told me once the waking up was hard,
The daylight beating at you like a board.
    Blood in my stomach sank.

Beside, you told him never to go out
    Along the river-side
Drinking and singing, clattering about.
You might have thrown a rock at me and cried
I was to blame, I let him fall in the road
    And pitch down on his side.

Well, I'll get hell enough when I get home
    For coming up this far,
Leaving the note, and running as I came.
I'll go and tell my father where you are.
You'd better go find Minnegan before
    Policemen hear and come.

Beany went home, and I got sick and ran,
    You old son of a bitch.
You better hurry down to Minnegan;
He's drunk or dying now, I don't know which,
Rolled in the roots and garbage like a fish,
    The poor old man.

At the Executed Murderer's Grave

For J. L. D.

> Why should we do this? What good is it to us?
> Above all, how can we do such a thing? How
> can it possibly be done?
> —Freud

1

My name is James A. Wright, and I was born
Twenty-five miles from this infected grave,
In Martins Ferry, Ohio, where one slave
To Hazel-Atlas Glass became my father.
He tried to teach me kindness. I return
Only in memory now, aloof, unhurried,
To dead Ohio, where I might lie buried,
Had I not run away before my time.
Ohio caught George Doty. Clean as lime,
His skull rots empty here. Dying's the best
Of all the arts men learn in a dead place.
I walked here once. I made my loud display,
Leaning for language on a dead man's voice.
Now sick of lies, I turn to face the past.
I add my easy grievance to the rest:

2

Doty, if I confess I do not love you,
Will you let me alone? I burn for my own lies.
The nights electrocute my fugitive,
My mind. I run like the bewildered mad
At St. Clair Sanitarium, who lurk,
Arch and cunning, under the maple trees,
Pleased to be playing guilty after dark.
Staring to bed, they croon self-lullabies.
Doty, you make me sick. I am not dead.
I croon my tears at fifty cents per line.

3

Idiot, he demanded love from girls,
And murdered one. Also, he was a thief.
He left two women, and a ghost with child.

The hair, foul as a dog's upon his head,
Made such revolting Ohio animals
Fitter for vomit than a kind man's grief.
I waste no pity on the dead that stink,
And no love's lost between me and the crying
Drunks of Belaire, Ohio, where police
Kick at their kidneys till they die of drink.
Christ may restore them whole, for all of me.
Alive and dead, those giggling muckers who
Saddled my nightmares thirty years ago
Can do without my widely printed sighing
Over their pains with paid sincerity.
I do not pity the dead, I pity the dying.

4

I pity myself, because a man is dead.
If Belmont County killed him, what of me?
His victims never loved him. Why should we?
And yet, nobody had to kill him either.
It does no good to woo the grass, to veil
The quicklime hole of a man's defeat and shame.
Nature-lovers are gone. To hell with them.
I kick the clods away, and speak my name.

5

This grave's gash festers. Maybe it will heal,
When all are caught with what they had to do
In fear of love, when every man stands still
By the last sea,
And the princes of the sea come down
To lay away their robes, to judge the earth
And its dead, and we dead stand undefended everywhere,
And my bodies — father and child and unskilled criminal —
Ridiculously kneel to bare my scars,
My sneaking crimes, to God's unpitying stars.

6

Staring politely, they will not mark my face
From any murderer's, buried in this place.
Why should they? We are nothing but a man.

7

Doty, the rapist and the murderer,
Sleeps in a ditch of fire, and cannot hear;
And where, in earth or hell's unholy peace,
Men's suicides will stop, God knows, not I.
Angels and pebbles mock me under trees.
Earth is a door I cannot even face.
Order be damned, I do not want to die,
Even to keep Belaire, Ohio, safe.
The hackles on my neck are fear, not grief.
(Open, dungeon! Open, roof of the ground!)
I hear the last sea in the Ohio grass,
Heaving a tide of gray disastrousness.
Wrinkles of winter ditch the rotted face
Of Doty, killer, imbecile, and thief:
Dirt of my flesh, defeated, underground.

Autumn Begins in Martins Ferry, Ohio

In the Shreve High football stadium,
I think of Polacks nursing long beers in Tiltonsville,
And gray faces of Negroes in the blast furnace at Benwood,
And the ruptured night watchman of Wheeling Steel,
Dreaming of heroes.

All the proud fathers are ashamed to go home.
Their women cluck like starved pullets,
Dying for love.

Therefore,
Their sons grow suicidally beautiful
At the beginning of October,
And gallop terribly against each other's bodies.

Lying in a Hammock at William Duffy's Farm
in Pine Island, Minnesota

Over my head, I see the bronze butterfly,
Asleep on the black trunk,
Blowing like a leaf in green shadow.
Down the ravine behind the empty house,
The cowbells follow one another
Into the distances of the afternoon.
To my right,
In a field of sunlight between two pines,
The droppings of last year's horses
Blaze up into golden stones.
I lean back, as the evening darkens and comes on.
A chicken hawk floats over, looking for home.
I have wasted my life.

Having Lost My Sons, I Confront the Wreckage
of the Moon: Christmas, 1960

After dark
Near the South Dakota border,
The moon is out hunting, everywhere,
Delivering fire,
And walking down hallways
Of a diamond.

Behind a tree,
It lights on the ruins
Of a white city:
Frost, frost.

Where are they gone,
Who lived there?

Bundled away under wings
And dark faces.

I am sick
Of it, and I go on,

Living, alone, alone,
Past the charred silos, past the hidden graves
Of Chippewas and Norwegians.

This cold winter
Moon spills the inhuman fire
Of jewels
Into my hands.

Dead riches, dead hands, the moon
Darkens,
And I am lost in the beautiful white ruins
Of America.

Willy Lyons

My uncle, a craftsman of hammers and wood,
Is dead in Ohio.
And my mother cries she is angry.
Willy was buried with nothing except a jacket
Stitched on his shoulder bones.
It is nothing to mourn for.
It is the other world.
She does not know how the roan horses, there,
Dead for a century,
Plod slowly.
Maybe they believe Willy's brown coffin, tangled heavily in
    moss,
Is a horse trough drifted to shore
Along that river under the willows and grass.
Let my mother weep on, she needs to, she knows of cold winds.
The long box is empty.
The horses turn back toward the river.
Willy planes limber trees by the waters,
Fitting his boat together.
We may as well let him go.
Nothing is left of Willy on this side
But one cracked ball-peen hammer and one suit,
Including pants, his son inherited,
For a small fee, from Hesslop's funeral home;

And my mother,
Weeping with anger, afraid of winter
For her brothers' sake:
Willy, and John, whose life and art, if any,
I never knew.

Two Postures Beside a Fire

1

Tonight I watch my father's hair,
As he sits dreaming near his stove.
Knowing my feather of despair,
He sent me an owl's plume for love,
Lest I not know, so I've come home.
Tonight Ohio, where I once
Hounded and cursed my loneliness,
Shows me my father, who broke stones,
Wrestled and mastered great machines,
And rests, shadowing his lovely face.

2

Nobly his hands fold together in his repose.
He is proud of me, believing
I have done strong things among men and become a man
Of place among men of place in the large cities.
I will not waken him.
I have come home alone, without wife or child
To delight him. Awake, solitary and welcome,
I too sit near his stove, the lines
Of an ugly age scarring my face, and my hands
Twitch nervously about.

Small Frogs Killed on the Highway

Still,
I would leap too
Into the light,
If I had the chance.
It is everything, the wet green stalk of the field
On the other side of the road.
They crouch there, too, faltering in terror
And take strange wing. Many
Of the dead never moved, but many
Of the dead are alive forever in the split second
Auto headlights more sudden
Than their drivers know.
The drivers burrow backward into dank pools
Where nothing begets
Nothing.

Across the road, tadpoles are dancing
On the quarter thumbnail
Of the moon. They can't see,
Not yet.

ANNE SEXTON

(1928 – 1974)

Her Kind

I have gone out, a possessed witch,
haunting the black air, braver at night;
dreaming evil, I have done my hitch
over the plain houses, light by light:
lonely thing, twelve-fingered, out of mind.
A woman like that is not a woman, quite.
I have been her kind.

I have found the warm caves in the woods,
filled them with skillets, carvings, shelves,
closets, silks, innumerable goods;
fixed the suppers for the worms and the elves:
whining, rearranging the disaligned.
A woman like that is misunderstood.
I have been her kind.

I have ridden in your cart, driver,
waved my nude arms at villages going by,
learning the last bright routes, survivor
where your flames still bite my thigh
and my ribs crack where your wheels wind.
A woman like that is not ashamed to die.
I have been her kind.

Ringing the Bells

And this is the way they ring
the bells in Bedlam
and this is the bell-lady
who comes each Tuesday morning
to give us a music lesson

and because the attendants make you go
and because we mind by instinct,
like bees caught in the wrong hive,
we are the circle of the crazy ladies
who sit in the lounge of the mental house
and smile at the smiling woman
who passes us each a bell,
who points at my hand
that holds my bell, E flat,
and this is the gray dress next to me
who grumbles as if it were special
to be old, to be old,
and this is the small hunched squirrel girl
on the other side of me
who picks at the hairs over her lip,
who picks at the hairs over her lip all day,
and this is how the bells really sound,
as untroubled and clean
as a workable kitchen,
and this is always my bell responding
to my hand that responds to the lady
who points at me, E flat;
and although we are no better for it,
they tell you to go. And you do.

With Mercy for the Greedy

For my friend, Ruth, who urges me to make an
appointment for the Sacrament of Confession

Concerning your letter in which you ask
me to call a priest and in which you ask
me to wear The Cross that you enclose;
your own cross,
your dog-bitten cross,
no larger than a thumb,
small and wooden, no thorns, this rose —

I pray to its shadow,
that gray place
where it lies on your letter . . . deep, deep.

I detest my sins and I try to believe
in The Cross. I touch its tender hips, its dark jawed face,
its solid neck, its brown sleep.

True. There is
a beautiful Jesus.
He is frozen to his bones like a chunk of beef.
How desperately he wanted to pull his arms in!
How desperately I touch his vertical and horizontal axes!
But I can't. Need is not quite belief.

All morning long
I have worn
your cross, hung with package string around my throat.
It tapped me lightly as a child's heart might,
tapping secondhand, softly waiting to be born.
Ruth, I cherish the letter you wrote.

My friend, my friend, I was born
doing reference work in sin, and born
confessing it. This is what poems are:
with mercy
for the greedy,
they are the tongue's wrangle,
the world's pottage, the rat's star.

Self in 1958

What is reality?
I am a plaster doll; I pose
with eyes that cut open without landfall or nightfall
upon some shellacked and grinning person,
eyes that open, blue, steel, and close.
Am I approximately an I. Magnin transplant?
I have hair, black angel,
black-angel-stuffing to comb,
nylon legs, luminous arms
and some advertised clothes.

I live in a doll's house
with four chairs,
a counterfeit table, a flat roof
and a big front door.
Many have come to such a small crossroad.
There is an iron bed,
(Life enlarges, life takes aim)
a cardboard floor,
windows that flash open on someone's city,
and little more.

Someone plays with me,
plants me in the all-electric kitchen,
Is this what Mrs. Rombauer said?
Someone pretends with me —
I am walled in solid by their noise —
or puts me upon their straight bed.
They think I am me!
Their warmth? Their warmth is not a friend!
They pry my mouth for their cups of gin
and their stale bread.

What is reality
to this synthetic doll
who should smile, who should shift gears,
should spring the doors open in a wholesome disorder,
and have no evidence of ruin or fears?
But I would cry,
rooted into the wall that
was once my mother,
if I could remember how
and if I had the tears.

For My Lover, Returning to His Wife

She is all there.
She was melted carefully down for you
and cast up from your childhood,
cast up from your one hundred favorite aggies.

She has always been there, my darling.
She is, in fact, exquisite.
Fireworks in the dull middle of February
and as real as a cast-iron pot.

Let's face it, I have been momentary.
A luxury. A bright red sloop in the harbor.
My hair rising like smoke from the car window.
Littleneck clams out of season.

She is more than that. She is your have to have,
has grown you your practical your tropical growth.
This is not an experiment. She is all harmony.
She sees to oars and oarlocks for the dinghy,

has placed wild flowers at the window at breakfast,
sat by the potter's wheel at midday,
set forth three children under the moon,
three cherubs drawn by Michelangelo,

done this with her legs spread out
in the terrible months in the chapel.
If you glance up, the children are there
like delicate balloons resting on the ceiling.

She has also carried each one down the hall
after supper, their heads privately bent,
two legs protesting, person to person,
her face flushed with a song and their little sleep.

I give you back your heart.
I give you permission —

for the fuse inside her, throbbing
angrily in the dirt, for the bitch in her
and the burying of her wound —
for the burying of her small red wound alive —

for the pale flickering flare under her ribs,
for the drunken sailor who waits in her left pulse,
for the mother's knee, for the stockings,
for the garter belt, for the call —

the curious call
when you will burrow in arms and breasts

and tug at the orange ribbon in her hair
and answer the call, the curious call.

She is so naked and singular.
She is the sum of yourself and your dream.
Climb her like a monument, step after step.
She is solid.

As for me, I am a watercolor.
I wash off.

Snow White and the Seven Dwarfs

No matter what life you lead
the virgin is a lovely number:
cheeks as fragile as cigarette paper,
arms and legs made of Limoges,
lips like Vin Du Rhône,
rolling her china-blue doll eyes
open and shut.
Open to say,
Good Day Mama,
and shut for the thrust
of the unicorn.
She is unsoiled.
She is as white as a bonefish.

Once there was a lovely virgin
called Snow White.
Say she was thirteen.
Her stepmother,
a beauty in her own right,
though eaten, of course, by age,
would hear of no beauty surpassing her own.
Beauty is a simple passion,
but, oh my friends, in the end
you will dance the fire dance in iron shoes.
The stepmother had a mirror to which she referred —
something like the weather forecast —
a mirror that proclaimed
the one beauty of the land.

She would ask,
Looking glass upon the wall,
who is fairest of us all?
And the mirror would reply,
You are fairest of us all.
Pride pumped in her like poison.

Suddenly one day the mirror replied,
Queen, you are full fair, 'tis true,
but Snow White is fairer than you.
Until that moment Snow White
had been no more important
than a dust mouse under the bed.
But now the queen saw brown spots on her hand
and four whiskers over her lip
so she condemned Snow White
to be hacked to death.
Bring me her heart, she said to the hunter,
and I will salt it and eat it.
The hunter, however, let his prisoner go
and brought a boar's heart back to the castle.
The queen chewed it up like a cube steak.
Now I am fairest, she said,
lapping her slim white fingers.

Snow White walked in the wildwood
for weeks and weeks.
At each turn there were twenty doorways
and at each stood a hungry wolf,
his tongue lolling out like a worm.
The birds called out lewdly,
talking like pink parrots,
and the snakes hung down in loops,
each a noose for her sweet white neck.
On the seventh week
she came to the seventh mountain
and there she found the dwarf house.
It was as droll as a honeymoon cottage
and completely equipped with
seven beds, seven chairs, seven forks
and seven chamber pots.
Snow White ate seven chicken livers
and lay down, at last, to sleep.

The dwarfs, those little hot dogs,
walked three times around Snow White,
the sleeping virgin. They were wise
and wattled like small czars.
Yes. It's a good omen,
they said, and will bring us luck.
They stood on tiptoes to watch
Snow White wake up. She told them
about the mirror and the killer-queen
and they asked her to stay and keep house.
Beware of your stepmother,
they said.
Soon she will know you are here.
While we are away in the mines
during the day, you must not
open the door.

Looking glass upon the wall . . .
The mirror told
and so the queen dressed herself in rags
and went out like a peddler to trap Snow White.
She went across seven mountains.
She came to the dwarf house
and Snow White opened the door
and bought a bit of lacing.
The queen fastened it tightly
around her bodice,
as tight as an Ace bandage,
so tight that Snow White swooned.
She lay on the floor, a plucked daisy.
When the dwarfs came home they undid the lace
and she revived miraculously.
She was as full of life as soda pop.
Beware of your stepmother,
they said.
She will try once more.

Looking glass upon the wall . . .
Once more the mirror told
and once more the queen dressed in rags
and once more Snow White opened the door.
This time she bought a poison comb,

a curved eight-inch scorpion,
and put it in her hair and swooned again.
The dwarfs returned and took out the comb
and she revived miraculously.
She opened her eyes as wide as Orphan Annie.
Beware, beware, they said,
but the mirror told,
the queen came,
Snow White, the dumb bunny,
opened the door
and she bit into a poison apple
and fell down for the final time.
When the dwarfs returned
they undid her bodice,
they looked for a comb,
but it did no good.
Though they washed her with wine
and rubbed her with butter
it was to no avail.
She lay as still as a gold piece.

The seven dwarfs could not bring themselves
to bury her in the black ground
so they made a glass coffin
and set it upon the seventh mountain
so that all who passed by
could peek in upon her beauty.
A prince came one June day
and would not budge.
He stayed so long his hair turned green
and still he would not leave.
The dwarfs took pity upon him
and gave him the glass Snow White —
its doll's eyes shut forever —
to keep in his far-off castle.
As the prince's men carried the coffin
they stumbled and dropped it
and the chunk of apple flew out
of her throat and she woke up miraculously.

And thus Snow White became the prince's bride.
The wicked queen was invited to the wedding feast
and when she arrived there were
red-hot iron shoes,
in the manner of red-hot roller skates,
clamped upon her feet.
First your toes will smoke
and then your heels will turn black
and you will fry upward like a frog,
she was told.
And so she danced until she was dead,
a subterranean figure,
her tongue flicking in and out
like a gas jet.
Meanwhile Snow White held court,
rolling her china-blue doll eyes open and shut
and sometimes referring to her mirror
as women do.

January 1st

Today is favorable for joint financial affairs but
do not take any chances with speculation.

My daddy played the market.
My mother cut her coupons.
The children ran in circles.
The maid announced, the soup's on.

The guns were cleaned on Sunday.
The family went out to shoot.
We sat in the blind for hours.
The ducks fell down like fruit.

The big fat war was going on.
So profitable for daddy.
She drove a pea green Ford.
He drove a pearl gray Caddy.

In the end they used it up.
All that pale green dough.
The rest I spent on doctors
who took it like gigolos.

My financial affairs are small.
Indeed they seem to shrink.
My heart is on a budget.
It keeps me on the brink.

I tell it stories now and then
and feed it images like honey.
I will not speculate today
with poems that think they're money.

ADRIENNE RICH
(1929 –)

The Middle-Aged

Their faces, safe as an interior
Of Holland tiles and Oriental carpet,
Where the fruit-bowl, always filled, stood in a light
Of placid afternoon — their voices' measure,
Their figures moving in the Sunday garden
To lay the tea outdoors or trim the borders,
Afflicted, haunted us. For to be young
Was always to live in other peoples' houses
Whose peace, if we sought it, had been made by others,
Was ours at second-hand and not for long.
The custom of the house, not ours, the sun
Fading the silver-blue Fortuny curtains,
The reminiscence of a Christmas party
Of fourteen years ago — all memory,
Signs of possession and of being possessed,
We tasted, tense with envy. They were so kind,
Would have given us anything; the bowl of fruit
Was filled for us, there was a room upstairs
We must call ours: but twenty years of living
They could not give. Nor did they ever speak
Of the coarse stain on that polished balustrade,
The crack in the study window, or the letters
Locked in a drawer and the key destroyed.
All to be understood by us, returning
Late, in our own time — how that peace was made,
Upon what terms, with how much left unsaid.

Snapshots of a Daughter-in-Law

1

You, once a belle in Shreveport,
with henna-colored hair, skin like a peachbud,
still have your dresses copied from that time,
and play a Chopin prelude
called by Cortot: *"Delicious recollections
float like perfume through the memory."*

Your mind now, moldering like wedding-cake,
heavy with useless experience, rich
with suspicion, rumor, fantasy,
crumbling to pieces under the knife-edge
of mere fact. In the prime of your life.

Nervy, glowering, your daughter
wipes the teaspoons, grows another way.

2

Banging the coffee-pot into the sink
she hears the angels chiding, and looks out
past the raked gardens to the sloppy sky.
Only a week since They said: *Have no patience.*

The next time it was: *Be insatiable.*
Then: *Save yourself; others you cannot save.*
Sometimes she's let the tapstream scald her arm,
a match burn to her thumbnail,

or held her hand above the kettle's snout
right in the woolly steam. They are probably angels,
since nothing hurts her anymore, except
each morning's grit blowing into her eyes.

3

A thinking woman sleeps with monsters.
The beak that grips her, she becomes. And Nature,
that sprung-lidded, still commodious
steamer-trunk of *tempora* and *mores*

gets stuffed with it all: the mildewed orange-flowers,
the female pills, the terrible breasts
of Boadicea beneath flat foxes' heads and orchids.

Two handsome women, gripped in argument,
each proud, acute, subtle, I hear scream
across the cut glass and majolica
like Furies cornered from their prey:
The argument *ad feminam,* all the old knives
that have rusted in my back, I drive in yours,
ma semblable, ma soeur!

4

Knowing themselves too well in one another:
their gifts no pure fruition, but a thorn,
the prick filed sharp against a hint of scorn . . .
Reading while waiting
for the iron to heat,
writing, *My Life had stood – a Loaded Gun –*
in that Amherst pantry while the jellies boil and scum,
or, more often,
iron-eyed and beaked and purposed as a bird,
dusting everything on the whatnot every day of life.

5

Dulce ridens, dulce loquens,
she shaves her legs until they gleam
like petrified mammoth-tusk.

6

When to her lute Corinna sings
neither words nor music are her own;
only the long hair dipping
over her cheek, only the song
of silk against her knees
and these
adjusted in reflections of an eye.

Poised, trembling and unsatisfied, before
an unlocked door, that cage of cages,
tell us, you bird, you tragical machine —

is this *fertilisante douleur?* Pinned down
by love, for you the only natural action,
are you edged more keen
to prise the secrets of the vault? has Nature shown
her household books to you, daughter-in-law,
that her sons never saw?

7

"To have in this uncertain world some stay
which cannot be undermined, is
of the utmost consequence."
                                        Thus wrote
a woman, partly brave and partly good,
who fought with what she partly understood.
Few men about her would or could do more,
hence she was labeled harpy, shrew and whore.

8

"You all die at fifteen," said Diderot,
and turn part legend, part convention.
Still, eyes inaccurately dream
behind closed windows blankening with steam.
Deliciously, all that we might have been,
all that we were — fire, tears,
wit, taste, martyred ambition —
stirs like the memory of refused adultery
the drained and flagging bosom of our middle years.

9

Not that it is done well, but
that it is done at all? Yes, think
of the odds! or shrug them off forever.
This luxury of the precocious child,
Time's precious chronic invalid, —
would we, darlings, resign it if we could?
Our blight has been our sinecure:
mere talent was enough for us —
glitter in fragments and rough drafts.

Sigh no more, ladies.
                       Time is male
and in his cups drinks to the fair.
Bemused by gallantry, we hear
our mediocrities over-praised,
indolence read as abnegation,
slattern thought styled intuition,
every lapse forgiven, our crime
only to cast too bold a shadow
or smash the mold straight off.

For that, solitary confinement,
tear gas, attrition shelling.
Few applicants for that honor.

10

                          Well,
she's long about her coming, who must be
more merciless to herself than history.
Her mind full to the wind, I see her plunge
breasted and glancing through the currents,
taking the light upon her
at least as beautiful as any boy
or helicopter,
                poised, still coming,
her fine blades making the air wince

but her cargo
no promise then:
delivered
palpable
ours.

Peeling Onions

Only to have a grief
equal to all these tears!

There's not a sob in my chest.
Dry-hearted as Peer Gynt

I pare away, no hero,
merely a cook.

Crying was labor, once
when I'd good cause.
Walking, I felt my eyes like wounds
raw in my head,
so postal-clerks, I thought, must stare.
A dog's look, a cat's, burnt to my brain—
yet all that stayed
stuffed in my lungs like smog.

These old tears in the chopping-bowl.

Necessities of Life

Piece by piece I seem
to re-enter the world: I first began

a small, fixed dot, still see
that old myself, a dark-blue thumbtack

pushed into the scene,
a hard little head protruding

from the pointillist's buzz and bloom.
After a time the dot

begins to ooze. Certain heats
melt it.
          Now I was hurriedly

blurring into ranges
of burnt red, burning green,

whole biographies swam up and
swallowed me like Jonah.

Jonah! I was Wittgenstein,
Mary Wollstonecraft, the soul

of Louis Jouvet, dead
in a blown-up photograph.

Till, wolfed almost to shreds,
I learned to make myself

unappetizing. Scaly as a dry bulb
thrown into a cellar

I used myself, let nothing use me.
Like being on a private dole,

sometimes more like kneading bricks in Egypt.
What life was there, was mine,

now and again to lay
one hand on a warm brick

and touch the sun's ghost
with economical joy,

now and again to name
over the bare necessities.

So much for those days. Soon
practice may make me middling-perfect, I'll

dare inhabit the world
trenchant in motion as an eel, solid

as a cabbage-head. I have invitations:
a curl of mist steams upward

from a field, visible as my breath,
houses along a road stand waiting

like old women knitting, breathless
to tell their tales.

"*I Am in Danger – Sir –* "

"Half-cracked" to Higginson, living,
afterward famous in garbled versions,

your hoard of dazzling scraps a battlefield,
now your old snood

mothballed at Harvard
and you in your variorum monument
equivocal to the end —
who are you?

Gardening the day-lily,
wiping the wine-glass stems,
your thought pulsed on behind
a forehead battered paper-thin,

you, woman, masculine
in single-mindedness,
for whom the word was more
than a symptom —

a condition of being.
Till the air buzzing with spoiled language
sang in your ears
of Perjury

and in your half-cracked way you chose
silence for entertainment,
chose to have it out at last
on your own premises.

Planetarium

Thinking of Caroline Herschel (1750 – 1848) astronomer,
sister of William; and others.

A woman in the shape of a monster
a monster in the shape of a woman
the skies are full of them

a woman   'in the snow
among the Clocks and instruments
or measuring the ground with poles'

in her 98 years to discover
8 comets

she whom the moon ruled
like us

levitating into the night sky
riding the polished lenses

Galaxies of women, there
doing penance for impetuousness
ribs chilled
in those spaces   of the mind

An eye,

   'virile, precise and absolutely certain'
   from the mad webs of Uranusborg

       encountering the NOVA

every impulse of light exploding
from the core
as life flies out of us

   Tycho whispering at last
   'Let me not seem to have lived in vain'

What we see, we see
and seeing is changing

the light that shrivels a mountain
and leaves a man alive

Heartbeat of the pulsar
heart sweating through my body

The radio impulse
pouring in from Taurus

   I am bombarded yet   I stand

I have been standing all my life in the
direct path of a battery of signals
the most accurately transmitted most
untranslatable language in the universe
I am a galactic cloud so deep   so invo-
luted that a light wave could take 15
years to travel through me   And has
taken   I am an instrument in the shape
of a woman trying to translate pulsations
into images   for the relief of the body
and the reconstruction of the mind.

from *Shooting Script*

3

The old blanket. The crumbs of rubbed wool turning up.

Where we lay and breakfasted. The stains of tea. The squares of winter light projected on the wool.

You, sleeping with closed windows. I, sleeping in the silver nitrate burn of zero air.

Where it can snow, I'm at home; the crystals accumulating spell out my story.

The cold encrustation thickening on the ledge.

The arrow-headed facts, accumulating, till a whole city is taken over.

Midwinter and the loss of love, going comes before gone, over and over the point is missed and still the blind will turns for its target.

5

Of simple choice they are the villagers; their clothes come with them like red clay roads they have been walking.

The sole of the foot is a map, the palm of the hand a letter, learned by heart and worn close to the body.

They seemed strange to me, till I began to recall their dialect.

Poking the spade into the dry loam, listening for the tick of broken pottery, hoarding the brown and black bits in a dented can.

Evenings, at the table, turning the findings out, pushing them around with a finger, beginning to dream of fitting them together.

Hiding all this work from them, although they might have helped me.

Going up at night, hiding the tin can in a closet, where the linoleum lies in shatters on a back shelf.

Sleeping to dream of the unformed, the veil of water pouring over the wet clay, the rhythms of choice, the lost methods.

9
Newsreel

This would not be the war we fought in. See, the foliage
is heavier, there were no hills of that size there.

But I find it impossible not to look for actual persons known to
me and not seen since; impossible not to look for myself.

The scenery angers me, I know there is something wrong, the
sun is too high, the grass too trampled, the peasants' faces
too broad, and the main square of the capital had no arcades
like those.

Yet the dead look right, and the roofs of the huts, and the
crashed fuselage burning among the ferns.

But this is not the war I came to see, buying my ticket,
stumbling through the darkness, finding my place among the
sleepers and masturbators in the dark.

I thought of seeing the General who cursed us, whose name
they gave to an expressway; I wanted to see the faces of the
dead when they were living.

Once I know they filmed us, back at the camp behind the
lines, taking showers under the trees and showing pictures of
our girls.

Somewhere there is a film of the war we fought in, and it
must contain the flares, the souvenirs, the shadows of the
netted brush, the standing in line of the innocent, the hills
that were not of this size.

Somewhere my body goes taut under the deluge, somewhere I
am naked behind the lines, washing my body in the water of
that war.

Someone has that war stored up in metal canisters, a memory
he cannot use, somewhere my innocence is proven with my
guilt, but this would not be the war I fought in.

10
—*for Valerie Glauber*

They come to you with their descriptions of your soul.

They come and drop their mementos at the foot of your bed; their feathers, ferns, fans, grasses from the western mountains.

They wait for you to unfold for them like a paper flower, a secret springing open in a glass of water.

They believe your future has a history and that it is themselves.

They have family trees to plant for you, photographs of dead children, old bracelets and rings they want to fasten onto you.

And, in spite of this, you live alone.

Your secret hangs in the open like Poe's purloined letter; their longing and their methods will never let them find it.

Your secret cries out in the dark and hushes; when they start out of sleep they think you are innocent.

You hang among them like the icon in a Russian play; living your own intenser life behind the lamp they light in front of you.

You are spilt here like mercury on a marble counter, liquefying into many globes, each silvered like a planet caught in a lens.

You are a mirror lost in a brook, an eye reflecting a torrent of reflections.

You are a letter written, folded, burnt to ash, and mailed in an envelope to another continent.

13

We are driven to odd attempts; once it would not have occurred to me to put out in a boat, not on a night like this.

Still, it was an instrument, and I had pledged myself to try any instrument that came my way. Never to refuse one from conviction of incompetence.

A long time I was simply learning to handle the skiff; I had no special training and my own training was against me.

I had always heard that darkness and water were a threat.

In spite of this, darkness and water helped me to arrive here.

I watched the lights on the shore I had left for a long time;
each one, it seemed to me, was a light I might have lit, in
the old days.

14

Whatever it was: the grains of the glacier caked in the
boot-cleats; ashes spilled on white formica.

The death-col viewed through power-glasses; the cube of ice
melting on stainless steel.

Whatever it was, the image that stopped you, the one on
which you came to grief, projecting it over & over on empty
walls.

Now to give up the temptations of the projector; to see instead
the web of cracks filtering across the plaster.

To read there the map of the future, the roads radiating from
the initial split, the filaments thrown out from that impasse.

To reread the instructions on your palm; to find there how
the lifeline, broken, keeps its direction.

To read the etched rays of the bullet-hole left years ago in the
glass; to know in every distortion of the light what fracture is.

To put the prism in your pocket, the thin glass lens, the map
of the inner city, the little book with gridded pages.

To pull yourself up by your own roots; to eat the last meal in
your old neighborhood.

Trying To Talk with a Man

Out in this desert we are testing bombs,

that's why we came here.

Sometimes I feel an underground river
forcing its way between deformed cliffs

an acute angle of understanding
moving itself like a locus of the sun
into this condemned scenery.

What we've had to give up to get here —
whole LP collections, films we starred in
playing in the neighborhoods, bakery windows
full of dry, chocolate-filled Jewish cookies,
the language of love-letters, of suicide notes,
afternoons on the riverbank
pretending to be children

Coming out to this desert
we meant to change the face of
driving among dull green succulents
walking at noon in the ghost town
surrounded by a silence

that sounds like the silence of the place
except that it came with us
and is familiar
and everything we were saying until now
was an effort to blot it out —
coming out here we are up against it

Out here I feel more helpless
with you than without you

You mention the danger
and list the equipment
we talk of people caring for each other
in emergencies — laceration, thirst —
but you look at me like an emergency

Your dry heat feels like power
your eyes are stars of a different magnitude
they reflect lights that spell out: EXIT
when you get up and pace the floor

talking of the danger
as if it were not ourselves
as if we were testing anything else.

Diving into the Wreck

First having read the book of myths,
and loaded the camera,
and checked the edge of the knife-blade,
I put on
the body-armor of black rubber
the absurd flippers
the grave and awkward mask.
I am having to do this
not like Cousteau with his
assiduous team
aboard the sun-flooded schooner
but here alone.

There is a ladder.
The ladder is always there
hanging innocently
close to the side of the schooner.
We know what it is for,
we who have used it.
Otherwise
it's a piece of maritime floss
some sundry equipment.

I go down.
Rung after rung and still
the oxygen immerses me
the blue light
the clear atoms
of our human air.
I go down.
My flippers cripple me,
I crawl like an insect down the ladder
and there is no one
to tell me when the ocean
will begin.

First the air is blue and then
it is bluer and then green and then
black I am blacking out and yet
my mask is powerful
it pumps my blood with power
the sea is another story

the sea is not a question of power
I have to learn alone
to turn my body without force
in the deep element.

And now: it is easy to forget
what I came for
among so many who have always
lived here
swaying their crenellated fans
between the reefs
and besides
you breathe differently down here.

I came to explore the wreck.
The words are purposes.
The words are maps.
I came to see the damage that was done
and the treasures that prevail.
I stroke the beam of my lamp
slowly along the flank
of something more permanent
than fish or weed

the thing I came for:
the wreck and not the story of the wreck
the thing itself and not the myth
the drowned face always staring
toward the sun
the evidence of damage
worn by salt and sway into this threadbare beauty
the ribs of the disaster
curving their assertion
among the tentative haunters.

This is the place.
And I am here, the mermaid whose dark hair
streams black, the merman in his armored body
We circle silently
about the wreck
we dive into the hold.
I am she: I am he

whose drowned face sleeps with open eyes
whose breasts still bear the stress

whose silver, copper, vermeil cargo lies
obscurely inside barrels
half-wedged and left to rot
we are the half-destroyed instruments
that once held to a course
the water-eaten log
the fouled compass

We are, I am, you are
by cowardice or courage
the one who find our way
back to this scene
carrying a knife, a camera
a book of myths
in which
our names do not appear.

Upper Broadway

The leafbud straggles forth
toward the frigid light of the airshaft   this is faith
this pale extension of a day
when looking up   you know   something is changing
winter has turned   though the wind is colder
Three streets away   a roof collapses   onto people
who thought they still had time   Time out of mind

I have written so many words
wanting to live inside you
to be of use to you

Now I must write for myself   for this blind
woman scratching the pavement   with her wand of thought
this slippered crone   inching on icy streets
reaching into wire trashbaskets   pulling out
what was thrown away   and infinitely precious

I look at my hands and see   they are still unfinished
I look at the vine and see the leafbud
inching towards life

I look at my face in the glass   and see
a halfborn woman

Grandmothers

1. Mary Gravely Jones

We had no petnames, no diminutives for you,
always the formal guest under my father's roof:
you were "Grandmother Jones" and you visited rarely.
I see you walking up and down the garden,
restless, southern-accented, reserved, you did not seem
my mother's mother or anyone's grandmother.
You were Mary, widow of William, and no matriarch,
yet smoldering to the end with frustrate life,
ideas nobody listened to, least of all my father.
One summer night you sat with my sister and me
in the wooden glider long after twilight,
holding us there with streams of pent-up words.
You could quote every poet I had ever heard of,
had read *The Opium Eater,* Amiel and Bernard Shaw,
your green eyes looked clenched against opposition.
You married straight out of the convent school,
your background was country, you left an unperformed
typescript of a play about Burr and Hamilton,
you were impotent and brilliant, no one cared
about your mind, you might have ended
elsewhere than in that glider
reciting your unwritten novels to the children.

2. Hattie Rice Rich

Your sweetness of soul was a mystery to me,
you who slip-covered chairs, glued broken china,
lived out of a wardrobe trunk in our guestroom
summer and fall, then took the Pullman train
in your darkblue dress and straw hat, to Alabama,
shuttling half-yearly between your son and daughter.
Your sweetness of soul was a convenience for everyone,
how you rose with the birds and children, boiled your own egg,
fished for hours on a pier, your umbrella spread,
took the street-car downtown shopping
endlessly for your son's whims, the whims of genius,
kept your accounts in ledgers, wrote letters daily.

All through World War Two the forbidden word
Jewish was barely uttered in your son's house;
your anger flared over inscrutable things.
Once I saw you crouched on the guestroom bed,
knuckles blue-white around the bedpost, sobbing
your one brief memorable scene of rebellion:
you didn't want to go back South that year.
You were never "Grandmother Rich" but "Anana";
you had money of your own but you were homeless,
Hattie, widow of Samuel, and no matriarch,
dispersed among the children and grandchildren.

3. Granddaughter

Easier to encapsulate your lives
in a slide-show of impressions given and taken,
to play the child or victim, the projectionist,
easier to invent a script for each of you,
myself still at the center,
than to write words in which you might have found
yourselves, looked up at me and said
"Yes, I was like that; but I was something more. . . ."
Danville, Virginia; Vicksburg, Mississippi;
the "war between the states" a living memory
its aftermath the plague-town closing
its gates, trying to cure itself with poisons.
I can almost touch that little town. . . .
a little white town rimmed with Negroes,
making a deep shadow on the whiteness.
Born a white woman, Jewish or of curious mind
— twice an outsider, still believing in inclusion —
in those defended hamlets of half-truth
broken in two by one strange idea,
"blood" the all-powerful, awful theme —
what were the lessons to be learned? If I believe
the daughter of one of you — Amnesia was the answer.

GARY SNYDER

(1930 –)

This Poem Is for Bear

"As for me I am a child of the god of the mountains."

A bear down under the cliff.
She is eating huckleberries.
They are ripe now
Soon it will snow, and she
Or maybe he, will crawl into a hole
And sleep. You can see
Huckleberries in bearshit if you
Look, this time of year
If I sneak up on the bear
It will grunt and run

The others had all gone down
From the blackberry brambles, but one girl
Spilled her basket, and was picking up her
Berries in the dark.
A tall man stood in the shadow, took her arm,
Led her to his home. He was a bear.
In a house under the mountain
She gave birth to slick dark children
With sharp teeth, and lived in the hollow
Mountain many years.
         snare a bear: call him out:
honey-eater
forest apple
light-foot
Old man in the fur coat, Bear! come out!
Die of your own choice!
Grandfather black-food!
         this girl married a bear
Who rules in the mountains, Bear!
         you have eaten many berries

you have caught many fish
you have frightened many people
Twelve species north of Mexico
Sucking their paws in the long winter
Tearing the high-strung caches down
Whining, crying, jacking off
(Odysseus was a bear)

Bear-cubs gnawing the soft tits
Teeth gritted, eyes screwed tight
                but she let them.
Til her brothers found the place
Chased her husband up the gorge
Cornered him in the rocks.
Song of the snared bear:
      "Give me my belt.
      "I am near death.
      "I came from the mountain caves
      "At the headwaters,
      "The small streams there
      "Are all dried up.

—I think I'll go hunt bears.
                "hunt.bears?
Why shit Snyder,
You couldn't hit a bear in the ass
           with a handful of rice!"

Riprap

Lay down these words
Before your mind like rocks.
           placed solid, by hands
In choice of place, set
Before the body of the mind
          in space and time:
Solidity of bark, leaf, or wall
          riprap of things:
Cobble of milky way,
        straying planets,

These poems, people,
                lost ponies with
Dragging saddles —
                and rocky sure-foot trails.
The worlds like an endless
                four-dimensional
Game of *Go.*
                ants and pebbles
In the thin loam, each rock a word
                a creek-washed stone
Granite: ingrained
                with torment of fire and weight
Crystal and sediment linked hot
                all change, in thoughts,
As well as things.

Riprap: a cobble of stone laid on steep slick rock
to make a trail for horses in the mountains.

Sixth-Month Song in the Foothills

In the cold shed sharpening saws.
                a swallow's nest hangs by the door
setting rakers in sunlight
falling from meadow through doorframe
                swallows flit under the eaves.

Grinding the falling axe
sharp for the summer
                a swallow shooting out over.
over the river, snow on low hills
sharpening wedges for splitting.

Beyond the low hills, white mountains
and now snow is melting. sharpening tools;
                pack horses grazing new grass
bright axes — and swallows
                fly in to my shed.

Trail Crew Camp at Bear Valley.
9000 Feet. Northern Sierra —
White Bone and Threads of Snowmelt Water

Cut branches back for a day—
trail a thin line through willow
      up buckbrush meadows,
        creekbed for twenty yards
   winding in boulders
      zigzags the hill
into timber, white pine.

gooseberry bush on the turns.
hooves clang on the riprap
      dust, brush, branches.
     a stone
  cairn at the pass—
strippt mountains hundreds of miles.

sundown went back
      the clean switchbacks to camp.
bell on the gelding,
stew in the cook tent,
black coffee in a big tin can.

I Went into the Maverick Bar

I went into the Maverick Bar
In Farmington, New Mexico.
And drank double shots of bourbon
      backed with beer.
My long hair was tucked up under a cap
I'd left the earring in the car.

Two cowboys did horseplay
      by the pool tables,
A waitress asked us
      where are you from?
a country-and-western band began to play
"We don't smoke Marijuana in Muskokie"
And with the next song,
      a couple began to dance.

They held each other like in High School dances
                in the fifties;
I recalled when I worked in the woods
                and the bars of Madras, Oregon.
That short-haired joy and roughness —
                America — your stupidity.
I could almost love you again.

We left — onto the freeway shoulders —
                under the tough old stars —
In the shadow of bluffs
                I came back to myself,
To the real work, to
                "What is to be done."

Two Fawns That Didn't See the Light This Spring

A friend in a tipi in the
Northern Rockies went out
hunting white tail with a
.22 and creeped up on a few
day-bedded, sleeping, shot
what he thought was a buck.
"It was a doe, and she was
carrying a fawn."
He cured the meat without
salt; sliced it following the
grain.

A friend in the Northern Sierra
hit a doe with her car. It
walked out calmly in the lights,
"And when we butchered her
there was a fawn — about so long —
so tiny — but all formed and right.
It had spots. And the little
hooves were soft and white."

SYLVIA PLATH

(1932 – 1963)

The Colossus

I shall never get you put together entirely,
Pieced, glued, and properly jointed.
Mule-bray, pig-grunt and bawdy cackles
Proceed from your great lips.
It's worse than a barnyard.

Perhaps you consider yourself an oracle,
Mouthpiece of the dead, or of some god or other.
Thirty years now I have labored
To dredge the silt from your throat.
I am none the wiser.

Scaling little ladders with gluepots and pails of Lysol
I crawl like an ant in mourning
Over the weedy acres of your brow
To mend the immense skull-plates and clear
The bald, white tumuli of your eyes.

A blue sky out of the Oresteia
Arches above us. O father, all by yourself
You are pithy and historical as the Roman Forum.
I open my lunch on a hill of black cypress.
Your fluted bones and acanthine hair are littered

In their old anarchy to the horizon-line.
It would take more than a lightning-stroke
To create such a ruin.
Nights, I squat in the cornucopia
Of your left ear, out of the wind,

Counting the red stars and those of plum-color.
The sun rises under the pillar of your tongue.
My hours are married to shadow.
No longer do I listen for the scrape of a keel
On the blank stones of the landing.

The Hanging Man

By the roots of my hair some god got hold of me.
I sizzled in his blue volts like a desert prophet.

The nights snapped out of sight like a lizard's eyelid:
A world of bald white days in a shadeless socket.

A vulturous boredom pinned me in this tree.
If he were I, he would do what I did.

Parliament Hill Fields

On this bald hill the new year hones its edge.
Faceless and pale as china
The round sky goes on minding its business.
Your absence is inconspicuous;
Nobody can tell what I lack.

Gulls have threaded the river's mud bed back
To this crest of grass. Inland, they argue,
Settling and stirring like blown paper
Or the hands of an invalid. The wan
Sun manages to strike such tin glints

From the linked ponds that my eyes wince
And brim; the city melts like sugar.
A crocodile of small girls
Knotting and stopping, ill-assorted, in blue uniforms,
Opens to swallow me. I'm a stone, a stick,

One child drops a barrette of pink plastic;
None of them seem to notice.
Their shrill, gravelly gossip's funneled off.
Now silence after silence offers itself.
The wind stops my breath like a bandage.

Southward, over Kentish Town, an ashen smudge
Swaddles roof and tree.
It could be a snowfield or a cloudbank.
I suppose it's pointless to think of you at all.
Already your doll grip lets go.

The tumulus, even at noon, guards its black shadow:
You know me less constant,
Ghost of a leaf, ghost of a bird.
I circle the writhen trees. I am too happy.
These faithful dark-boughed cypresses

Brood, rooted in their heaped losses.
Your cry fades like the cry of a gnat.
I lose sight of you on your blind journey,
While the heath grass glitters and the spindling rivulets
Unspool and spend themselves. My mind runs with them,

Pooling in heel-prints, fumbling pebble and stem.
The day empties its images
Like a cup or a room. The moon's crook whitens,
Thin as the skin seaming a scar.
Now, on the nursery wall,

The blue night plants, the little pale blue hill
In your sister's birthday picture start to glow.
The orange pompons, the Egyptian papyrus
Light up. Each rabbit-eared
Blue shrub behind the glass

Exhales an indigo nimbus,
A sort of cellophane balloon.
The old dregs, the old difficulties take me to wife.
Gulls stiffen to their chill vigil in the drafty half-light;
I enter the lit house.

Morning Song

Love set you going like a fat gold watch.
The midwife slapped your footsoles, and your bald cry
Took its place among the elements.

Our voices echo, magnifying your arrival. New statue.
In a drafty museum, your nakedness
Shadows our safety. We stand round blankly as walls.

I'm no more your mother
Than the cloud that distills a mirror to reflect its own slow
Effacement at the wind's hand.

All night your moth-breath
Flickers among the flat pink roses. I wake to listen:
A far sea moves in my ear.

One cry, and I stumble from bed, cow-heavy and floral
In my Victorian nightgown.
Your mouth opens clean as a cat's. The window square

Whitens and swallows its dull stars. And now you try
Your handful of notes;
The clear vowels rise like balloons.

Blackberrying

Nobody in the lane, and nothing, nothing but blackberries,
Blackberries on either side, though on the right mainly,
A blackberry alley, going down in hooks, and a sea
Somewhere at the end of it, heaving. Blackberries
Big as the ball of my thumb, and dumb as eyes
Ebon in the hedges, fat
With blue-red juices. These they squander on my fingers.
I had not asked for such a blood sisterhood; they must love me.
They accommodate themselves to my milkbottle, flattening
    their sides.

Overhead go the choughs in black, cacophonous flocks —
Bits of burnt paper wheeling in a blown sky.
Theirs is the only voice, protesting, protesting.
I do not think the sea will appear at all.
The high, green meadows are glowing, as if lit from within.
I come to one bush of berries so ripe it is a bush of flies,
Hanging their bluegreen bellies and their wing panes in a
    Chinese screen.
The honey-feast of the berries has stunned them; they believe
    in heaven.
One more hook, and the berries and bushes end.

The only thing to come now is the sea.
From between two hills a sudden wind funnels at me,
Slapping its phantom laundry in my face.
These hills are too green and sweet to have tasted salt.

I follow the sheep path between them. A last hook brings me
To the hills' northern face, and the face is orange rock
That looks out on nothing, nothing but a great space
Of white and pewter lights, and a din like silversmiths
Beating and beating at an intractable metal.

Crossing the Water

Black lake, black boat, two black, cut-paper people.
Where do the black trees go that drink here?
Their shadows must cover Canada.

A little light is filtering from the water flowers.
Their leaves do not wish us to hurry:
They are round and flat and full of dark advice.

Cold worlds shake from the oar.
The spirit of blackness is in us, it is in the fishes.
A snag is lifting a valedictory, pale hand;

Stars open among the lilies.
Are you not blinded by such expressionless sirens?
This is the silence of astounded souls.

The Bee Meeting

Who are these people at the bridge to meet me? They are the
     villagers ——
The rector, the midwife, the sexton, the agent for bees.
In my sleeveless summery dress I have no protection,
And they are all gloved and covered, why did nobody tell me?
They are smiling and taking out veils tacked to ancient hats.

I am nude as a chicken neck, does nobody love me?
Yes, here is the secretary of bees with her white shop smock,
Buttoning the cuffs at my wrists and the slit from my neck to
     my knees.
Now I am milkweed silk, the bees will not notice.
They will not smell my fear, my fear, my fear.

Which is the rector now, is it that man in black?
Which is the midwife, is that her blue coat?
Everybody is nodding a square black head, they are knights in
    visors,
Breastplates of cheesecloth knotted under the armpits.
Their smiles and their voices are changing. I am led through a
    beanfield.

Strips of tinfoil winking like people,
Feather dusters fanning their hands in a sea of bean flowers,
Creamy bean flowers with black eyes and leaves like bored hearts.
Is it blood clots the tendrils are dragging up that string?
No, no, it is scarlet flowers that will one day be edible.

Now they are giving me a fashionable white straw Italian hat
And a black veil that molds to my face, they are making me
    one of them.
They are leading me to the shorn grove, the circle of hives.
Is it the hawthorn that smells so sick?
The barren body of hawthorn, etherizing its children.

Is it some operation that is taking place?
It is the surgeon my neighbors are waiting for,
This apparition in a green helmet,
Shining gloves and white suit.
Is it the butcher, the grocer, the postman, someone I know?

I cannot run, I am rooted, and the gorse hurts me
With its yellow purses, its spiky armory.
I could not run without having to run forever.
The white hive is snug as a virgin,
Sealing off her brood cells, her honey, and quietly humming.

Smoke rolls and scarves in the grove.
The mind of the hive thinks this is the end of everything.
Here they come, the outriders, on their hysterical elastics.
If I stand very still, they will think I am cow-parsley,
A gullible head untouched by their animosity,

Not even nodding, a personage in a hedgerow.
The villagers open the chambers, they are hunting the queen.
Is she hiding, is she eating honey? She is very clever.
She is old, old, old, she must live another year, and she knows it.
While in their fingerjoint cells the new virgins

Dream of a duel they will win inevitably,
A curtain of wax dividing them from the bride flight,
The upflight of the murderess into a heaven that loves her.
The villagers are moving the virgins, there will be no killing.
The old queen does not show herself, is she so ungrateful?

I am exhausted, I am exhausted——
Pillar of white in a blackout of knives.
I am the magician's girl who does not flinch.
The villagers are untying their disguises, they are shaking hands.
Whose is that long white box in the grove, what have they
    accomplished, why am I cold.

The Arrival of the Bee Box

I ordered this, this clean wood box
Square as a chair and almost too heavy to lift.
I would say it was the coffin of a midget
Or a square baby
Were there not such a din in it.

The box is locked, it is dangerous.
I have to live with it overnight
And I can't keep away from it.
There are no windows, so I can't see what is in there.
There is only a little grid, no exit.

I put my eye to the grid.
It is dark, dark,
With the swarmy feeling of African hands
Minute and shrunk for export,
Black on black, angrily clambering.

How can I let them out?
It is the noise that appalls me most of all,
The unintelligible syllables.
It is like a Roman mob,
Small, taken one by one, but my god, together!

I lay my ear to furious Latin.
I am not a Caesar.

I have simply ordered a box of maniacs.
They can be sent back.
They can die, I need feed them nothing, I am the owner.

I wonder how hungry they are.
I wonder if they would forget me
If I just undid the locks and stood back and turned into a tree.
There is the laburnum, its blond colonnades,
And the petticoats of the cherry.

They might ignore me immediately
In my moon suit and funeral veil.
I am no source of honey
So why should they turn on me?
Tomorrow I will be sweet God, I will set them free.

The box is only temporary.

Daddy

You do not do, you do not do
Any more, black shoe
In which I have lived like a foot
For thirty years, poor and white,
Barely daring to breathe or Achoo.

Daddy, I have had to kill you.
You died before I had time——
Marble-heavy, a bag full of God,
Ghastly statue with one gray toe
Big as a Frisco seal

And a head in the freakish Atlantic
Where it pours bean green over blue
In the waters off beautiful Nauset.
I used to pray to recover you.
Ach, du.

In the German tongue, in the Polish town
Scraped flat by the roller
Of wars, wars, wars.
But the name of the town is common.
My Polack friend

Says there are a dozen or two.
So I never could tell where you
Put your foot, your root,
I never could talk to you.
The tongue stuck in my jaw.

It stuck in a barb wire snare.
Ich, ich, ich, ich,
I could hardly speak.
I thought every German was you.
And the language obscene

An engine, an engine
Chuffing me off like a Jew.
A Jew to Dachau, Auschwitz, Belsen.
I began to talk like a Jew.
I think I may well be a Jew.

The snows of the Tyrol, the clear beer of Vienna
Are not very pure or true.
With my gipsy ancestress and my weird luck
And my Taroc pack and my Taroc pack
I may be a bit of a Jew.

I have always been scared of *you,*
With your Luftwaffe, your gobbledygoo.
And your neat mustache
And your Aryan eye, bright blue.
Panzer-man, panzer-man, O You———

Not God but a swastika
So black no sky could squeak through.
Every woman adores a Fascist,
The boot in the face, the brute
Brute heart of a brute like you.

You stand at the blackboard, daddy,
In the picture I have of you,
A cleft in your chin instead of your foot
But no less a devil for that, no not
Any less the black man who

Bit my pretty red heart in two.
I was ten when they buried you.

At twenty I tried to die
And get back, back, back to you.
I thought even the bones would do.

But they pulled me out of the sack,
And they stuck me together with glue.
And then I knew what to do.
I made a model of you,
A man in black with a Meinkampf look

And a love of the rack and the screw.
And I said I do, I do.
So daddy, I'm finally through.
The black telephone's off at the root,
The voices just can't worm through.

If I've killed one man, I've killed two——
The vampire who said he was you
And drank my blood for a year,
Seven years, if you want to know.
Daddy, you can lie back now.

There's a stake in your fat black heart
And the villagers never liked you.
They are dancing and stamping on you.
They always *knew* it was you.
Daddy, daddy, you bastard, I'm through.

Ariel

Stasis in darkness.
Then the substanceless blue
Pour of tor and distances.

God's lioness,
How one we grow,
Pivot of heels and knees! — The furrow

Splits and passes, sister to
The brown arc
Of the neck I cannot catch,

Nigger-eye
Berries cast dark
Hooks——

Black sweet blood mouthfuls,
Shadows.
Something else

Hauls me through air——
Thighs, hair;
Flakes from my heels.

White
Godiva, I unpeel——
Dead hands, dead stringencies.

And now I
Foam to wheat, a glitter of seas.
The child's cry

Melts in the wall.
And I
Am the arrow,

The dew that flies
Suicidal, at one with the drive
Into the red

Eye, the cauldron of morning.

Poppies in October

Even the sun-clouds this morning cannot manage such skirts.
Nor the woman in the ambulance
Whose red heart blooms through her coat so astoundingly——

A gift, a love gift
Utterly unasked for
By a sky

Palely and flamily
Igniting its carbon monoxides, by eyes
Dulled to a halt under bowlers.

O my God, what am I
That these late mouths should cry open
In a forest of frost, in a dawn of cornflowers.

Lady Lazarus

I have done it again.
One year in every ten
I manage it——

A sort of walking miracle, my skin
Bright as a Nazi lampshade,
My right foot

A paperweight,
My face a featureless, fine
Jew linen.

Peel off the napkin
O my enemy.
Do I terrify?——

The nose, the eye pits, the full set of teeth?
The sour breath
Will vanish in a day.

Soon, soon the flesh
The grave cave ate will be
At home on me

And I a smiling woman.
I am only thirty.
And like the cat I have nine times to die.

This is Number Three.
What a trash
To annihilate each decade.

What a million filaments.
The peanut-crunching crowd
Shoves in to see

Them unwrap me hand and foot——
The big strip tease.
Gentlemen, ladies

These are my hands
My knees.
I may be skin and bone,

Nevertheless, I am the same, identical woman.
The first time it happened I was ten.
It was an accident.

The second time I meant
To last it out and not come back at all.
I rocked shut

As a seashell.
They had to call and call
And pick the worms off me like sticky pearls.

Dying
Is an art, like everything else.
I do it exceptionally well.

I do it so it feels like hell.
I do it so it feels real.
I guess you could say I've a call.

It's easy enough to do it in a cell.
It's easy enough to do it and stay put.
It's the theatrical

Comeback in broad day
To the same place, the same face, the same brute
Amused shout:

'A miracle!'
That knocks me out.
There is a charge

For the eyeing of my scars, there is a charge
For the hearing of my heart——
It really goes.

And there is a charge, a very large charge
For a word or a touch
Or a bit of blood

Or a piece of my hair or my clothes.
So, so, Herr Doktor.
So, Herr Enemy.

I am your opus,
I am your valuable,
The pure gold baby

That melts to a shriek.
I turn and burn.
Do not think I underestimate your great concern.

Ash, ash—
You poke and stir.
Flesh, bone, there is nothing there——

A cake of soap,
A wedding ring,
A gold filling.

Herr God, Herr Lucifer
Beware
Beware.

Out of the ash
I rise with my red hair
And I eat men like air.

Sheep in Fog

The hills step off into whiteness.
People or stars
Regard me sadly, I disappoint them.

The train leaves a line of breath.
O slow
Horse the color of rust,

Hooves, dolorous bells——
All morning the
Morning has been blackening,

A flower left out.
My bones hold a stillness, the far
Fields melt my heart.

They threaten
To let me through to a heaven
Starless and fatherless, a dark water.

Words

Axes
After whose stroke the wood rings,
And the echoes!
Echoes traveling
Off from the center like horses.

The sap
Wells like tears, like the
Water striving
To re-establish its mirror
Over the rock

That drops and turns,
A white skull,
Eaten by weedy greens.
Years later I
Encounter them on the road——

Words dry and riderless,
The indefatigable hoof-taps.
While
From the bottom of the pool, fixed stars
Govern a life.

Edge

The woman is perfected.
Her dead

Body wears the smile of accomplishment,
The illusion of a Greek necessity

Flows in the scrolls of her toga,
Her bare

Feet seem to be saying:
We have come so far, it is over.

Each dead child coiled, a white serpent,
One at each little

Pitcher of milk, now empty.
She has folded

Them back into her body as petals
Of a rose close when the garden

Stiffens and odors bleed
From the sweet, deep throats of the night flower.

The moon has nothing to be sad about,
Staring from her hood of bone.

She is used to this sort of thing.
Her blacks crackle and drag.

Winter Trees

The wet dawn inks are doing their blue dissolve.
On their blotter of fog the trees
Seem a botanical drawing—
Memories growing, ring on ring,
A series of weddings.

Knowing neither abortions nor bitchery,
Truer than women,
They seed so effortlessly!
Tasting the winds, that are footless,
Waist-deep in history—

Full of wings, otherworldliness.
In this, they are Ledas.
O mother of leaves and sweetness
Who are these pietàs?
The shadows of ringdoves chanting, but easing nothing.

Child

Your clear eye is the one absolutely beautiful thing.
I want to fill it with color and ducks,
The zoo of the new

Whose names you meditate —
April snowdrop, Indian pipe,
Little

Stalk without wrinkle,
Pool in which images
Should be grand and classical

Not this troublous
Wringing of hands, this dark
Ceiling without a star.

MARK STRAND

(1934 –)

Keeping Things Whole

In a field
I am the absence
of field.
This is
always the case.
Wherever I am
I am what is missing.

When I walk
I part the air
and always
the air moves in
to fill the spaces
where my body's been.

We all have reasons
for moving.
I move
to keep things whole.

Coming to This

We have done what we wanted.
We have discarded dreams, preferring the heavy industry
of each other, and we have welcomed grief
and called ruin the impossible habit to break.

And now we are here.
The dinner is ready and we cannot eat.
The meat sits in the white lake of its dish.
The wine waits.

Coming to this
has its rewards: nothing is promised, nothing is taken away.
We have no heart or saving grace,
no place to go, no reason to remain.

Breath

When you see them
tell them I am still here,
that I stand on one leg while the other one dreams,
that this is the only way,

that the lies I tell them are different
from the lies I tell myself,
that by bcing both here and beyond
I am becoming a horizon,

that as the sun rises and sets I know my place,
that breath is what saves me,
that even the forced syllables of decline are breath,
that if the body is a coffin it is also a closet of breath,

that breath is a mirror clouded by words,
that breath is all that survives the cry for help
as it enters the stranger's ear
and stays long after the word is gone,

that breath is the beginning again, that from it
all resistance falls away, as meaning falls
away from life, or darkness falls from light,
that breath is what I give them when I send my love.

Courtship

There is a girl you like so you tell her
your penis is big, but that you cannot get yourself
to use it. Its demands are ridiculous, you say,
even self-defeating, but to be honored somehow,
briefly, inconspicuously in the dark.

When she closes her eyes in horror,
you take it all back. You tell her you're almost
a girl yourself and can understand why she is shocked.
When she is about to walk away, you tell her
you have no penis, that you don't

know what got into you. You get on your knees.
She suddenly bends down to kiss your shoulder and you know
you're on the right track. You tell her you want
to bear children and that is why you seem confused.
You wrinkle your brow and curse the day you were born.

She tries to calm you, but you lose control.
You reach for her panties and beg forgiveness as you do.
She squirms and you howl like a wolf. Your craving
seems monumental. You know you will have her.
Taken by storm, she is the girl you will marry.

"The Dreadful Has Already Happened"

The relatives are leaning over, staring expectantly.
They moisten their lips with their tongues. I can feel
them urging me on. I hold the baby in the air.
Heaps of broken bottles glitter in the sun.

A small band is playing old fashioned marches.
My mother is keeping time by stamping her foot.
My father is kissing a woman who keeps waving
to somebody else. There are palm trees.

The hills are spotted with orange flamboyants and tall
billowy clouds move behind them. "Go on, Boy,"
I hear somebody say, "Go on."
I keep wondering if it will rain.

The sky darkens. There is thunder.
"Break his legs," says one of my aunts,
"Now give him a kiss." I do what I'm told.
The trees bend in the bleak tropical wind.

The baby did not scream, but I remember that sigh
when I reached inside for his tiny lungs and shook them

out in the air for the flies. The relatives cheered.
It was about that time I gave up.

Now, when I answer the phone, his lips
are in the receiver; when I sleep, his hair is gathered
around a familiar face on the pillow; wherever I search
I find his feet. He is what is left of my life.

Elegy for My Father
(Robert Strand, 1908 – 1968)

1. The Empty Body

The hands were yours, the arms were yours,
But you were not there.
The eyes were yours, but they were closed and would not open.
The distant sun was there.
The moon poised on the hill's white shoulder was there.
The wind on Bedford Basin was there.
The pale green light of winter was there.
Your mouth was there,
But you were not there.
When somebody spoke, there was no answer.
Clouds came down
And buried the buildings along the water,
And the water was silent.
The gulls stared.
The years, the hours, that would not find you
Turned in the wrists of others.
There was no pain. It had gone.
There were no secrets. There was nothing to say.
The shade scattered its ashes.
The body was yours, but you were not there.
The air shivered against its skin.
The dark leaned into its eyes.
But you were not there.

2. *Answers*

Why did you travel?
Because the house was cold.
Why did you travel?
Because it is what I have always done between sunset and sunrise.
What did you wear?
I wore a blue suit, a white shirt, yellow tie, and yellow socks.
What did you wear?
I wore nothing. A scarf of pain kept me warm.
Who did you sleep with?
I slept with a different woman each night.
Who did you sleep with?
I slept alone. I have always slept alone.
Why did you lie to me?
I always thought I told the truth.
Why did you lie to me?
Because the truth lies like nothing else and I love the truth.
Why are you going?
Because nothing means much to me anymore.
Why are you going?
I don't know. I have never known.
How long shall I wait for you?
Do not wait for me. I am tired and I want to lie down.
Are you tired and do you want to lie down?
Yes, I am tired and I want to lie down.

3. *Your Dying*

Nothing could stop you.
Not the best day. Not the quiet. Not the ocean rocking.
You went on with your dying.
Not the trees
Under which you walked, not the trees that shaded you.
Not the doctor
Who warned you, the white-haired young doctor who saved
 you once.
You went on with your dying.
Nothing could stop you. Not your son. Not your daughter
Who fed you and made you into a child again.
Not your son who thought you would live forever.
Not the wind that shook your lapels.

Not the stillness that offered itself to your motion.
Not your shoes that grew heavier.
Not your eyes that refused to look ahead.
Nothing could stop you.
You sat in your room and stared at the city
And went on with your dying.
You went to work and let the cold enter your clothes.
You let blood seep into your socks.
Your face turned white.
Your voice cracked in two.
You leaned on your cane.
But nothing could stop you.
Not your friends who gave you advice.
Not your son. Not your daughter who watched you grow small.
Not fatigue that lived in your sighs.
Not your lungs that would fill with water.
Not your sleeves that carried the pain of your arms.
Nothing could stop you.
You went on with your dying.
When you played with children you went on with your dying.
When you sat down to eat,
When you woke up at night, wet with tears, your body sobbing,
You went on with your dying.
Nothing could stop you.
Not the past.
Not the future with its good weather.
Not the view from your window, the view of the graveyard.
Not the city. Not the terrible city with its wooden buildings.
Not defeat. Not success.
You did nothing but go on with your dying.
You put your watch to your ear.
You felt yourself slipping.
You lay on the bed.
You folded your arms over your chest and you dreamed of the
    world without you,
Of the space under the trees,
Of the space in your room,
Of the spaces that would now be empty of you,
And you went on with your dying.
Nothing could stop you.
Not your breathing. Not your life.

Not the life you wanted.
Not the life you had.
Nothing could stop you.

4. *Your Shadow*

You have your shadow.
The places where you were have given it back.
The hallways and bare lawns of the orphanage have given it back.
The Newsboys Home has given it back.
The streets of New York have given it back and so have the
    streets of Montreal.
The rooms in Belém where lizards would snap at mosquitos
    have given it back.
The dark streets of Manaus and the damp streets of Rio have
    given it back.
Mexico City where you wanted to leave it has given it back.
And Halifax where the harbor would wash its hands of you has
    given it back.
You have your shadow.
When you traveled the white wake of your going sent your
    shadow below, but when you arrived it was there to greet
    you. You had your shadow.
The doorways you entered lifted your shadow from you and
    when you went out, gave it back. You had your shadow.
Even when you forgot your shadow, you found it again; it had
    been with you.
Once in the country the shade of a tree covered your shadow
    and you were not known.
Once in the country you thought your shadow had been cast
    by somebody else. Your shadow said nothing.
Your clothes carried your shadow inside; when you took them
    off, it spread like the dark of your past.
And your words that float like leaves in an air that is lost, in a
    place no one knows, gave you back your shadow.
Your friends gave you back your shadow.
Your enemies gave you back your shadow. They said it was
    heavy and would cover your grave.
When you died your shadow slept at the mouth of the furnace
    and ate ashes for bread.
It rejoiced among ruins.

It watched while others slept.
It shone like crystal among the tombs.
It composed itself like air.
It wanted to be like snow on water.
It wanted to be nothing, but that was not possible.
It came to my house.
It sat on my shoulders.
Your shadow is yours. I told it so. I said it was yours.
I have carried it with me too long. I give it back.

5. *Mourning*

They mourn for you.
When you rise at midnight,
And the dew glitters on the stone of your cheeks,
They mourn for you.
They lead you back into the empty house.
They carry the chairs and tables inside.
They sit you down and teach you to breathe.
And your breath burns,
It burns the pine box and the ashes fall like sunlight.
They give you a book and tell you to read.
They listen and their eyes fill with tears.
The women stroke your fingers.
They comb the yellow back into your hair.
They shave the frost from your beard.
They knead your thighs.
They dress you in fine clothes.
They rub your hands to keep them warm.
They feed you. They offer you money.
They get on their knees and beg you not to die.
When you rise at midnight they mourn for you.
They close their eyes and whisper your name over and over.
But they cannot drag the buried light from your veins.
They cannot reach your dreams.
Old man, there is no way.
Rise and keep rising, it does no good.
They mourn for you the way they can.

6. The New Year

It is winter and the new year.
Nobody knows you.
Away from the stars, from the rain of light,
You lie under the weather of stones.
There is no thread to lead you back.
Your friends doze in the dark
Of pleasure and cannot remember.
Nobody knows you. You are the neighbor of nothing.
You do not see the rain falling and the man walking away,
The soiled wind blowing its ashes across the city.
You do not see the sun dragging the moon like an echo.
You do not see the bruised heart go up in flames,
The skulls of the innocent turn into smoke.
You do not see the scars of plenty, the eyes without light.
It is over. It is winter and the new year.
The meek are hauling their skins into heaven.
The hopeless are suffering the cold with those who have
    nothing to hide.
It is over and nobody knows you.
There is starlight drifting on the black water.
There are stones in the sea no one has seen.
There is a shore and people are waiting.
And nothing comes back.
Because it is over.
Because there is silence instead of a name.
Because it is winter and the new year.

The Coming of Light

Even this late it happens:
the coming of love, the coming of light.
You wake and the candles are lit as if by themselves,
stars gather, dreams pour into your pillows,
sending up warm bouquets of air.
Even this late the bones of the body shine
and tomorrow's dust flares into breath.

The Late Hour

A man walks towards town,
a slack breeze smelling of earth
and the raw green of trees blows at his back.

He drags the weight of his passion as if nothing were over,
as if the woman, now curled in bed beside her lover,
still cared for him.

She is awake and stares at scars of light
trapped in the panes of glass.
He stands under her window, calling her name;

he calls all night and it makes no difference.
It will happen again, he will come back wherever she is.
Again he will stand outside and imagine

her eyes opening in the dark
and see her rise to the window and peer down.
Again she will lie awake beside her lover

and hear the voice from somewhere in the dark.
Again the late hour, the moon and stars,
the wounds of night that heal without sound,

again the luminous wind of morning that comes before the sun.
And, finally, without warning or desire,
the lonely and the feckless end.

Where Are the Waters of Childhood?

See where the windows are boarded up,
where the gray siding shines in the sun and salt air
and the asphalt shingles on the roof have peeled or fallen off,
where tiers of oxeye daisics float on a sea of grass?
That's the place to begin.

Enter the kingdom of rot,
smell the damp plaster, step over the shattered glass,
the pockets of dust, the rags, the soiled remains of a mattress,
look at the rusted stove and sink, at the rectangular stain
on the wall where Winslow Homer's *Gulf Stream* hung.

Go to the room where your father and mother
would let themselves go in the drift and pitch of love,
and hear, if you can, the creak of their bed,
then go to the place where you hid.

Go to your room, to all the rooms whose cold, damp air you
    breathed,
to all the unwanted places where summer, fall, winter, spring,
seem the same unwanted season, where the trees you knew
    have died
and other trees have risen. Visit that other place
you barely recall, that other house half hidden.

See the two dogs burst into sight. When you leave,
they will cease, snuffed out in the glare of an earlier light.
Visit the neighbors down the block; he waters his lawn,
she sits on her porch, but not for long.
When you look again they are gone.

Keep going back, back to the field, flat and sealed in mist.
On the other side, a man and a woman are waiting;
they have come back, your mother before she was gray,
your father before he was white.

Now look at the North West Arm, how it glows a deep
    cerulean blue.
See the light on the grass, the one leaf burning, the cloud
that flares. You're almost there, in a moment your parents
will disappear, leaving you under the light of a vanished star,
under the dark of a star newly born. Now is the time.

Now you invent the boat of your flesh and set it upon the waters
and drift in the gradual swell, in the laboring salt.
Now you look down. The waters of childhood are there.

A Morning

I have carried it with me each day: that morning I took
my uncle's boat from the brown water cove
and headed for Mosher Island.
Small waves splashed against the hull
and the hollow creak of oarlock and oar
rose into the woods of black pine crusted with lichen.
I moved like a dark star, drifting over the drowned
other half of the world until, by a distant prompting,
I looked over the gunwale and saw beneath the surface
a luminous room, a light-filled grave, saw for the first time
the one clear place given to us when we are alone.

CHARLES WRIGHT
(1935 –)

The New Poem

It will not resemble the sea.
It will not have dirt on its thick hands.
It will not be part of the weather.

It will not reveal its name.
It will not have dreams you can count on.
It will not be photogenic.

It will not attend our sorrow.
It will not console our children.
It will not be able to help us.

Northhanger Ridge

Half-bridge over nothingness,
White sky of the palette knife; blot orange,
Vertical blacks; blue, birdlike,
Drifting up from the next life,
The heat-waves, like consolation, wince—
One cloud, like a trunk, stays shut
Above the horizon; off to the left, dream-wires,
Hill-snout like a crocodile's.

Or so I remember it,
Their clenched teeth in their clenched mouths,
Their voices like shards of light,
Brittle, unnecessary.
Ruined shoes, roots, the cabinet of lost things:
This is the same story,
Its lips in flame, its throat a dark water,
The page stripped of its meaning.

Sunday, and Father Dog is turned loose:
Up the long road the children's feet
Snick in the dust like raindrops; the wind
Excuses itself and backs off; inside, heat
Lies like a hand on each head;
Slither and cough. Now Father Dog
Addles our misconceptions, points, preens,
His finger a white flag, run up, run down.

Bow-wow and arf, the Great Light;
O, and the Great Yes, and the Great No;
Redemption, the cold kiss of release,
&c.; sentences, sentences.
(Meanwhile, docile as shadows, they stare
From their four corners, looks set:
No glitter escapes
This evangelical masonry.)

Candleflame; vigil and waterflow:
Like dust in the night the prayers rise:
From 6 to 6, under the sick Christ,
The children talk to the nothingness,
Crossrack and wound; the dark room
Burns like a coal, goes
Ash to the touch, ash to the tongue's tip;
Blood turns in the wheel:

Something drops from the leaves; the drugged moon
Twists and turns in its sheets; sweet breath
In a dry corner, the black widow reknits her dream.
Salvation again declines,
And sleeps like a skull in the hard ground,
Nothing for ears, nothing for eyes;
It sleeps as it's always slept, without
Shadow, waiting for nothing.

Bible Camp, 1949

Tattoos

1 *

Necklace of flame, little dropped hearts,
Camellias: I crunch you under my foot.
And here comes the wind again, bad breath
Of thirty-odd years, and catching up. Still,
I crunch you under my foot.

Your white stalks sequester me,
Their roots a remembered solitude.
Their mouths of snow keep forming my name.
Programmed incendiaries,
Fused flesh, so light your flowering,

So light the light that fires you
—Petals of horn, scales of blood—
Where would you have me return?
What songs would I sing,
And the hymns . . . What garden of wax statues . . .

                                                    1973

* Camellias; Mother's Day; St. Paul's Episcopal Church, Kingsport, Tennessee.

2 *

The pin oak has found new meat,
The linkworm a bone to pick.
Lolling its head, slicking its blue tongue,
The nightflower blooms on its one stem;
The crabgrass hones down its knives:

Between us again there is nothing. And since
The darkness is only light
That has not yet reached us,
You slip it on like a glove.
Duck soup, you say. *This is duck soup.*

And so it is.
                    Along the far bank
Of Blood Creek, I watch you turn
In that light, and turn, and turn,
Feeling it change on your changing hands,
Feeling it take. Feeling it.

                                                    1972

* Death of my father.

3 *

Body fat as my forearm, blunt-arrowed head
And motionless, eyes
Sequin and hammer and nail
In the torchlight, he hangs there,
Color of dead leaves, color of dust,

Dumbbell and hourglass — copperhead.
Color of bread dough, color of pain, the hand
That takes it, that handles it
—The snake now limp as a cat—
Is halfway to heaven, and in time.

Then Yellow Shirt, twitching and dancing,
Gathers it home, handclap and heartstring,
His habit in ecstasy.
Current and godhead, hot coil,
Grains through the hourglass glint and spring.

1951

* Snake-handling religious service; East Tennessee.

4 *

Silt fingers, silt stump and bone.
And twice now, in the drugged sky,
White moons, black moons.
And twice now, in the gardens,
The great seed of affection.

Liplap of Zuan's canal, blear
Footfalls of Tintoretto; the rest
Is brilliance: Turner at 3 a.m.; moth lamps
Along the casements. O blue
Feathers, this clear cathedral . . .

And now these stanchions of joy,
Radiant underpinning:
Old scaffolding, old arrangements,
All fall in a rain of light.
I have seen what I have seen.

1968

* Venice, Italy.

5 *

Hungering acolyte, pale body,
The sunlight — through St Paul of the 12 Sorrows —
Falls like Damascus on me:
I feel the gold hair of Paradise rise through my skin
Needle and thread, needle and thread;

I feel the worm in the rose root.
I hear the river of heaven
Fall from the air, I hear it enter the wafer
And sink me, the whirlpool stars
Spinning me down, and down. O . . .

Now I am something else, smooth,
Unrooted, with no veins and no hair, washed
In the waters of nothingness;
Anticoronal, released . . .
And then I am risen, the cup, new sun, at my lips.

1946

* Acolyte; fainting at the altar; Kingsport, Tennessee.

6 *

Skyhooked above the floor, sucked
And mummied by salt towels, my left arm
Hangs in the darkness, bloodwood, black gauze,
The slow circle of poison
Coming and going through the same hole . . .

Sprinkle of rain through the pine needles,
Shoosh pump shoosh pump of the heart;
Bad blood, bad blood . . .
                        Chalk skin like a light,
Eyes thin dimes, whose face
Comes and goes at the window?

Whose face . . .
                For I would join it,
And climb through the nine-and-a-half footholds of fever
Into the high air,
and shed these clothes and renounce,
Burned over, repurified.

1941

* Blood-poisoning; hallucination; Hiwassee, North Carolina.

*7 ***

This one's not like the other, pale, gingerly —
Like nothing, in fact, to rise, as he does,
In three days, his blood clotted,
His deathsheet a feather across his chest,
His eyes twin lenses, and ready to unroll.

Arm and a leg, nail hole and knucklebone,
He stands up. In his right hand,
The flagstaff of victory;
In his left, the folds of what altered him.
And the hills spell V, and the trees V . . .

Nameless, invisible, what spins out
From this wall comes breath by breath,
And pulls the vine, and the ringing tide,
The scorched syllable from the moon's mouth.
And what pulls them pulls me.

1963

* *The Resurrection,* Piero della Francesca, Borgo San Sepolcro, Italy.

*8 ***

A tongue hangs in the dawn wind, a wind
That trails the tongue's voice like a banner, star
And whitewash, the voice
Sailing across the 14 mountains, snap and drift,
To settle, a last sigh, here.

That tongue is his tongue, the voice his voice:
Lifting out of the sea
Where the tongue licks, the voice starts,
Monotonous, out of sync,
Yarmulke, tfillin, tallis.

His nude body waist deep in the waves,
The book a fire in his hands, his movements
Reedflow and counter flow, the chant light
From his lips, the prayer rising to heaven,
And everything brilliance, brilliance, brilliance.

1959

* Harold Schimmel's morning prayers; Positano, Italy.

9 *

In the fixed crosshairs of evening,
In the dust-wallow of certitude,
Where the drop drops and the scalding starts,
Where the train pulls out and the light winks,
The tracks go on, and go on:

The flesh pulls back and snaps,
The fingers are ground and scraped clean,
Reed whistles in a green fire.
The bones blow on, singing their bald song.
It stops. And it starts again.

Theologians, Interpreters:
Song, the tracks, crosshairs, the light;
The drop that is always falling.
Over again I feel the palm print,
The map that will take me there.

1952

* Temporary evangelical certitude; Christ School, Arden, North Carolina.

10 *

It starts here, in a chair, sunflowers
Inclined from an iron pot, a soiled dishcloth
Draped on the backrest. A throat with a red choker
Throbs in the mirror. High on the wall,
Flower-like, disembodied,

A wren-colored evil eye stares out
At the white blooms of the oleander, at the white
Gobbets of shadow and shade,
At the white lady and white parasol, at this
Dichogamous landscape, this found chord

(And in the hibiscus and moonflowers,
In the smoke trees and spider ferns,
The unicorn crosses his thin legs,
The leopard sips at her dish of blood,
And the vines strike and the vines recoil).

1973

* Visions of heaven.

11 *

So that was it, the rush and the take-off,
The oily glide of the cells
Bringing it up — ripsurge, refraction,
The inner spin
Trailing into the cracked lights of oblivion . . .

Re-entry is something else, blank, hard:
Black stretcher straps; the peck, peck
And click of a scalpel; glass shards
Eased one by one from the flesh;
Recisions; the long bite of the veins . . .

And what do we do with this,
Rechuted, reworked into our same lives, no one
To answer to, no one to glimpse and sing,
The cracked light flashing our names?
We stand fast, friend, we stand fast.

1958

* Automobile wreck; hospital; Baltimore, Maryland.

12 *

Oval oval oval oval push pull push pull . . .
Words unroll from our fingers.
A splash of leaves through the windowpanes,
A smell of tar from the streets:
Apple, arrival, the railroad, shoe.

The words, like bees in a sweet ink, cluster and drone,
Indifferent, indelible,
A hum and a hum:
Back stairsteps to God, ropes to the glass eye:
Vineyard, informer, the chair, the throne.

Mojo and numberless, breaths
From the wet mountains and green mouths; rustlings,
Sure sleights of hand,
The news that arrives from nowhere:
Angel, omega, silence, silence . . .

1945

* Handwriting class; Palmer Method; words as 'things'; Kingsport, Tennessee.

13 *

What I remember is fire, orange fire,
And his huge cock in his hand,
Touching my tiny one; the smell
Of coal dust, the smell of heat,
Banked flames through the furnace door.

Of him I remember little, if anything:
Black, overalls splotched with soot,
His voice, *honey, O, honey* . . .
And then he came, his left hand
On my back, holding me close.

Nothing was said, of course — one
Terrible admonition, and that was all . . .
And if that hand, like loosed lumber, fell
From grace, and stayed there? We give,
And we take it back. We give again . . .

1940

* The janitor; kindergarten; Corinth, Mississippi.

14 *

Now there is one, and still masked;
White death's face, sheeted and shoeless, eyes shut
Behind the skull holes.
She stands in a field, her shadow no shadow,
The clouds no clouds. Call her Untitled.

.

And now there are four, white shoes, white socks;
They stand in the same field, the same clouds
Vanishing down the sky. Cat masks and mop hair
Cover their faces. Advancing, they hold hands.

.

Nine. Now there are nine, their true shadows
The judgments beneath their feet.
Black masks, white nightgowns. A wind
Is what calls them, that field, those same clouds
Lisping one syllable *I, I, I.*

1970

* Dream.

*15 * *

And the saw keeps cutting,
Its flashy teeth shredding the mattress, the bedclothes,
The pillow and pillow case.
Plugged in to a socket in your bones,
It coughs, and keeps on cutting.

It eats the lamp and the bedpost.
It licks the clock with its oiled tongue,
And keeps on cutting.
It leaves the bedroom, and keeps on cutting.
It leaves the house, and keeps on cutting . . .

—Dogwood, old feathery petals,
Your black notches burn in my blood;
You flutter like bandages across my childhood.
Your sound is a sound of good-bye.
Your poem is a poem of pain.

1964

* The day of my mother's funeral, in Tennessee; Rome, Italy.

*16 * *

All gloss, gothic and garrulous, staked
To her own tree, she takes it off,
Half-dollar an article. With each
Hike of the price, the gawkers
Diminish, spitting, rubbing their necks.

Fifteen, and staked to *my* tree,
Sap-handled, hand in my pocket, head
Hot as the carnival tent, I see it out — as does
The sheriff of Cherokee County,
Who fondles the payoff, finger and shaft.

Outside, in the gathering dark, all
Is fly buzz and gnat hum and whine of the wires;
Quick scratch of the match, cicadas,
Jackhammer insects; drone, drone
Of the blood-suckers, sweet dust, last sounds . . .

1950

* Sideshow stripper; Cherokee County Fair, Cherokee, North Carolina.

17 *

I dream that I dream I wake
The room is throat-deep and brown with dead moths
I throw them back like a quilt
I peel them down from the wall
I kick them like leaves I shake them I kick them again

The bride on the couch and the bridegroom
Under their gauze dust-sheet
And cover up turn to each other
Top hat and tails white veil and say as I pass
It's mother again just mother the window open

On the 10th floor going up
Is Faceless and under steam his mask
Hot-wired my breath at his heels in sharp clumps
Darkness and light darkness and light
Faceless come back O come back

1955 ff.

* Recurrent dream.

18 *

Flash click tick, flash click tick, light
Through the wavefall — electrodes, intolerable curlicues;
Splinters along the skin, eyes
Flicked by the sealash, spun, pricked;
Terrible vowels from the sun.

And everything dry, wrung, the land flaked
By the wind, bone dust and shale;
And hills without names or numbers,
Bald coves where the sky harbors.
The dead grass whistles a tune, strangely familiar.

And all in a row, seated, their mouths biting the empty air,
Their front legs straight, and their backs straight,
Their bodies pitted, eyes wide,
The rubble quick glint beneath their feet,
The lions stare, explaining it one more time.

1959

* The Naxian lions; Delos, Greece.

19 *

The hemlocks wedge in the wind.
Their webs are forming something—questions:
Which shoe is the alter ego?
Which glove inures the fallible hand?
Why are the apple trees in draped black?

And I answer them. In words
They will understand, I answer them:
The left shoe.
The left glove.
Someone is dead; someone who loved them is dead.

Regret is what anchors me;
I wash in a water of odd names.
White flakes from next year sift down, sift down.
I lie still, and dig in,
Snow-rooted, ooze-rooted, cold blossom.

                                        1972

* Death of my father.

20 *

You stand in your shoes, two shiny graves
Dogging your footsteps;
You spread your fingers, ten stalks
Enclosing your right of way;
You yip with pain in your little mouth.

And this is where the ash falls.
And this is the time it took to get here—
And yours, too, is the stall, the wet wings
Arriving, and the beak.
And yours the thump, and the soft voice:

The octopus on the reef's edge, who slides
His fat fingers among the cracks,
Can use you. You've prayed to him,
In fact, and don't know it.
You *are* him, and think yourself yourself.

                                        1973

* The last stanza is an adaptation of lines from Eugenio Montale's *Serenata Indiana.*

from *Skins*

6

Under the rock, in the sand and the gravel run;
In muck bank and weed, at the heart of the river's edge:
Instar, and again, instar,
The wing cases visible. Then
Emergence: leaf drift and detritus; skin split,
The image forced from the self.
And rests, wings drying, eyes compressed,
Legs compressed, constricted
Beneath the dun and the watershine —
Incipient spinner, set for the take-off . . .
And does, in clean tear: imago rising out of herself
For the last time, slate-winged and many-eyed.
And joins, and drops to her destiny,
Flesh to the surface, wings flush on the slate film.

20

You've talked to the sun and moon,
Those idols of stitched skin, bunch grass and twigs
Stuck on their poles in the fall rain;
You've prayed to Sweet Medicine;
You've looked at the Hanging Road, its stars
The stepstones and river bed where you hope to cross;
You've followed the cricket's horn
To sidestep the Lake of Pain . . .
And what does it come to, Pilgrim,
This walking to and fro on the earth, knowing
That nothing changes, or everything:
And only, to tell it, these sad marks,
Phrases half-parsed, ellipses and scratches across the dirt?
It comes to a point. It comes and it goes.

Edvard Munch

We live in houses of ample weight,
Their windows a skin-colored light, pale and unfixable.
Our yards are large and windraked, their trees bent to the storm.
People we don't know are all around us.

Or else there is no one, and all day
We stand on a bridge, or a cliff's edge, looking down.
Our mothers stare at our shoes.

Hands to our ears, our mouths open, we're pulled on
By the flash black, flash black flash of the lighthouse
We can't see on the rock coast,
Notes in a bottle, our lines the ink from the full moon.

Stone Canyon Nocturne

Ancient of Days, old friend, no one believes you'll come back.
No one believes in his own life anymore.

The moon, like a dead heart, cold and unstartable, hangs by a
    thread
At the earth's edge,
Unfaithful at last, splotching the ferns and the pink shrubs.

In the other world, children undo the knots in their tally strings.
They sing songs, and their fingers blear.

And here, where the swan hums in his socket, where bloodroot
And belladonna insist on our comforting,
Where the fox in the canyon wall empties our hands, ecstatic
    for more,

Like a bead of clear oil the Healer revolves through the night
    wind,
Part eye, part tear, unwilling to recognize us.

Spider Crystal Ascension

The spider, juiced crystal and Milky Way, drifts on his web
    through the night sky
And looks down, waiting for us to ascend . . .

At dawn he is still there, invisible, short of breath, mending
    his net.

All morning we look for the white face to rise from the lake
    like a tiny star.
And when it does, we lie back in our watery hair and rock.

from *Homage to Paul Cézanne*

The dead are a cadmium blue.
We spread them with palette knives in broad blocks and planes.

We layer them stroke by stroke
In steps and ascending mass, in verticals raised from the earth.

We choose, and layer them in,
Blue and a blue and a breath,

Circle and smudge, cross-beak and buttonhook,
We layer them in. We squint hard and terrace them line by line.

And so we are come between, and cry out,
And stare up at the sky and its cloudy panes,

And finger the cypress twists.
The dead understand all this, and keep in touch,

Rustle of hand to hand in the lemon trees,
Flags, and the great sifts of anger

To powder and nothingness.
The dead are a cadmium blue, and they understand.

Dead Color

I lie for a long time on my left side and my right side
And eat nothing,
                    but no voice comes on the wind
And no voice drops from the cloud.
Between the grey spiders and the orange spiders,
                         no voice comes on the wind . . .

Later, I sit for a long time by the waters of Har,
And no face appears on the face of the deep.

Meanwhile, the heavens assemble their dark map.
The traffic begins to thin.
Aphids munch on the sweet meat of the lemon trees.
The lawn sprinklers rise and fall . . .

And here's a line of brown ants cleaning a possum's skull.
And here's another, come from the opposite side.

Over my head, star-pieces dip in their yellow scarves toward
   their black desire.

Windows, rapturous windows!

Hawaii Dantesca

White-sided flowers are thrusting up on the hillside,
                         blank love letters from the dead.
It's autumn, and nobody seems to mind.

Or the broken shadows of those missing for hundreds of years
Moving over the sugar cane
                    like storks, which nobody marks or mends.

This is the story line.

And the viridescent shirtwaists of light the trees wear.
And the sutra-circles of cattle egrets wheeling out past the rain
   showers.
And the spiked marimbas of dawn rattling their amulets . . .

Soon it will be time for the long walk under the earth toward
   the sea.

And time to retrieve the yellow sunsuit and little shoes
                              they took my picture in
In Knoxville, in 1938.

Time to gather the fire in its quartz bowl.

I hope the one with the white wings will come.
I hope the island of reeds is as far away as I think it is.

When I get there, I hope they forgive me if the knot I tie is
   the wrong knot.

MICHAEL HARPER
(1938 –)

American History

Those four black girls blown up
in that Alabama church
remind me of five hundred
middle passage blacks,
in a net, under water
in Charleston harbor
so *redcoats* wouldn't find them.
Can't find what you can't see
can you?

Martin's Blues

He came apart in the open,
the slow motion cameras
falling quickly
neither alive nor kicking;
stone blind dead
on the balcony
that old melody
etched his black lips
in a pruned echo:
*We shall overcome
some day —*
Yes we did!
Yes we did!

Last Affair: Bessie's Blues Song

Disarticulated
arm torn out,
large veins cross
her shoulder intact,
her tourniquet
her blood in all-white big bands:

Can't you see
what love and heartache's done to me
I'm not the same as I used to be
this is my last affair

Mail truck or parked car
in the fast lane,
afloat at forty-three
on a Mississippi road,
Two-hundred-pound muscle on her ham bone,
'nother nigger dead 'fore noon:

Can't you see
what love and heartache's done to me
I'm not the same as I used to be
this is my last affair

Fifty-dollar record
cut the vein in her neck,
fool about her money
toll her black train wreck,
white press missed her fun'ral
in the same stacked deck:

Can't you see
what love and heartache's done to me
I'm not the same as I used to be
this is my last affair

Loved a little blackbird
heard she could sing,
Martha in her vineyard
pestle in her spring,
Bessie had a bad mouth
made my chimes ring:

Can't you see
what love and heartache's done to me
I'm not the same as I used to be
this is my last affair

Nightmare Begins Responsibility

I place these numbed wrists to the pane
watching white uniforms whisk over
him in the tube-kept
prison
fear what they will do in experiment
watch my gloved stickshifting gasolined hands
breathe *boxcar-information-please* infirmary tubes
distrusting white-pink mending paperthin
silkened end hairs, distrusting tubes
shrunk in his *trunk-skincapped*
shaven head, in thighs
distrusting-white-hands-picking-baboon-light
on this son who will not make his second night
of this wardstrewn intensive airpocket
where his father's asthmatic
hymns of *night-train,* train done gone
his mother can only know that he has flown
up into essential calm unseen corridor
going boxscarred home, *mamaborn, sweetsonchild*
gonedowntown into *researchtestingwarehousebatteryacid*
*mama-son-done-gone/*me telling her 'nother
train tonight, no music, no breathstroked
heartbeat in my infinite distrust of them:

and of my distrusting self
white-doctor-who-breathed-for-him-all-night
say it for two sons gone,
say nightmare, say it loud
panebreaking heartmadness:
nightmare begins responsibility.

Tongue-Tied in Black and White

"I had a most marvelous piece of luck. I died."
[John Berryman]

In Los Angeles
while the mountains cleared of smog
your songs dreamed
Jefferson and Madison
walking hand in hand
as my grandfather walked to Canada.
What eyes met the black student
next to me, her hands fanning
your breezy neck from this veranda,
but Henry's Mr. Bones.

Home from Mexico and you in LIFE,
I walk dead center into the image
of LBJ cloistered by the draping
flags of Texas and the confederacy,
and as my aunt of Oklahoma told me
I understand your father's impulse
to force you into Crane's nightmare.

After the Roethke reading in Seattle
you stroked the stout legs of an ex-
student's wife while he sketched
you in adoration and as you cautioned
your audience, '45 minutes and no longer,'
how Harvard paid in prestige not money,
how a man at Harvard read for four hours,
that he ought to be set down in the Roman
courtyard and have rocks set upon him
until death—your audience laughed.

You admired my second living son
as you loved the honeyed dugs of his mother,
your spotless tan suit weaving in the arch
where goalposts supported you in foyer
for you would not fall.

At your last public reading,
let out for fear of incident without a drink,
your foot bandaged from fire you'd
stamped out in a wastebasket of songs,

your solitary voice speckled in Donne,
in Vermont where the stories of Bread
Loaf, Brown, another broken leg abandoned
in monotones of your friends studying you;

Now I must take up our quarrel:
never dangerous with women
though touched by their nectared hair,
you wrote in that needful black idiom
offending me, for only your inner voices
spoke such tongues, your father's soft prayers
in an all black town in Oklahoma; your ear lied.
That slave in you was white blood forced to derision,
those seventeenth-century songs saved you from review.

Naked, in a bottle of Wild Turkey,
the bridge you dived over was your source:
St. Paul to St. Louis to New Orleans,
the *asiento,* Toussaint, border ruffians,
signature of Lincoln, porters bringing
messages to white widows of Europe,
a classics major, and black, taking your classes,
the roughpage of your bird legs and beard
sanitizing your hospital room,
the last image of your bandaged foot
stamping at flames on the newborn bridge.

This is less than the whole truth
but it is the blacker story
and what you asked to be told:
'lay off the sauce when you write'
you said to me, winking at the brownskinned
actress accompanying me to the lectern;
and how far is Texas from Canada
and our shared relatives in blacktown
on the outskirts of your tongue, tied still.

CHARLES SIMIC

(1938 –)

Fear

Fear passes from man to man
Unknowing,
As one leaf passes its shudder
To another.

All at once the whole tree is trembling
And there is no sign of the wind.

Hearing Steps

Someone is walking through the snow:
An ancient sound. Perhaps the Mongols are migrating again?
Perhaps, once more we'll go hanging virgins
From bare trees, plundering churches,
Raping widows in the deep snow?

Perhaps, the time has come again
To go back into forests and snow fields,
Live alone killing wolves with our bare hands,
Until the last word and the last sound
Of this language I am speaking is forgotten.

Fork

This strange thing must have crept
Right out of hell.
It resembles a bird's foot
Worn around the cannibal's neck.

As you hold it in your hand,
As you stab with it into a piece of meat,
It is possible to imagine the rest of the bird:
Its head which like your fist
Is large, bald, beakless and blind.

My Shoes

Shoes, secret face of my inner life:
Two gaping toothless mouths,
Two partly decomposed animal skins
Smelling of mice-nests.

My brother and sister who died at birth
Continuing their existence in you,
Guiding my life
Toward their incomprehensible innocence.

What use are books to me
When in you it is possible to read
The Gospel of my life on earth
And still beyond, of things to come?

I want to proclaim the religion
I have devised for your perfect humility
And the strange church I am building
With you as the altar.

Ascetic and maternal, you endure:
Kin to oxen, to Saints, to condemned men,
With your mute patience, forming
The only true likeness of myself.

Charon's Cosmology

With only his feeble lantern
To tell him where he is
And every time a mountain
Of fresh corpses to load up

Take them to the other side
Where there are plenty more
I'd say by now he must be confused
As to which side is which

I'd say it doesn't matter
No one complains he's got
Their pockets to go through
In one a crust of bread in another a sausage

Once in a long while a mirror
Or a book which he throws
Overboard into the dark river
Swift cold and deep

The Lesson

It occurs to me now
that all these years
I have been
the idiot pupil
of a practical joker.

Diligently
and with foolish reverence
I wrote down
what I took to be
his wise pronouncements
concerning
my life on earth.
Like a parrot
I rattled off the dates
of wars and revolutions.
I rejoiced
at the death of my tormentors
I even became convinced
that their number
was diminishing.

It seemed to me
that gradually

my teacher was revealing to me
a pattern,
that what I was being told
was an intricate plot
of a picaresque novel
in installments,
the last pages of which
would be given over
entirely
to lyrical evocations
of nature.

Unfortunately,
with time,
I began to detect in myself
an inability
to forget even
the most trivial detail.
I lingered more and more
over the beginnings:
The haircut of a soldier
who was urinating
against our fence;
shadows of trees on the ceiling,
the day
my mother and I
had nothing to eat . . .

Somehow,
I couldn't get past
that prison train
that kept waking me up
every night.
I couldn't get that whistle
that rumble
out of my head . . .

In this classroom
austerely furnished
by my insomnia,
at the desk consisting
of my two knees,

for the first time
in this long and terrifying
apprenticeship,
I burst out laughing.
Forgive me, all of you!
At the memory of my uncle
charging a barricade
with a homemade bomb,
I burst out laughing.

A Wall

That's the only image
That turns up.

A wall, all by itself,
Poorly lit, beckoning,
But no sense of the room,
Not even a hint
Of why it is I remember
That fragment so clearly:

The fly I was watching,
The details of its wings
Glowing like turquoise,
Its feet, to my amusement
Following a minute crack —
An eternity
Around that simple event.

And nothing else, and nowhere
To go back to,
And no one else
As far as I know to verify.

Shirt

To get into it
As it lies
Crumpled on the floor
Without disturbing a single crease

Respectful
Of the way I threw it down
Last night
The way it happened to land

Almost managing
The impossible contortions
Doubling back now
Through a knotted sleeve

The Cold

As if in a presence of an intelligence
Concentrating, I thought myself
Scrutinized and measured closely
By the barrens of sky and earth,

And then algebraized and entered
In a notebook page blank and white
Except for the parallel blue lines
Which might have been bars,

For I kept walking and walking,
And it got darker and then there was
A flicker of a light or two
Far above and beyond the large cage.

Winter Night

The church is an iceberg.

It's the wind. It must be gusting tonight
Out of those galactic orchards,
Copernican pits and stones.

The monster created by mad Dr. Frankenstein
Sailed for the New World,
And ended up some place like New Hampshire.

Actually, it's just a local drunk,
Knocking with a snow-shovel,
Wanting to go in and sit.

An iceberg is a large, drifting
Piece of ice, broken off a glacier.

Old Couple

They're waiting to be murdered,
Or evicted. Soon
They expect to have nothing to eat.
As far as I know, they never go out.

A vicious pain's coming, they think.
It will start in the head
And spread down to the bowels.
They'll be carried off on stretchers, howling.

In the meantime, they watch the street
From their fifth floor window.
It has rained, and now it looks
Like it's going to snow a little.

I see him get up to lower the shades.
If their window stays dark,
I know that his hand has reached hers
Just as she was about to turn on the lights.

FRANK BIDART

(1939 –)

Self-Portrait, 1969

He's *still* young—; thirty, but looks younger—
or does he? . . . In the eyes and cheeks, tonight,
turning in the mirror, he saw his mother,—
puffy; angry; bewildered . . . Many nights
now, when he stares there, he gets angry: —
something *unfulfilled* there, something dead
to what he once thought he surely could be—
Now, just the glamour of habits . . .

                            Once, instead,
he thought insight would remake him, he'd reach
—what? The thrill, the exhilaration
unravelling disaster, that seemed to teach
necessary knowledge . . . became just jargon.

Sick of being decent, he craves another
crash. What *reaches* him except disaster?

Another Life

Peut-être n'es-tu pas suffisamment mort.
C'est ici la limite de notre domaine. Ðevant
toi coule un fleuve. — *Valéry*

"—In a dream I never *exactly* dreamed,
but that is, somehow, the quintessence
of what I *might* have dreamed,
                    Kennedy is in Paris

again; it's '61; once again
some new national life seems possible,
though desperately, I try to remain unduped,
even cynical . . .

          He's standing in an open car,·

brilliantly lit, bright orange
next to a grey de Gaulle, and they stand
not far from me, slowly moving up the Champs-Elysées . . .

Bareheaded in the rain, he gives a short
choppy wave, smiling like a sun god.

—I stand and
look, suddenly at peace; once again mindlessly
moved,
        as they bear up the fields of Elysium

the possibility of Atlantic peace,

reconciliation between all that power, energy,
optimism, —
        and an older wisdom, without
illusions, without force, the austere source
of nihilism, corrupted only by its dream of Glory . . .

But no —; as I
watch, the style is

              not quite right —;

              Kennedy is *too* orange . . .

And de Gaulle, white, dead
white, ghost white, not even grey . . .

                  As my heart
began to grieve for my own awkwardness and
ignorance, which would never be
soothed by the informing energies
              of whatever
wisdom saves, —

        I saw a young man, almost
my twin, who had written
          'MONSTER'
in awkward lettering with a crayon across
the front of his sweat shirt.
          He was gnawing on his arm,

in rage and anger gouging up

pieces of flesh —; but as I moved to stop him, somehow
help him,
            suddenly he looked up,

and began, as I had, to look at Kennedy and de Gaulle:

and then abruptly, almost as if I were seeing him
through a camera lens, his figure
split in two, —
            or doubled, —

and all the fury
            drained from his stunned, exhausted face . . .

But only for a moment. Soon his eyes turned down
to the word on his chest. The two figures
again became one,

and with fresh energy he attacked the mutilated arm . . .

—Fascinated, I watched as this
pattern, this cycle,
            repeated several times.

Then he reached out and touched me.

—Repelled,
            I pulled back . . . But he became
frantic, demanding that I become
the body he split into:
            'It's harder
to manage *each* time! Please,
give me your energy; — *help me!*'

                        —I said it was impossible,
there was *no part* of us the same:
we were just watching a parade together:
(and then, as he reached for my face)
                        leave me *alone!*

He smirked, and said
I was never alone.

            I told him to go to hell.

He said that this was hell.

—I said it was impossible,
there was *no part* of us the same:
we were just watching a parade together:
                            when I saw

Grief, avenging Care, pale
Disease, Insanity, Age, and Fear,
                            —all the raging desolations

which I had come to learn were my patrimony;
the true progeny of my parents' marriage;
the gifts hidden within the mirror;

—standing guard at the gate of this place,
triumphant,
        striking poses
                    eloquent of the disasters they embodied . . .

—I took several steps to the right, and saw
Kennedy was paper-thin,
                            as was de Gaulle;
mere cardboard figures
whose possible real existence
lay buried beneath a million tumbling newspaper
                                    photographs . . .

—I turned, and turned, but now all that was left
was an enormous
            fresco; — on each side, the unreadable
                            fresco of my life . . ."

Happy Birthday

Thirty-three, goodbye —
the awe I feel

is not that you won't come again, or why —

or even that after
a time, we think of those who are dead

with a sweetness that cannot be explained —

but that I've read the trading-cards:
RALPH TEMPLE CYCLIST CHAMPION TRICK RIDER

WILLIE HARRADON CYCLIST
THE YOUTHFUL PHENOMENON

F. F. IVES CYCLIST
100 MILES 6 H. 25 MIN. 30 SEC.

—as the fragile metal of their
wheels stopped turning, as they

took on wives, children, accomplishments, all those
predilections which also insisted on ending,

they could not tell themselves from what they had done.

Terrible to dress in the clothes
of a period that must end.

They didn't plan it that way—
they didn't plan it that way.

from *Elegy*

IV. Light

I am asleep, dreaming a terrible dream, so I awake,
and want to call my father to ask if, just
for a short time, the dog can come to stay with me.

But the light next to my bed won't light:
I press and press the switch. Touching the phone,
I can't see to dial the numbers. Can I learn how to keep

the dog in my apartment? In the dark, trying
a second light, I remember
I always knew these machines would fail me.

                                        Then I awake,

remember my father and the dog are dead,
the lights in that room do not go on.

V. Lineage

"I went to a mausoleum today, and found
what I want. Eye-level.
Don't forget:
I want to be buried in a mausoleum at eye-level."

She feels she never quite recovered
from her mother's, my grandmother's, death.

Her mother died by falling from a
third floor hospital window.

"—I'm *sure* she didn't want to kill herself;

after the stroke, sometimes she got confused, and
maybe she thought
     she saw grandpa at the window . . .

She wanted to be at home. After the stroke,
we *had* to put her in a nursing home, —

she hated it, but you couldn't
get help to stay with her, and she needed
someone twenty-four hours a day, —

she begged me to take her out;
       the cruel,
unreasonable things she said to me! Her doctor

told me I was doing the right thing, but
what she said
    almost drove me crazy . . .

it's astonishing how clearly I can still hear her voice.

I still dream I can see her falling
three stories, her arms stretching out . . .

For forty years, she counted
on grandpa, —
    after he died, she still
talked to him.

I know I made a lot of
mistakes with you, but I couldn't count on anyone—

I had to be both father *and* mother . . ."

As the subject once again changes from my grandmother

to my father, or the dog —
to my stepfather, or me —
                              her obsessive, baffled voice

says that when she allowed herself to love

she let something into her head which will
never be got out — ;
                        which could only betray her
or *be* betrayed, but never appeased — ;
whose voice

            death and memory have made
into a razor-blade without a handle . . .

"Don't forget:
I want to be buried in a mausoleum at eye-level."

ROBERT PINSKY
(1940 –)

from *Essay on Psychiatrists*

II. *Some Terms*

"Shrink" is a misnomer. The religious
Analogy is all wrong, too, and the old,
Half-forgotten jokes about Viennese accents

And beards hardly apply to the good-looking woman
In boots and a knit dress, or the man
Seen buying the Sunday *Times* in mutton-chop

Whiskers and expensive jogging shoes.
In a way I suspect that even the terms "doctor"
And "therapist" are misnomers; the patient

Is not necessarily "sick." And one assumes
That no small part of the psychiatrist's
Role is just that: to point out misnomers.

III. *Proposition*

These are the first citizens of contingency.
Far from the doctrinaire past of the old ones,
They think in their prudent meditations

Not about ecstasy (the soul leaving the body)
Nor enthusiasm (the god entering one's person)
Nor even about sanity (which means

Health, an impossible perfection)
But ponder instead relative truth and the warm
Dusk of amelioration. The cautious

Young augurs with their family-life, good books
And records and foreign cars believe
In amelioration — in that, and in suffering.

X. *Dionysus as Psychiatrist*

In a more hostile view, the psychiatrists
Are like Bacchus — the knowing smirk of his mask,
His patients, his confident guidance of passion,

And even his little jokes, as when the great palace
Is hit by lightning which blazes and stays,
Bouncing among the crumpling stone walls . . .

And through the burning rubble he comes,
With his soft ways picking along lightly
With a calm smile for the trembling Chorus

Who have fallen to the ground, bowing
In the un-Greek, Eastern way — What, Asian women,
He asks, Were you disturbed just now when Bacchus

Jostled the palace? He warns Pentheus to adjust,
To learn the ordinary man's humble sense of limits,
Violent limits, to the rational world. He cures

Pentheus of the grand delusion that the dark
Urgencies can be governed simply by the mind,
And the mind's will. He teaches Queen Agave to look

Up from her loom, up at the light, at her tall
Son's head impaled on the stiff spear clutched
In her own hand soiled with dirt and blood.

Memorial
(J. E. and N. M. S.)

Here lies a man. And here, a girl. They live
In the kind of artificial life we give

To birds or statues: imagining what they feel,
Or that like birds the dead each had one call,

Repeated, or a gesture that suspends
Their being in a forehead or the hands.

A man comes whistling from a house. The screen
Snaps shut behind him. Though there is no man

And no house, memory sends him to get tools
From a familiar shed, and so he strolls

Through summer shade to work on the family car.
He is my uncle, and fresh home from the war,

With little for me to remember him doing yet.
The clock of the cancer ticks in his body, or not,

Depending if it is there, or waits. The search
Of memory gains and fails like surf: the porch

And trim are painted cream, the shakes are stained.
The shadows could be painted (so little wind

Is blowing there) or stains on the crazy-paving
Of the front walk. . . . Or now, the shadows are moving:

Another house, unrelated; a woman says,
Is this your special boy, and the girl says, yes,

Moving her hand in mine. The clock in her, too —
As someone told me a month or two ago,

Months after it finally took her. A public building
Is where the house was: though a surf, unyielding

And sickly, seethes and eddies at the stones
Of the foundation. The dead are made of bronze,

But dying they were like birds with clocklike hearts —
Unthinkable, how much pain the tiny parts

Of even the smallest bird might yet contain.
We become larger than life in how much pain

Our bodies may encompass . . . all Titans in that,
Or heroic statues. Although there is no heat

Brimming in the fixed, memorial summer, the brows
Of lucid metal sweat a faint warm haze

As I try to think the pain I never saw.
Though there is no pain there, the small birds draw

Together in crowds above the houses — and cry
Over the surf: as if there were a day,

Memorial, marked on the calendar for dread
And pain and loss — although among the dead

Are no hurts, but only emblematic things;
No hospital beds, but a lifting of metal wings.

Dying

Nothing to be said about it, and everything—
The change of changes, closer or further away:
The Golden Retriever next door, Gussie, is dead,

Like Sandy, the Cocker Spaniel from three doors down
Who died when I was small; and every day
Things that were in my memory fade and die.

Phrases die out: first, everyone forgets
What doornails are; then after certain decades
As a dead metaphor, *"dead as a doornail"* flickers

And fades away. But someone I know is dying—
And though one might say glibly, "everyone is,"
The different pace makes the difference absolute.

The tiny invisible spores in the air we breathe,
That settle harmlessly on our drinking water
And on our skin, happen to come together

With certain conditions on the forest floor,
Or even a shady corner of the lawn—
And overnight the fleshy, pale stalks gather,

The colorless growth without a leaf or flower;
And around the stalks, the summer grass keeps growing
With steady pressure, like the insistent whiskers

That grow between shaves on a face, the nails
Growing and dying from the toes and fingers
At their own humble pace, oblivious

As the nerveless moths, that live their night or two—
Though like a moth a bright soul keeps on beating,
Bored and impatient in the monster's mouth.

Song of Reasons

Because of the change of key midway in "Come Back to
  Sorrento"
The little tune comes back higher, and everyone feels

A sad smile beginning. Also customary is the forgotten reason
Why the Dukes of Levis-Mirepoix are permitted to ride
  horseback

Into the Cathedral of Notre Dame. Their family is so old
They killed heretics in Languedoc seven centuries ago;

Yet they are somehow Jewish, and therefore the Dukes claim
Collateral descent from the family of the Virgin Mary.

And the people in magazines and on television are made
To look exactly the way they do for some reason, too:

Every angle of their furniture, every nuance of their doors
And the shapes of their eyebrows and shirts has its history

Or purpose arcane as the remote Jewishness of those far Dukes,
In the great half-crazy tune of the song of reasons.

A child has learned to read, and each morning before leaving
For school she likes to be helped through The Question Man

In the daily paper: Your Most Romantic Moment? Your Family
  Hero?
Your Worst Vacation? Your Favorite Ethnic Group? — and
  pictures

Of the five or six people, next to their answers. She likes it;
The exact forms of the ordinary each morning seem to show

An indomitable charm to her; even the names and occupations.
It is like a bedtime story in reverse, the unfabulous doorway

Of the day that she canters out into, businesslike as a dog
That trots down the street. The street: sunny pavement, plane
  trees,

The flow of cars that come guided by with a throaty music
Like the animal shapes that sing at the gates of sleep.

DAVE SMITH

(1942–)

On a Field Trip at Fredericksburg

The big steel tourist shield says maybe
fifteen thousand got it here. No word
of either Whitman or one uncle
I barely remember in the smoke
that filled his tiny mountain house.

If each finger were a thousand of them
I could clap my hands and be dead
up to my wrists. It was quick
though not so fast as we can do it
now, one bomb, atomic or worse,
one silly pod slung on wing-tip,
high up, an egg cradled
by some rapacious mockingbird.

Hiroshima canned nine times their number
in a flash. Few had the time
to moan or feel the feeling
ooze back in the groin.

In a ditch I stand
above Marye's Heights, the book-
boned faces of Brady's fifteen-year-old
drummers, before battle, rigid
as August's dandelions
all the way to the Potomac
rolling in my skull.

If Audubon came here, the names
of birds would gush, the marvel
single feathers make
evoke a cloud, a nation,
a gray blur preserved
on a blue horizon, but

there is only a wandering child,
one dark stalk snapped off
in her hand, held out to me.
Taking it, I try to help her
hold its obscure syllables
one instant in her mouth,
like a drift of wind
at the forehead, the front door,
the black, numb fingernails.

Cumberland Station

Gray brick, ash, hand-bent railings, steps so big
it takes hours to mount them, polished oak
pews holding the slim hafts of sun, and one
splash of the *Pittsburgh Post-Gazette.* The man
who left Cumberland gone, come back, no job
anywhere. I come here alone, shaken
the way I came years ago to ride down
mountains in Big Daddy's cab. He was
the first set cold in the black meadow.

Six rows of track gleam, thinned, rippling
like water on walls where famous engines steam, half
submerged in frothing crowds with something
to celebrate and plenty to eat. One engineer takes
children for a free ride, a frolic
like an earthquake. Ash cakes their hair.
I am one of those who walked uphill
through flowers of soot to zing
scared to death into the world.

Now whole families afoot cruise South Cumberland
for something to do, no jobs, no money for bars,
the old stories cracked like wallets.

This time there's no fun in coming back. The second
death. My roundhouse uncle coughed his youth
into a gutter. His son, the third, slid on the ice,
losing his need to drink himself

stupidly dead. In this vaulted hall
I think of all the dirt poured down
from shovels and trains and empty pockets.
I stare into the huge malignant headlamps
circling the gray walls and catch a stuttered
glimpse of faces stunned like deer on a track,
children getting drunk, shiny as Depression apples.

Churning through the inner space of this godforsaken
wayside, I feel the ground try to upchuck and I dig
my fingers in my temples to bury a child
diced on a cowcatcher, a woman smelling
alkaline from washing out the soot.
Where I stood in that hopeless, hateful room
will not leave me. The scarf of smoke I saw
over a man's shoulder runs through me
like the sored Potomac River.

Grandfather, you ask why I don't visit you
now you have escaped the ticket-seller's cage
to fumble hooks and clean the Shakespeare reels.
What could we catch? I've been sitting in the pews
thinking about us a long time, long enough to see
a man can't live in jobless, friendless Cumberland
anymore. The soot owns even the fish.

I keep promising I'll come back, we'll get out,
you and me, like brothers, and I mean it.
A while ago a man with the look of a demented cousin
shuffled across this skittery floor and snatched up
the *Post-Gazette* and stuffed it in his coat
and nobody gave a damn because nobody cares
who comes or goes here or even who steals
what nobody wants: old news, photographs
of dead diesels behind chipped glass
swimming into Cumberland Station.

I'm the man who stole it and I wish you were here
to beat the hell out of me for it because
what you said a long time ago welts my face
and won't go away. I admit
it isn't mine even if it's nobody else's.

Anyway, that's all I catch this trip — bad
news. I can't catch my nephew's life, my uncle's,
Big Daddy's, yours, or the ash-haired kids'
who fell down to sleep here after the war.

Outside new families pick their way along tracks
you and I have walked home on many nights.
Every face on the walls goes on smiling,
and, Grandfather, I wish I had the guts
to tell you this is a place I hope
I never have to go through again.

Looking for the Melungeon

Rounding a slip of the marsh, the boat skids
under me and the propeller whines naked,
then digs and shoots me forward. A clapper rail
disappears in reeds and one crane, shaken
from his nap blinks, and holds.

He makes me think of the Lost Tribe of Virginia,
as if the scree of insects were the Jew's
harp in John Jacob Niles's mouth.

A creek opens its throat and I enter, dragging
down to hear my wake's slip-slop,
thinking of the man who warned me people
were the same everywhere, lost and wondering

how they came to the life no one else wanted.
Sweet Jesus, he was right. Now he lies
in this sodden ground for the first time
in his life and I do not know even where.

Today is no different, the waters flood hulks
of empty houses, leaving beer cans to gleam
in the indifferent moon. The first stalks of
narcissus break the ground with gold
though March still means tonight to freeze.

I know this place, its small mustering of facts
wind-worn and useless, real and repeated, the same
anywhere. At the end the creek leads to a room,
one placid boat swinging at a stick, pines sieving

air, the cleat ringing like small jewelry.

Hawktree

Tonight in the hills there was a light
that leaped out of the head
and yellow longing of a young boy.
It was spring and he had walked
through the toy-littered yards
to the edge of town, and beyond.
In the tall spare shadow of a pine
he saw her standing, she of skin
whiter than the one cloud
each day loaned to the long sky,
whiter even than the pure moon.
But she would not speak to one
who kept her name to himself
when boys laughed in the courtyard.
He watched her burn like a candle
in the cathedral of needles.
After a while he saw the other light,
the sun's leveling blister, bring
its change to her wheaten hair.
In growing dark he waited, certain
she would hear the pine's whisper,
counting on nature's mediation.
But she would not speak and even
as he watched she vanished.
Slowly he knew his arms furred
with a fragrant green darkness
and as the moon cut its swaths
on the ground, as trucks rooted
along the road of colored pleasures,
he felt his feet pushing through
his shoes, his hair go sharply stiff.

He could hear her laugh, could see
her long finger loop a man's ear,
but this did not matter. Already
he felt himself sway a little
in the desert wind, in the wordless
emptied gnarling he had become.

Rain Forest

The green mothering of moss knits shadow and light,
silence and call of each least bird where
we walk and find there are only a few words
we want to say: water, root, light, and love,
like the names of time. Stunned from ourselves,
we are at tour's tail end, our guide long gone,
dawdling deep in what cannot be by any human
invented, a few square miles of the concentric
universe intricate as the whorls of fingertips.
The frailest twigs puff and flag in the giantism
of this elaborate grotto, and we are the dream,
before we know better, of an old grotesque
stonecutter who squats under a brow of sweat,
the afternoon a long glowing stalk of marble.
We have entered the huge inward drift behind
his eyes and wait to become ourselves. We stare
through limpid eyes into the vapor-lit past
where breath, wordlessly, like a near river
seams up, seams in and out and around darkness.
Somewhere far back in the hunch of shadows,
we stood by this wall of vines, and he, angry,
froze us in our tracks and the blade of belief.
That tree there bore the same long slithering
of light from a sky he owned. Disfigured now,
its trunk rises thick and black as a monument
that rings when struck. Here the hiking path,
a crease, stops, then spirals around into stumps.
Our party has gone that way, stumbling quietly.
From time to time, someone calls out but we know
only the words whispered from the wall of leaves:

water, root, light, and love. We stand silent
in the earliest air remembered, hearing at last
the distant and precise taps of the mallet
until our clothes, as if rotted, fall away
and the feckless light fixes us on the column
of our spines. Without warning, we begin to dance,
a bird cries, and another. Our feet seem to spark
on the hard dirt as we go round the black tree ,
and for no reason we know we see ourselves
throwing our heads back to laugh, our gums
and teeth shiny as cut wood, our eyes marbled,
straining to see where it comes from, that
hoarse rasp of joy, that clapping of hands
before which we may not speak or sing or ever stop.

Desks

Piled on a loading dock where I walked,
    student desks battered, staggered
by the dozens, as if all our talk
    of knowledge was over,

as if there'd be no more thin blondes
    with pigtails, no math, no art,
no birds to stare at. Surplus now, those moulds
    we tried to sleep in, always hard

so it wouldn't be pleasant and we'd fall
    awake in time for the one question
with no answer. Quiet as a study hall,
    this big place, this final destination,

oblivious to whatever the weather is,
    hearing the creak of the wind's weight.
The desks are leg-naked, empty, as if
    we might yet come, breathless, late.

And all that time I thought of the flames
    I hadn't guessed, of a blonde
I had loved for years, how the names
    carved one into another would

all scar out the same, blunt, hard, in blue
    searing, like love's first pain.
I stood there like a child, scared, new,
    bird-eyed, not knowing why I came.

Reading the Books Our Children Have Written

They come into this room while the quail are crying to huddle
    up,
the canyon winds just beginning. They pass my big brown desk,
their faces damp and glistening like the first peaches washed,
and offer themselves to be kissed. I am their father still,
I kiss them, I say *See you tomorrow!* Their light steps fade
down the stairs, what they are saying like the far stars
shrill, hard to understand. They are saying their father
writes a book and they are in it, for they are his children.
Then they lie in their beds waiting for sleep, sometimes singing.

Later I get up and go down in darkness and find the hour they
    played
before they were scrubbed, before they brought me those faces.
There on the floor I find the stapled pages, the strange mild
countenances of animals no one has ever seen, the tall dark man
who writes an endless story of birds homeless in the night. They
    have
numbered every page, they have named each colorful wing.
They have done all this to surprise me, surprising themselves.
On the last lined yellow page, one has written *This is a poem.*
Under this the other one has answered. *See tomorrow.*

Sea Owl

Unlike the hawk he has no dream of height,
his shadow is what he cannot remember.
In the wide and unlit room of the night
he waits. It is always December,

with the floor of the pines full of silver.
His toys move but his claws go tight
as soundlessly he descends the stair.
Nothing knows his cradle, where the white

drone of the day hides him. The flesh-bright
ribbons tear in his grip. He dismembers
the shore's secrets. The iron spike
of the sun is all he remembers.

Smithfield Ham

Aged, bittersweet, in salt crusted, the pink meat
lined with the sun's flare, fissured
as a working man's skin at hat level,
I see far back the flesh fall
as the honed knife goes
through to the plate, the lost
voice saying " . . . it cuts easy as butter. . . ."

Brown sugar and grease tries to hold itself
still beneath the sawed knee's white.
Around the table the clatter of china
kept in the highboy echoes,
children squeal in a near room.

The hand sawing is grandfather's, knuckled,
steadily starting each naked plate
heaped when it ends. Mine
waits shyly to receive
under the tall ceiling
all aunts, uncles have gathered to hold.

My shirt white as the creased linen, I shine
before the wedge of cherry pie, coffee
black as the sugarless future.
My mother, proud in his glance,
whispers he has called for me and for ham.

Tonight I come back to eat in that house the sliced
muscle that fills me with an old thirst.

With each swallow, unslaked, I feel
his hand fall more upon mine,
that odd endless blessing
I cannot say the name of . . .
it comes again with her family
tale, the dead recalled, Depression,
the jobless, china sold, low sobs, sickness.

Chewing, I ask how he is. Close your mouth, she says.
This time, if he saw me, maybe he'd remember
himself, who thanklessly carved us
that cured meat. The Home has to
let us in, we've paid, maybe we
have to go. I gnaw a roll
left too long on the table.
When my knife screeches the plate,
my mother shakes her head, whining like a child.

Nothing's sharp anymore, I can't help it, she says.
Almost alone, I lift the scalded coffee
steeped black and bitter.
My mouth, as if incontinent,
dribbles and surprises us.
Her face is streaked with summer
dusk where katydids drill and die.

Wanting to tell her there's always tomorrow,
I say you're sunburned, beautiful as ever.
Gardening has put the smell of dirt on her.
Like a blade, her hand touches mine.
More? she whispers. Then, " . . . you think
you'll never get enough, so sweet,
until the swelling starts, the ache . . .
it's that thirst that wants
to bust a person open late at night."
I fill my cup again, drink, nod, listen.

LOUISE GLÜCK
(1943 –)

All Hallows

Even now this landscape is assembling.
The hills darken. The oxen
sleep in their blue yoke,
the fields having been
picked clean, the sheaves
bound evenly and piled at the roadside
among cinquefoil, as the toothed moon rises:

This is the barrenness
of harvest or pestilence.
And the wife leaning out the window
with her hand extended, as in payment,
and the seeds
distinct, gold, calling
Come here
Come here, little one

And the soul creeps out of the tree.

Messengers

You have only to wait, they will find you.
The geese flying low over the marsh,
glittering in black water.
They find you.

And the deer —
how beautiful they are,
as though their bodies did not impede them.
Slowly they drift into the open
through bronze panels of sunlight.

Why would they stand so still
if they were not waiting?
Almost motionless, until their cages rust,
the shrubs shiver in the wind,
squat and leafless.

You have only to let it happen:
that cry—*release, release*—like the moon
wrenched out of earth and rising
full in its circle of arrows

until they come before you
like dead things saddled with flesh,
and you above them, wounded and dominant.

Poem

In the early evening, as now, a man is bending
over his writing table.
Slowly he lifts his head; a woman
appears, carrying roses.
Her face floats to the surface of the mirror,
marked with the green spokes of rose stems.

It is a form
of suffering: then always the transparent page
raised to the window until its veins emerge
as words finally filled with ink.

And I am meant to understand
what binds them together
or to the gray house held firmly in place by dusk

because I must enter their lives:
it is spring, the pear tree
filming with weak, white blossoms.

The School Children

The children go forward with their little satchels.
And all morning the mothers have labored
to gather the late apples, red and gold,
like words of another language.

And on the other shore
are those who wait behind great desks
to receive these offerings.

How orderly they are — the nails
on which the children hang
their overcoats of blue or yellow wool.

And the teachers shall instruct them in silence
and the mothers shall scour the orchards for a way out,
drawing to themselves the gray limbs of the fruit trees
bearing so little ammunition.

The Apple Trees

Your son presses against me
his small intelligent body.

I stand beside his crib
as in another dream
you stood among trees hung
with bitten apples
holding out your arms.
I did not move
but saw the air dividing
into panes of color — at the very last
I raised him to the window saying
See what you have made
and counted out the whittled ribs,
the heart on its blue stalk
as from among the trees
the darkness issued:

In the dark room your son sleeps.
The walls are green, the walls
are spruce and silence.
I wait to see how he will leave me.
Already on his hand the map appears
as though you carved it there,
the dead fields, women rooted to the river.

The Drowned Children

You see, they have no judgment.
So it is natural that they should drown,
first the ice taking them in
and then, all winter, their wool scarves
floating behind them as they sink
until at last they are quiet.
And the pond lifts them in its manifold dark arms.

But death must come to them differently,
so close to the beginning.
As though they had always been
blind and weightless. Therefore
the rest is dreamed, the lamp,
the good white cloth that covered the table,
their bodies.

And yet they hear the names they used
like lures slipping over the pond:
What are you waiting for
come home, come home, lost
in the waters, blue and permanent.

The Garden

1. The Fear of Birth

One sound. Then the hiss and whir
of houses gliding into their places.

And the wind
leafs through the bodies of animals —

But my body that could not content itself
with health — why should it be sprung back
into the chord of sunlight?

It will be the same again.
This fear, this inwardness,
until I am forced into a field
without immunity
even to the least shrub that walks
stiffly out of the dirt, trailing
the twisted signature of its root,
even to a tulip, a red claw.

And then the losses,
one after another,
all supportable.

2. The Garden

The garden admires you.
For your sake it smears itself with green pigment,
the ecstatic reds of the roses,
so that you will come to it with your lovers.

And the willows —
see how it has shaped these green
tents of silence. Yet
there is still something you need,
your body so soft, so alive, among the stone animals.

Admit that it is terrible to be like them,
beyond harm.

3. The Fear of Love

That body lying beside me like obedient stone —
once its eyes seemed to be opening,
we could have spoken.

At that time it was winter already.
By day the sun rose in its helmet of fire
and at night also, mirrored in the moon.

Its light passed over us freely,
as though we had lain down
in order to leave no shadows,
only these two shallow dents in the snow.
And the past, as always, stretched before us,
still, complex, impenetrable.

How long did we lie there
as, arm in arm in their cloaks of feathers,
the gods walked down
from the mountain we built for them?

4. *Origins*

As though a voice were saying
You should be asleep by now —
But there was no one. Nor
had the air darkened,
though the moon was there,
already filled in with marble.

As though, in a garden crowded with flowers,
a voice had said
How dull they are, these golds,
so sonorous, so repetitious
until you closed your eyes,
lying among them, all
stammering flame:

And yet you could not sleep,
poor body, the earth
still clinging to you —

5. *The Fear of Burial*

In the empty field, in the morning,
the body waits to be claimed.
The spirit sits beside it, on a small rock —
nothing comes to give it form again.

Think of the body's loneliness.
At night pacing the sheared field,
its shadow buckled tightly around.
Such a long journey.

And already the remote, trembling lights of the village
not pausing for it as they scan the rows.
How far away they seem,
the wooden doors, the bread and milk
laid like weights on the table.

Lamentations

1. The Logos

They were both still,
the woman mournful, the man
branching into her body.

But god was watching.
They felt his gold eye
projecting flowers on the landscape.

Who knew what he wanted?
He was god, and a monster.
So they waited. And the world
filled with his radiance,
as though he wanted to be understood.

Far away, in the void that he had shaped,
he turned to his angels.

2. Nocturne

A forest rose from the earth.
O pitiful, so needing
God's furious love —

Together they were beasts.
They lay in the fixed
dusk of his negligence;
from the hills, wolves came, mechanically
drawn to their human warmth,
their panic.

Then the angels saw
how He divided them:
the man, the woman, and the woman's body.

Above the churned reeds, the leaves let go
a slow moan of silver.

3. *The Covenant*

Out of fear, they built a dwelling place.
But a child grew between them
as they slept, as they tried
to feed themselves.

They set it on a pile of leaves,
the small discarded body
wrapped in the clean skin
of an animal. Against the black sky
they saw the massive argument of light.

Sometimes it woke. As it reached its hands
they understood they were the mother and father,
there was no authority above them.

4. *The Clearing*

Gradually, over many years,
the fur disappeared from their bodies
until they stood in the bright light
strange to one another.
Nothing was as before.
Their hands trembled, seeking
the familiar.

Nor could they keep their eyes
from the white flesh
on which wounds would show clearly
like words on a page.

And from the meaningless browns and greens
at last God arose, His great shadow
darkening the sleeping bodies of His children,
and leapt into heaven.

How beautiful it must have been,
the earth, that first time
seen from the air.

ALBERT GOLDBARTH

(1948 –)

A History of Civilization

In the dating bar, the potted ferns lean down
conspiratorially, little spore-studded
elopement ladders. The two top buttons
of every silk blouse have already half-undone all
introduction. Slices of smile, slices of sweet brie,
dark and its many white wedges. In back

of the bar, the last one-family grocer's is necklaced
over and over: strings of leeks, greek olives, sardines.
The scoops stand at attention in the millet barrel,
the cordovan sheen of the coffee barrel, the kidney beans.
And a woman whose pride is a clean linen apron polishes
a register as intricate as a Sicilian shrine. In back

of the grocery, dozing and waking in fitful starts
by the guttering hearth, a ring of somber-gabardined grandpas
plays dominoes. Their stubble picks up the flicker like filaments
still waiting for the bulb or the phone to be invented. Even their
coughs, their phlegms, are in an older language. They move
    the simple
pieces of matching numbers. In back

of the back room, in the unlit lengths of storage, it's
that season: a cat eyes a cat. The sacks and baskets
are sprayed with the sign of a cat's having eyed a cat, and
everything to do with rut and estrus comes down to a few
sure moves. The dust motes drift, the continents.
In the fern bar a hand tries a knee, as if unplanned.

The World of Expectations

What starts with F and ends with U-C-K? starts
another stupid high school joke. We also
snapped the thick resilient straps of Maria
Alfonso's bra. I don't know what we expected.
Annoyance, perhaps — though a kind of annoyance
that opened the way for attention — then maybe
intimacy, though we wouldn't have phrased it that way.
We called it F-ing. An alarm goes off,

the expectations are serial and easy: the clumsy
effecting of fire-drill practice, arrival of miles of hose.
And maybe Dennis or Leo or I would get to stand
near Maria, and maybe she'd even bend in her
provocative way that showed the first shadowy
rampway into her cleavage. When I finally did get
effed, of course it had nothing to do with the world
of expectations we mapped round and flat

where the condom ate wallet for years. Now I hear
Leo's divorced; drunk enough, it's as if a large hand
crumples him like a Coors can. The point is, even
Dennis's happiness, what kids mean and a sexual
axis, never struck our daydreams. The point is, not
even sex, necessarily — what did they see
in Station 19 when the bell went crazy? Flames
like cartoon devils? Their heroics, axe and ladder,

tested successfully? Glory? Pain? Some calls to glory
and pain are real, of course. But back then
we pulled levers for hijinks, for stupid jokes. And it came
long, red and clamorous. Firetruck.

FAMILY/ *Grove*

1

It's common to say of bad acting, or family photos like these,
the expressions are "wooden." It's true, I suppose: my father's
grimace is fitted into his face like the polymer moonslice of a
cheap keychain charm, and my mother's arms — even at the

most intimate — are raised and angled as if she were practicing umpire signals or fake hieroglyphic poses. That's sad — these aren't bad acting, but everyday honesties caught bad, in the everyday light. Here, at the arboretum, is a pose I know was meant to say fun, and love, and yet it looks as if they're about to strike me brutally — that smile, those arms. Maybe this is an honesty, that even they weren't aware of — a dozen times a day, it must have been, I rubbed against their grain. You see? — my lips stiff in a petulance. But I remember, before and beyond that, the dark the impolite glare of photography never really caught at all — an hour or so past bedtime, while I waited under the covers for sleep and they tiptoed noisily up to my room, on the way to theirs and whatever they shared in the double bed below the parquet picture — they'd stop, they'd strain their ears at the night like burglars against a safe, listening for my breathing, "checking," is how they always called it, "to make sure." So here it's twenty years ago, we're in an arboretum Chicago surrounds with its urban blatter, if we're wooden that's because we're a grove of our own; three rootknit family trees. See? — they face, and compete for, the flash of the camera like any trees and any light. In certain seasons, I remember, they were beautiful.

2

A number of researchers theorize that sleep developed, at least in part, to keep our mammalian ancestors safe in the hours given over to the great reptilian predators. In those wooded places dinosaurs couldn't enter without an announcing crash, they'd burrow and curl and let sleep make them silent for once, unnoticeable. Many of our nightmares are likely a deep mammalian memory of those scaled hunters tearing the earth; and probably served as a doublecheck system, waking the animal intermittently, blood hot, primed for flight — it would search the trunks around it for dangerous faces, sniffing, focusing, find no threat, so stretch and yawn and drowse off feeling safe again. I love being a mammal — that is, I love women's breasts, by which we get that name. And I love my sleep. I always have. In the hour or so while I waited to hear my parents' sentinel tiptoeing, there in the house on Washtenaw Avenue, I'd hug myself under the covers and squint, and

populate the whorls of the planks in the walls with a squadron
of heroes — Flash Gordon, Roy Rogers, some guy who could
breathe like a fish. These were necessary comfort because of
the others, who visited first — devil faces, terrible lizard
creatures, a man from the ten o'clock news who did something
bad with a knife to good boys and then left them in the forest
preserve. Looking, frightened, finally calmed of fright, in the
wood, in the woods, around me.

3

And now on my bedroom wall I have that old parquet picture,
a gift from my parents — they handed it over so casually. They
must not understand that it's a time machine; you look, it
takes you back. You're ten. A girl in a puff-sleeved peasant
dress is leaning to drink from a small round chink that trickles
coolly. Her breasts just brush the rumple of her blouse — the
lightest, pinking touch! Her eyes are closed (the one we see is a
dark v, like a bird in distant sky), and her feet are tensed in
support, accenting her difficult angle and her total
concentration on the thrill of tongue, to water. The pose
seems impossible to hold for even a minute — though of
course she's held it for over two generations now. My father
would say, with a strangely insistent pride, "Every shape is a
different piece of wood!" (I think he truly found this
wondrous — it was their only parquet.) "Each foot, a different
piece! Her hair, this leaf . . . each its own piece! And every
piece *is the natural color except her lips!* These they had to paint
red." They're very red. I look, I'm very ten. Most days I don't
look, though. I wake, I enter the world, it has a story to tell
me in dollar signs. I shake a hundred hands until a small
erosion wears away some of the lifeline, then I have lunch, and
then I lie, and then I'm lied straight back to, and then I come
home, it takes a while to drink away a sour taste, to think well
of myself, to be sleepy. I look. And when I do she's there, held
sure, the very light we see by held steady, longer than even a
life, in the grain.

The Tip

It's so dark now,
there's this streetlamp
packing light
like an iceberg.

It says: *like an iceberg*
I'm only one-tenth, look up.
And, vaguely, yes
there are stars.

And caught in the lamplight, leaning,
still, like a creature
the ice age is carrying thousands of miles
—a man just recovered from illness.

You see? — that daze
of special knowledge, clearer
and colder than ours. Yes he's death's, he's
eternity's, one-tenth.

MICHAEL BLUMENTHAL
(1949 –)

I Have Lived This Way for Years and Do Not Wish To Change

I hope you'll forgive the black paint
on my windows, the smell of cat litter
in the kitchen. Guests complain sometimes
that my collection of Minoan cadavers spoils
their appetite, or that having the shower
in the living room creates too much moisture,
but I think you'll grow used to it
if we get to be friends.

Yes, it is kind of inconvenient
having the bed strapped to the ceiling,
but I've grown so accustomed to the view
of my Max Ernst carpet that I hardly think
I could sleep with gravity anymore.

Why thank you, it was a gift from my lover's husband
after our honeymoon in Cincinnati. I do think
it goes well with the orange bedroom set, the burgundy curtains.

See, you're feeling quite at home already.
Don't be shy.
Help yourself to the jellyfish, the goose down,
the chocolate-covered cotton balls.

Washington Heights, 1959

Even the bad news came slowly and was afraid.
Grandmothers tapped their way up the steep hill
to Bennett Park, gradual as mealybugs along
the stem of a coleus. A pink rubber ball, some

small boy's humble playground, would roll by,
and some gray girl would lift to where the mind
said step but the old legs wouldn't answer.

Trees danced their lonely dance in fields of concrete.
Each one we came to, we called: country. What grass
we knew lived by the river, a place our mothers called:
don't play there, it isn't safe anymore. Safety
was the day's dull wisdom, their past a net we swam
against, a high tide. Risk was small and fragile, tied
to a wave called future, sinking every laugh it came upon.

Fishing, our bait was bubble gum and daydreams,
our creels filled with old beer cans wished to bass,
prophylactics weaving like white eels in a Hudson
we dreamt clean as a mountain river. Five old bottles
meant a chance to find your hero and a piece of bubble
gum besides, snow a chance to claim your arms again.

Childhood reading was obituaries in *Aufbau:* name,
maiden name, place of birth, surviving relatives,
death the one occasion we were sure of. Black ties
meant another neighbor wouldn't be there anymore,
candles that memory would find us. Scarred bricks
held auditions for home plate, lines on pavement
drew a floor for dancing.

Saturday was Sabbath and the slow turned slower.
Those who couldn't carry with their arms grew heavy
with their faith. Each year, we set the table
for a man who never came, ate bitter herbs,
read aloud some dreams that never quite rang true.

Constancy was Mario, tapping his Cats Paw heels to walk
on old cloth shoes stretched wide with aching. His
deep black hair turned gray with years, but the sound
of hammer to rubber to steel stayed firm with a sense
of praying. Friends died and aging backs bent towards
the earth, slow and predictable as corn husks in November.
As long as the mail kept coming, we smiled, waited
for the ice truck, buried the dead, called it home.

Wishful Thinking
for Cynthia

I like to think that ours will be more than just another story
of failed love and the penumbras of desire. I like to think
that the moon that day was in whatever house the astrologists
would have it in for a kind of quiet, a trellis lust could climb
easily and then subside, resting against the sills and ledges,
giving way like shore to an occasional tenderness, coddling
the cold idiosyncrasies of impulse and weather that pound it
as it holds to its shape against the winds and duststorms of
temptation and longing. I like to think that some small canister
of hope and tranquillity washed ashore that day and we, in
the right place, found it. These are the things I imagine
all lovers wish for amid the hot commencements of love
and promises, their histories and failures washing ashore
like flotsam, their innards girthed against those architects
of misery, desire and restlessness, their hopes rising
against the air as it fondles the waves and frolics them skywards.
I like to think that, if the heart pauses awhile in a single place,
it finds a home somewhere, like a vagabond lured by fatigue
to an unlikely town and, with a sudden peacefulness, deciding
to stay there. I like to think these things because, whether
or not they reach fruition, they provide the heart with a kind
of solace, the way poetry does, or all forms of tenderness
that issue out amid the deserts of failed love and petulant desire.
I like to think them because, meditated on amid this pattern
of off-white and darkness, they lend themselves to a kind of
music, not unlike the music a dove makes as it circles the trees,
not unlike the sun and the earth and their orbital brothers,
the planets, as they chant to the heavens their longing for hope
and repetition amid orderly movement, not unlike the music
these humble wishes make with their cantata of willfulness
and good intentions, looking for some pleasant abstractions
amid our concretized lives, something tender and lovely to
defy the times with, quiet and palpable amid the flickers of flux
and the flames of longing: a bird rising over the ashes, a dream.

JORIE GRAHAM

(1951–)

The Geese

Today as I hang out the wash I see them again, a code
as urgent as elegant,
tapering with goals.
For days they have been crossing. We live beneath these geese

as if beneath the passage of time, or a most perfect heading.
Sometimes I fear their relevance.
Closest at hand,
between the lines,

the spiders imitate the paths the geese won't stray from,
imitate them endlessly to no avail:
things will not remain connected,
will not heal,

and the world thickens with texture instead of history,
texture instead of place.
Yet the small fear of the spiders
binds and binds

the pins to the lines, the lines to the eaves, to the pincushion
    bush,
as if, at any time, things could fall further apart
and nothing could help them
recover their meaning. And if these spiders had their way,

chainlink over the visible world,
would we be in or out? I turn to go back in.
There is a feeling the body gives the mind
of having missed something, a bedrock poverty, like falling

without the sense that you are passing through one world,
that you could reach another
anytime. Instead the real
is crossing you,

your body an arrival
you know is false but can't outrun. And somewhere in between
these geese forever entering and
these spiders turning back,

this astonishing delay, the everyday, takes place.

Over and Over Stitch

Late in the season the world digs in, the fat blossoms
hold still for just a moment longer.
Nothing looks satisfied,
but there is no real reason to move on much further:
this isn't a bad place;
why not pretend

we wished for it?
The bushes have learned to live with their haunches.
The hydrangea is resigned
to its pale and inconclusive utterances.
Towards the end of the season
it is not bad

to have the body. To have experienced joy
as the mere lifting of hunger
is not to have known it
less. The tobacco leaves
don't mind being removed
to the long racks — all uses are astounding

to the used.
There are moments in our lives which, threaded, give us
    heaven —
noon, for instance, or all the single victories
of gravity, or the kudzu vine,
most delicate of manias,
which has pressed its luck

this far this season.
It shines a gloating green.
Its edges darken with impatience, a kind of wind.

Nothing again will ever be this easy, lives
being snatched up like dropped stitches, the dry stalks of daylilies
marking a stillness we can't keep.

Mind

The slow overture of rain,
each drop breaking
without breaking into
the next, describes
the unrelenting, syncopated
mind. Not unlike
the hummingbirds
imagining their wings
to be their heart, and swallows
believing the horizon
to be a line they lift
and drop. What is it
they cast for? The poplars,
advancing or retreating,
lose their stature
equally, and yet stand firm,
making arrangements
in order to become
imaginary. The city
draws the mind in streets,
and streets compel it
from their intersections
where a little
belongs to no one. It is
what is driven through
all stationary portions
of the world, gravity's
stake in things. the leaves,
pressed against the dank
window of November
soil, remain unwelcome
till transformed, parts
of a puzzle unsolvable

till the edges give a bit
and soften. See how
then the picture becomes clear,
the mind entering the ground
more easily in pieces,
and all the richer for it.

San Sepolcro

In this blue light
    I can take you there,
snow having made me
    a world of bone
seen through to. This
    is my house,

my section of Etruscan
    wall, my neighbor's
lemontrees, and, just below
    the lower church,
the airplane factory.
    A rooster

crows all day from mist
    outside the walls.
There's milk on the air,
    ice on the oily
lemonskins. How clean
    the mind is,

holy grave. It is this girl
    by Piero
della Francesca, unbuttoning
    her blue dress,
her mantle of weather,
    to go into

labor. Come, we can go in.
    It is before
the birth of god. No-one
    has risen yet

to the museums, to the assembly
    line — bodies

and wings — to the open air
    market. This is
what the living do: go in.
    It's a long way.
And the dress keeps opening
    from eternity

to privacy, quickening.
    Inside, at the heart,
is tragedy, the resent moment
    forever stillborn,
but going in, each breath
    is a button

coming undone, something terribly
    nimble-fingered
finding all of the stops.

My Garden, My Daylight

My neighbor brings me bottom fish —
    tomcod, rockcod —
a fist of ocean. He comes out
    from the appletrees between us
holding his gift like a tight
    spool of thread.

Once a week he brings me fresh-catch,
    boned and skinned
and rolled up like a tongue. I freeze them,
    speechless, angelic
instruments. I have a choir of them.
    Alive, they feed

driving their bodies through the mud,
    mud through their flesh.
See how white they become. High above,
    the water thins

to blue, then air, then less. . . .
        These aren't as sweet

as those that shine up there,
        quick schools
forever trying to slur over, become water.
        But these belong to us
who cannot fall out of this world
        but only deeper

into it, driving it into the white
        of our eyes. Muddy
daylight, we utter it, we drown in it.
        You can stay dry
if you can step between the raindrops
        mother's mother

said. She's words now you can't hear.
        I try to wind my way
between what's here: chalk, lily, milk,
        titanium, snow —
as far as I can say
        these appleblossoms house

five shades of white, and yet
        I know there's more.
Between my held breath and its small hot
        death, a garden,
Whiteness, grows. Its icy fruit
        seems true,

it glows. *For free* he says
        so that I can't refuse.

At Luca Signorelli's Resurrection of the Body

See how they hurry
        to enter
their bodies,
        these spirits.
Is it better, flesh,
        that they

should hurry so?
    From above
the green-winged angels
    blare down
trumpets and light. But
    they don't care,

they hurry to congregate,
    they hurry
into speech, until
    it's a marketplace,
it is humanity. But still
    we wonder

in the chancel
    of the dark cathedral,
is it better, back?
    The artist
has tried to make it so: each tendon
    they press

to re-enter
    is perfect. But is it
perfection
    they're after,
pulling themselves up
    through the soil

into the weightedness, the color,
    into the eye
of the painter? Outside
    it is 1500,
all round the cathedral
    streets hurry to open

through the wild
    silver grasses. . . .
The men and women
    on the cathedral wall
do not know how,
    having come this far,

to stop their
    hurrying. They amble off

in groups, in
    couples. Soon
some are clothed, there is
    distance, there is

perspective. Standing below them
    in the church
in Orvieto, how can we
    tell them
to be stern and brazen
    and slow,

that there is no
    entrance,
only entering. They keep on
    arriving,
wanting names,
    wanting

happiness. In his studio
    Luca Signorelli
in the name of God
    and Science
and the believable
    broke into the body

studying arrival.
    But the wall
of the flesh
    opens endlessly,
its vanishing point so deep
    and receding

we have yet to find it,
    to have it
stop us. So he cut
    deeper,
graduating slowly
    from the symbolic

to the beautiful. How far
    is true?
When his one son
    died violently,

he had the body brought to him
    and laid it

on the drawing-table,
    and stood
at a certain distance
    awaiting the best
possible light, the best depth
    of day,

then with beauty and care
    and technique
and judgement, cut into
    shadow, cut
into bone and sinew and every
    pocket

in which the cold light
    pooled.
It took him days
    that deep
caress, cutting,
    unfastening,

until his mind
    could climb into
the open flesh and
    mend itself.

RITA DOVE
(1952–)

Geometry

I prove a theorem and the house expands:
the windows jerk free to hover near the ceiling,
the ceiling floats away with a sigh.

As the walls clear themselves of everything
but transparency, the scent of carnations
leaves with them. I am out in the open

and above the windows have hinged into butterflies,
sunlight glinting where they've intersected.
They are going to some point true and unproven.

Adolescence — II

Although it is night, I sit in the bathroom, waiting.
Sweat prickles behind my knees, the baby-breasts are alert.
Venetian blinds slice up the moon; the tiles quiver in pale strips.

Then they come, the three seal men with eyes as round
As dinner plates and eyelashes like sharpened tines.
They bring the scent of licorice. One sits in the washbowl,

One on the bathtub edge; one leans against the door.
"Can you feel it yet?" they whisper.
I don't know what to say, again. They chuckle,

Patting their sleek bodies with their hands.
"Well, maybe next time." And they rise,
Glittering like pools of ink under moonlight,

And vanish. I clutch at the ragged holes
They leave behind, here at the edge of darkness.
Night rests like a ball of fur on my tongue.

Ö

Shape the lips to an *o*, say *a*.
That's *island*.

One word of Swedish has changed the whole neighborhood.
When I look up, the yellow house on the corner
is a galleon stranded in flowers. Around it

the wind. Even the high roar of a leaf-mulcher
could be the horn-blast from a ship
as it skirts the misted shoals.

We don't need much more to keep things going.
Families complete themselves
and refuse to budge from the present,
the present extends its glass forehead to sea
(backyard breezes, scattered cardinals)

and if, one evening, the house on the corner
took off over the marshland,
neither I nor my neighbor
would be amazed. Sometimes

a word is found so right it trembles
at the slightest explanation.
You start out with one thing, end
up with another, and nothing's
like it used to be, not even the future.

Dusting

Every day a wilderness — no
shade in sight. Beulah
patient among knickknacks,
the solarium a rage
of light, a grainstorm
as her gray cloth brings
dark wood to life.

Under her hand scrolls
and crests gleam

darker still. What
was his name, that
silly boy at the fair with
the rifle booth? And his kiss and
the clear bowl with one bright
fish, rippling
wound!

Not Michael—
something finer. Each dust
stroke a deep breath and
the canary in bloom.
Wavery memory: home
from a dance, the front door
blown open and the parlor
in snow, she rushed
the bowl to the stove, watched
as the locket of ice
dissolved and he
swam free.

That was years before
Father gave her up
with her name, years before
her name grew to mean
Promise, then
Desert-in-Peace.
Long before the shadow and
sun's accomplice, the tree.

Maurice.

The Fish in the Stone

The fish in the stone
would like to fall
back into the sea.

He is weary
of analysis, the small
predictable truths.

He is weary of waiting
in the open,
his profile stamped
by a white light.

In the ocean the silence
moves and moves

and so much is unnecessary!
Patient, he drifts
until the moment comes
to cast his
skeletal blossom.

The fish in the stone
knows to fail is
to do the living
a favor.

He knows why the ant
engineers a gangster's
funeral, garish
and perfectly amber.
He knows why the scientist
in secret delight
strokes the fern's
voluptuous braille.

Parsley

1. The Cane Fields

There is a parrot imitating spring
in the palace, its feathers parsley green.
Out of the swamp the cane appears

to haunt us, and we cut it down. El General
searches for a word; he is all the world
there is. Like a parrot imitating spring,

On October 2, 1957, Rafael Trujillo (1891–1961), dictator of the Dominican
Republic, ordered 20,000 blacks killed because they could not pronounce the letter
"r" in *perejil*, the Spanish word for parsley.

we lie down screaming as rain punches through
and we come up green. We cannot speak an R—
out of the swamp, the cane appears

and then the mountain we call in whispers *Katalina*.
The children gnaw their teeth to arrowheads.
There is a parrot imitating spring.

El General has found his word: *perejil*.
Who says it, lives. He laughs, teeth shining
out of the swamp. The cane appears

in our dreams, lashed by wind and streaming.
And we lie down. For every drop of blood
there is a parrot imitating spring.
Out of the swamp the cane appears.

2. *The Palace*

The word the general's chosen is parsley.
It is fall, when thoughts turn
to love and death; the general thinks
of his mother, how she died in the fall
and he planted her walking cane at the grave
and it flowered, each spring stolidly forming
four-star blossoms. The general

pulls on his boots, he stomps to
her room in the palace, the one without
curtains, the one with a parrot
in a brass ring. As he paces he wonders
Who can I kill today. And for a moment
the little knot of screams
is still. The parrot, who has traveled

all the way from Australia in an ivory
cage, is, coy as a widow, practising
spring. Ever since the morning
his mother collapsed in the kitchen
while baking skull-shaped candies
for the Day of the Dead, the general
has hated sweets. He orders pastries
brought up for the bird; they arrive

dusted with sugar on a bed of lace.
The knot in his throat starts to twitch;
he sees his boots the first day in battle
splashed with mud and urine
as a soldier falls at his feet amazed —
how stupid he looked! — at the sound
of artillery. *I never thought it would sing*
the soldier said, and died. Now

the general sees the fields of sugar
cane, lashed by rain and streaming.
He sees his mother's smile, the teeth
gnawed to arrowheads. He hears
the Haitians sing without R's
as they swing the great machetes:
Katalina, they sing, *Katalina,*

mi madle, mi amol en muelte. God knows
his mother was no stupid woman; she
could roll an R like a queen. Even
a parrot can roll an R! In the bare room
the bright feathers arch in a parody
of greenery, as the last pale crumbs
disappear under the blackened tongue. Someone

calls out his name in a voice
so like his mother's, a startled tear
splashes the tip of his right boot.
My mother, my love in death.
The general remembers the tiny green sprigs
men of his village wore in their capes
to honor the birth of a son. He will
order many, this time, to be killed

for a single, beautiful word.

Biographies
Credits
Index of First Lines
Index of Titles

Biographies

A. R. AMMONS (1926–)

Archibald Randolph Ammons was born and raised on a farm in North Carolina. He began writing poetry while serving in the navy in World War II; afterward he enrolled at Wake Forest College, concentrating in the sciences. As an M.A. candidate in English at Berkeley, he was encouraged in writing by the poet Josephine Miles. He left Berkeley in 1952 without taking a degree and worked in a glass-manufacturing company for ten years. In 1955 Ammons published a first book, *Ommateum,* at his own expense; in 1964 his second book, *Expressions of Sea Level* (1964), was published with the help of the poet John Logan, and Ammons joined the faculty at Cornell, where he is now professor of English. He recently was awarded a MacArthur fellowship. Ammons, because of his scientific training, is one of the few modern poets capable of writing easily within modern physical conceptions of the universe. Though his poetry reveals influences as diverse as Emerson, Moore, Stevens, Frost, and Williams, it has achieved a concise strength of its own, both in the shapeliness of the small nature lyrics and in the monumental force of the long poems, including "Sphere" and "Hibernaculum." His *Selected Poems* came out in 1977, the *Selected Longer Poems* in 1980.

JOHN ASHBERY (1927–)

John Ashbery grew up on his father's farm in upstate New York. In 1949 he graduated from Harvard and then took an M.A. in English at Columbia. In 1956, W. H. Auden selected Ashbery as the Yale Younger Poet. He received a Fulbright scholarship and moved to Paris, where he became art critic for the *Herald Tribune* in 1958. After returning to America, he served as executive editor of *Art News* (1965–1972). Ashbery writes art criticism for *Newsweek* and has taught at Brooklyn College and Bard. His recent poetry includes *Self-Portrait in a Convex Mirror* (1975), *As We Know* (1979), *Shadow Train* (1981), and *A Wave* (1984). Ashbery's poems of process often represent themselves as linear or circular journeys. They are written at a second order of experience (like the poetry of Eliot's *Quartets* or Stevens' longer poems), but they deliberately include the banal, the colloquial, and the popular. His art criticism has been collected as *Reported Sightings* (1989). He has been a MacArthur fellow.

JOHN BERRYMAN (1914–1972)

John Berryman, born John Smith, was a remarkable scholar, critic, teacher, and poet, who committed suicide after a long struggle with alcoholism and addiction to medicinal drugs. His father shot himself when Berryman was twelve; his mother remarried and Berryman took his stepfather's name. He received a B.A. from Columbia in 1936; after study at Cambridge University, he returned to Columbia to take a Ph.D. with a thesis on Stephen Crane. Berryman taught at Wayne State, Harvard, Princeton, and the University of Minnesota, where he taught until his death. His essays have been collected as *The Freedom of the Poet*. *The Dream Songs*, through their protagonist Henry, give voice to the impulsive and uncensored side of Berryman; the songs are shaped, however, by the poet who examines his own unruly impulses.

FRANK BIDART (1939–)

Frank Bidart, a native Californian, attended the University of California at Riverside before enrolling in the graduate program at Harvard, where he studied with Robert Lowell. Bidart has taught at Brandeis and the University of California, Berkeley; he is now professor of English at Wellesley College. The first Bernard F. Conners Prize was awarded by the *Paris Review* in 1981 to Bidart for his long poem "The War of Vaslav Nijinsky"; this is one of the dramatic poems of cinematic cross-cutting and operatic vocal range for which Bidart is best known. He has published *Golden State* (1973), *The Book of the Body* (1977), and *The Sacrifice* (1983); *In the Western Night* appeared in 1990.

ELIZABETH BISHOP (1911–1979)

Elizabeth Bishop's childhood was spent with her grandparents in Nova Scotia, after her father died and her mother was declared insane. Later she lived with an aunt in Massachusetts and graduated from Vassar College. The librarian at Vassar introduced Bishop to Marianne Moore, who encouraged her to continue writing. Bishop had a small private income; after graduation, she lived in Key West, France, and Mexico. On a visit to Brazil she met Lota de Macedo Soares, with whom she lived for nineteen years, until her return to the United States. During the last years of her life Bishop taught at Harvard and lived in Boston. Bishop had once wanted to be a painter, and her work is rich in observed detail. George Herbert was the poet she most admired, and her purity of line may derive from his example. Her *Complete Poems, 1927–1979* was published in 1983; the *Collected Prose* in 1984.

MICHAEL BLUMENTHAL (1949–)

Michael Blumenthal was raised in Manhattan by German-speaking refugee parents. After studying philosophy at the University of New

York, Binghamton, he taught briefly, then took a law degree at Cornell but gave up the practice of law to write poetry. He has been an editor at Time-Life Books, and an arts administrator, and is now a lecturer in poetry at Harvard. He has published *Sympathetic Magic* (1980), *Days We Would Rather Know* (1984), and *Against Romance* (1987); his third book of poetry, *Laps* (1984), was awarded the Juniper Prize by the University of Massachusetts, and he has held a Guggenheim fellowship. Blumenthal's verse is buoyantly inventive, comic in tone but aware of the ironies of hope.

AMY CLAMPITT (1920 –)

Amy Clampitt was raised in the rural town of New Providence, Iowa; her father was a "Quaker activist." She attended Grinnell College, worked for Oxford University Press and as a reference librarian for the Audubon Society, and then became a free-lance writer and editor. She was awarded a Guggenheim fellowship in poetry in 1982 and currently lives in New York City. Her books include *The Kingfisher* (1983), *What the Light Was Like* (1985), and *Westward* (1990). Her poetry, influenced by poets as diverse as Keats and Marianne Moore, has treated with fine detail her early life in Iowa, travels in England and Greece, and the landscape of the Maine coast. Persistent social concerns — including gender questions, the danger of war, and ethical obligations — also enter her work.

JAMES DICKEY (1923 –)

James Dickey was born in Atlanta, Georgia; at twenty-one he enlisted in the air force after a year's study at Clemson College in South Carolina. After the war he attended Vanderbilt, where he began writing poetry; his experiences during World War II are recorded in the striking early poems of *Drowning with Others* (1962) and *Helmets* (1964). Dickey's talents are various: he wrote the novel *Deliverance* (1970), adapted it for motion pictures, and acted in it; he has published forceful literary criticism (*Babel to Byzantium,* 1968). His later poetry (as in *The Zodiac,* 1976) has become increasingly experimental, concerned with a dispersal rather than a concentration of linguistic energy.

RITA DOVE (1952 –)

Rita Dove was raised in Akron, Ohio, where her family had moved from the south. She attended Miami University as a presidential scholar, graduating *summa cum laude* in English. She received a Fulbright to study modern European literature at the University of Tübingen, Germany, and later took an M.F.A. at the University of Iowa. She is professor of English at the University of Virginia, and has also been a Guggenheim fellow. Dove often writes historical poems about the black experience in America. *The Yellow House on the Corner* (1980) and *Museum* (1983) contain as well poems about her own life here and in Germany. *Thomas and Beulah* (1986) was awarded the Pulitzer Prize.

ALLEN GINSBERG (1926–)

Allen Ginsberg was born in Newark, New Jersey. His father Louis was a poet and highschool teacher of English; his mother Naomi was born in Russia. Ginsberg's childhood was spent in an atmosphere of socialist rhetoric and political activism. His mother's madness and death occasioned the long elegy, "Kaddish" (the Hebrew prayer for the dead). Ginsberg attended Columbia but was expelled for writing an obscenity on his dormitory window; after living for a while with the writers William Burroughs and Jack Kerouac, he reentered Columbia, graduating in 1948. He was implicated in a friend's thefts, pled insanity to avoid imprisonment, and spent eight months in a psychiatric institute. Ginsberg and others (Kerouac, Gregory Corso, Snyder) became known as the Beat Generation and made San Francisco their center. Later Ginsberg traveled to India to study Zen Buddhism. His exuberant poetry, influenced by Blake, Whitman, and Williams (who encouraged his early work), has taken up many social and political issues. Ginsberg has been a controversial figure since the publication of *Howl* in 1956. He has been actively involved in civil rights, homosexual rights, and the peace movement. The *Collected Poems* were published in 1985.

LOUISE GLÜCK (1943–)

Louise Glück was born in New York City; she attended Sarah Lawrence College and Columbia University, studying there with Stanley Kunitz. Glück taught at Goddard College in Vermont before joining the faculty at Warren Wilson College. Among her books are *Firstborn* (1969), *The House on Marshland* (1976), and *Descending Figure* (1980). Her poetry has shown an individual use of generalized western myth, especially in her longer sequences; she writes in a veiled and almost disembodied style at once austere and sensuous.

ALBERT GOLDBARTH (1948–)

Albert Goldbarth was born, of a religious Jewish family, in Chicago. He graduated from the University of Illinois, took an M.F.A. at the University of Iowa, and has taught at the University of Utah, Cornell, and the University of Texas; he is now professor of English at the University of Kansas, Wichita, and has been a Guggenheim fellow. Goldbarth's historical imagination has led him to imaginative reconstructions, in long poems like *Opticks* (1974), of past artists and their work; he has also written autobiographical domestic poems. His *Original Light: New and Selected Poems* appeared in 1983, and *Popular Culture* in 1990.

JORIE GRAHAM (1950–)

Jorie Graham was raised in Italy by her American parents. She went to a French *lycée* in Rome and grew up speaking French, Italian, and English. She attended the Sorbonne to study philosophy, then entered the program of cinema studies at New York University. She worked in television before taking an M.F.A. at the University of Iowa. Her poetry pursues philosophical questions of consciousness and creativity; she frequently uses landscapes or paintings as her vehicles for such questions, especially in her second collection, *Erosion* (1983), and her most recent, *The End of Beauty* (1987). She has been a Guggenheim fellow and a MacArthur fellow, and is now professor of English at the University of Iowa.

MICHAEL HARPER (1938–)

Michael Harper was born and raised in Brooklyn and educated at California State College in Los Angeles and the University of Iowa. He has taught at California State College in Hayward, Reed College, Lewis and Clark College, Contra Costa College, and Brown University, where he is professor of English and director of the writing program. He was a fellow at the Center for Advanced Study, University of Illinois (1970–71), when his first volume of poetry, *Dear John, Dear Coltrane,* was published. Harper has recently edited *Chant of Saints* (1973), an anthology of black art and writing. His poetry, deeply influenced by the rhythms of jazz and the blues, aims at a synoptic view of black history and personal history.

ROBERT HAYDEN (1913–1980)

Robert Hayden received a B.A. from Detroit City College. He won the Hopwood Award for Poetry at the University of Michigan in 1938 and 1942 and published his first book, *Heart-Shape in the Dust,* in 1940. After receiving an M.A. at Michigan, he taught at Fisk University, then became professor of English at the University of Michigan, where he remained until he died. Hayden's distinguished work, incorporating the modernist idiom of Eliot and Pound, brought black poetry into the mainstream of contemporary American verse. His *Complete Poems* appeared posthumously in 1985.

LANGSTON HUGHES (1902–1967)

Langston Hughes, whose father rejected the social status of American blacks and moved to Mexico, was raised by his mother. During his adolescence Hughes lived with his father but returned to America to attend Columbia. He dropped out after a year but eventually received his B.A. from Lincoln University. He was a central figure in the Harlem Renaissance of the 1920s, with his musical sequences of poems combining lyricism and social protest. In addition to poetry, Hughes wrote short stories, novels, children's stories, nonfiction, musical lyrics, plays, and opera libretti, and translated García Lorca and Gabriela Mistral.

RANDALL JARRELL (1914–1965)

Randall Jarrell was born in Nashville, but his early years were spent in California, for which he felt a lifelong nostalgia. He returned to Nashville at the age of twelve and attended Vanderbilt University, receiving an M.A. in psychology in 1938. After his military service (1942–1946), he served on the faculties of Kenyon, the University of Texas, Sarah Lawrence, Princeton, and the Women's College of the University of North Carolina. In 1965 Jarrell suffered a nervous breakdown for which he was hospitalized; later that year he walked in front of a car on a highway and was killed. Jarrell was the liveliest critic of poetry of his generation; his essays are collected in *Poetry and the Age* (1953), *A Sad Heart at the Supermarket* (1962), and *The Third Book of Criticism* (1971). His *Complete Poems* appeared posthumously in 1969.

ROBERT LOWELL (1917–1977)

Robert Lowell was born into a family that had included many famous Americans (a Revolutionary general, a governor of Massachusetts, a president of Harvard, two poets). Lowell left Harvard after two years and, following the advice of Ford Madox Ford, enrolled at Kenyon to study under John Crowe Ransom. At Kenyon he met Tate, Jarrell, and Peter Taylor; he graduated *summa cum laude* in classics. After college, Lowell rebelled against family tradition: he converted to Catholicism (later abandoned) and was imprisoned as a conscientious objector. After a series of manic-depressive breakdowns, he had psychoanalytic therapy; the analytic sessions may have helped to shape *Life Studies* (1960). Other volumes of his poetry include *Lord Weary's Castle* (1946), *For the Union Dead* (1964), *History* (1973), *For Lizzie and Harriet* (1973), *The Dolphin* (1973), and *Day by Day* (1977). Lowell's poetry—"my autobiography in verse"—includes commentary on his family, his three wives (Jean Stafford, Elizabeth Hardwick, and Caroline Blackwood), his daughter Harriet and his son Sheridan; it also extends, especially in *History,* to a synoptic view of cultural history. For the last several years of his life he taught at Harvard.

JAMES MERRILL (1926–)

James Merrill, the son of a stockbroker, was born in New York City and graduated from Amherst College. He published *First Poems* in 1951, while living in New York. He later moved to Stonington, Connecticut, and began to spend several months of each year in Greece. *From the First Nine* (1983) is a selection of poems from his first nine books; *The*

Changing Light at Sandover (1982) collects the verse trilogy—the Ouijaboard books—earlier published in three volumes (*The Book of Ephraim, Mirabell,* and *Scripts for the Pageant*). Merrill's work, in the tradition of Byron, Keats, and Auden, has been a poetry of sensuality and worldliness; he writes both mythological and autobiographical poems, and a narrative impulse can often be seen, notably in the long trilogy. His most recent volume is *The Inner Room* (1988).

W. S. MERWIN (1927–)

W. S. Merwin, the son of a Presbyterian minister, was born in Pennsylvania and graduated from Princeton in 1947. W. H. Auden selected him as the Yale Younger Poet for 1952. Merwin's several volumes of poetry include *A Mask for Janus* (1952), *The Dancing Bears* (1954), *The Moving Target* (1963), *The Lice* (1968), and *The Compass Flower* (1977). Merwin has also written prose poems (*The Miner's Pale Children,* 1970) and has translated many foreign authors into English. His poetry, though austere and abstractly formulated, nevertheless has often concerned itself with war *(The Lice)* and ecological questions. Merwin now lives and teaches in Hawaii.

HOWARD NEMEROV (1920–)

Howard Nemerov grew up in New York; he attended Harvard where he won the Bowdoin Prize in 1940. After graduation he enlisted in the Royal Canadian Air Force and, three years later, the U.S. Air Force. Before joining the faculty of Washington University in St. Louis, where he is now professor of English, Nemerov taught at Hollis, Bennington, and Brandeis. In 1977 his *Collected Poems* won both the National Book Award and the Pulitzer Prize. Nemerov's poems are philosophical and grave but with the sting of wit. His most recent volume is *War Stories* (1987); he served as Library of Congress Poet Laureate from 1988 to 1990.

FRANK O'HARA (1926–1966)

Frank O'Hara attended Harvard after his two-year service in the navy. He graduated in 1950, took an M.A. from the University of Michigan where he received the Hopwood Award for Poetry in 1951, then went to New York to work as a curator for the Museum of Modern Art; he also worked for two years at *Art News.* In New York, O'Hara was at the center of the Abstract Expressionist movement; his acquaintances included de Kooning, Motherwell, Frankenthaler, Pollock, and Kline among the painters; his closest friends were the poets John Ashbery, James Schuyler, and Kenneth Koch. O'Hara wrote candidly about homosexuality as well as about popular culture, the movies, jazz, art, and the city. Before his premature death in a car accident, rather little of O'Hara's verse had been collected; in 1980 the *Collected Poems* appeared, revealing his full stature as a poet of invention, irreverence, and colloquial energy.

ROBERT PINSKY (1940–)

Robert Pinsky was born in New Jersey and educated at Rutgers (B.A. 1962) and at Stanford, where he studied with Yvor Winters, taking a Ph.D. in English. Pinsky taught at Wellesley College and the University of California, Berkeley, before joining the faculty at Boston University, where he is now professor of English. In addition to books of verse, Pinsky has published a study of Walter Savage Landor, *The Situation of Poetry* (1976), and *Poetry and the World* (1988). His writing, still Wintersian in its emphasis on the discursive, is witty and serious, and concerned with the social as well as the private self. His most recent book is *The Want Bone* (1990).

SYLVIA PLATH (1932–1963)

Sylvia Plath was raised in Massachusetts; her father was a German-speaking professor, a student of bees, and her mother was a teacher of secretarial skills. She had her first poem published at the age of eight; as an undergraduate at Smith College she was published in *Seventeen* and *Mademoiselle*. Throughout her adult life, Plath suffered from manic-depressive illness; although she underwent many treatments, her symptoms persisted. She married the Yorkshire poet Ted Hughes and, after teaching briefly at Smith, emigrated to England, continued writing, and had two children. After separating from Hughes, Plath committed suicide. Her autobiographical novel, *The Bell Jar,* was published at first pseudonymously but posthumously under her own name. Plath was influenced by Roethke and Hughes, but the later poetry is vigorously her own — forceful, driven, exact, and rich in observation. The *Collected Poems* appeared in 1981.

ADRIENNE RICH (1929–)

Adrienne Rich grew up in Baltimore, the daughter of a professor of medicine at Johns Hopkins. While attending Radcliffe she published her first book, *A Change of World* (1951), selected by W. H. Auden for the Yale Series of Younger Poets. Her marriage to Alfred Conrad, a professor of economics at Harvard Business School, ended in divorce; they had three sons. Rich often writes about events in her own life, but in the context of the general condition of women. She has been active in the political movements for peace, women's rights, and gay rights, which she joined after declaring herself a lesbian. Her volumes of poetry include *Snapshots of a Daughter-in-Law* (1963), *Leaflets* (1969), *The Will to Change* (1971), *Diving into the Wreck* (1973), *The Dream of a Common Language* (1978), *The Fact of a Doorframe: Poems Selected and New* (1984), and *Time's Power* (1989). She has also published a book on the institution of motherhood, *Of Woman Born* (1976), and a collection of essays (*On Lies, Secrets, and Silence,* 1979). Rich's poetry aims at a "common language" and, though committed and political, is also meditative, elegiac, and historical. She teaches at Stanford University.

THEODORE ROETHKE (1908–1963)

Theodore Roethke's childhood acquaintance with the world of his father's Michigan greenhouse is recalled in *The Lost Son* (1948), *Praise to the End!* (1951), and *The Waking* (1953), winner of a Pulitzer Prize. He taught at the University of Washington in Seattle, where he became mentor to a generation of west-coast poets. His life was marred by a succession of mental breakdowns, for which he was intermittently confined, and by alcoholism. But his vivid early poems, reproducing a child's terrors and preconscious intimations of growth and vitality, proved to be a powerful influence on other poets, from Berryman to Plath. His posthumous *The Far Field* received a National Book Award in 1965.

ANNE SEXTON (1928–1974)

Born in Newton, Massachusetts, Anne Sexton studied with Robert Lowell at Boston University after her therapist suggested she write poetry. Before this she had been a child model, member of a jazz band, and suburban housewife and mother. She suffered a breakdown, was hospitalized for a time, and found a new hope in writing; these and other events of her life became the lyric subjects of her poetry. Later her work took on an increasingly satirical edge, notably in *Transformations* (1971), her rewritings in savage verse of fairy tales from Grimm. Sexton's life ended in suicide after dependence on alcohol had begun to affect her ability to write. At the time of her death she was a teacher of creative writing at Boston University. Her *Complete Poems* were published in 1981.

CHARLES SIMIC (1938–)

Charles Simic was born in Yugoslavia and educated in the United States, at the University of Chicago and New York University. He taught at California State College in Hayward and then joined the faculty at the University of New Hampshire, where he is now professor of English and director of the creative writing program. He has received a Guggenheim and a MacArthur fellowship. In addition to writing his own poetry, Simic has translated French, Russian, and Yugoslav poets into English. Simic's verse draws on macabre aspects of folk tale and myth for its dark power: it is a spare, reduced poetry often evoking the war years of his childhood, especially in *Return to a Place Lit by a Glass of Milk* (1974) and *Charon's Cosmology* (1980). His volume of prose poems, *The World Doesn't End* (1989), was awarded the Pulitzer Prize.

DAVE SMITH (1942–)

Dave Smith was born in Portsmouth, Virginia, and educated at the University of Virginia (B.A. 1965), Southern Illinois University (M.A. 1969), and Ohio University (Ph.D. 1976). He has taught most recently at the University of Utah, the University of Florida in Gainesville, and Virginia Commonwealth University in Richmond. He has received numerous awards, including a National Endowment for the Arts grant, a Guggenheim, and an award from the American Academy and Institute of Arts and Letters. Smith's poetry often issues from a strong regionalism and has described landscapes of the south as well as of Utah. Influenced by Robert Penn Warren, he likes a powerful narrative line in his verse; at the same time, there is a strain of mythic, romantic, and even hallucinatory imagery justifying the title of *Homage to Edgar Allan Poe* (1981). Other books include *Dream Flights* (1981), *In the House of the Judge* (1984), and *Cuba Night* (1990).

GARY SNYDER (1930–)

Gary Snyder's family moved to a small farm near Seattle soon after his birth in San Francisco. Snyder studied at Reed College and Indiana University before entering the doctoral program in Japanese at Berkeley, where he completed all requirements but a thesis. In the fifties Snyder was part of the Beat movement in San Francisco which included Kerouac and Ginsberg. Snyder spent twelve years in Japan, living chiefly in Buddhist monasteries. He now lives with his wife and children in the Sierra Nevada foothills. In 1974 his book *Turtle Island* won a National Book Award; like his other books, it draws on his interests in anthropology and ecology, and his definition of himself as belonging to a "Pacific basin culture" that includes Indians, Eskimos, and Asians.

WALLACE STEVENS (1879–1955)

Wallace Stevens was the son of a lawyer in Reading, Pennsylvania. He attended Harvard (where he was president of the literary magazine *The Advocate*) for three years, then entered New York Law School. Stevens eventually became successful as a surety lawyer and, at the time of his death, was a vice-president of an insurance company in Hartford, Connecticut. Stevens was married to Elsie Kachel; they had one child, Holly Bright. He lived in Hartford from 1916 to 1955, when he died of cancer. His fame as a poet began relatively late in life: his first book, *Harmonium,* was published in 1923. His poetic theory appears in the collection of essays, *The Necessary Angel* (1951), and in additional essays appearing in *Opus Posthumous* (1957). Stevens organized his *Collected Poems* (1954) the year before he died; his daughter later published *The Palm at the End of the Mind* (1971) in which she arranges a selection of the poems chronologically. Stevens' poetry powerfully modified his Romantic and Emersonian inheritance, investigating at first the theoretical base for an American poetics and then expanding its inquiry into the processes by which man constructs changing views of himself and his world.

MARK STRAND (1934–)

Mark Strand was born in Prince Edward Island, Canada, but has lived most of his life in the United States. He took a B.F.A. at Yale and an M.A. at the University of Iowa. Strand has taught at Columbia, Princeton, the University of Virginia, the University of Washington, and Brandeis; he is now director of the creative writing program at the University of Utah. Besides his poetry, Strand has published several volumes of translations, children's books, essays on literature and painting, and short stories. He received a Fulbright to Italy, the Edgar Allan Poe Award, and a Guggenheim fellowship. His poetry, influenced by Stevens, moves usually at a high degree of abstraction; its elegiac and plain tones describe a surreal and unfathomable universe. The *Selected Poems* appeared in 1980. Strand was named Library of Congress Poet Laureate in 1990.

RICHARD WILBUR (1921–)

Richard Wilbur attended Amherst College, where he met and was influenced by Robert Frost. His admiration for a formal, "European" style began during military service in Italy and France in World War II. He has translated Molière into English verse and was one of the lyricists for Leonard Bernstein's *Candide* (1956). Wilbur taught at Harvard, Wellesley, and Wesleyan before joining the faculty at Smith College, where he is now professor of English. Wilbur's subjects are sometimes domestic, but they more often draw on images from nature used for a moral purpose. Wilbur is light and witty in his observations; his musicality and grace are tempered by detachment and irony. His *New and Collected Poems* appeared in 1989.

CHARLES WRIGHT (1935–)

Charles Wright was born in Tennessee; he attended Davidson College and the University of Iowa. Wright performed his military service as an army intelligence agent in Verona (1957–1961) and returned to Italy as a Fulbright student in Rome (1963–1965). He taught at the University of California, Irvine, in 1966–1983 and is now professor of English at the University of Virginia. Among his many awards and fellowships are the Edgar Allan Poe Award (1976), a grant from the American Academy and Institute of Arts and Letters (1977), and the American Book Award for poetry (1983). His *Selected Poems* appeared in 1982. Wright has written extraordinary sequences, influenced by both Pound and Stevens, in which historical events and remembered landscapes take on an abstract and expressionist form, most recently in *Zone Journals* (1989).

JAMES WRIGHT (1927–1980)

James Wright was born in Martins Ferry, Ohio; his father worked for a glass factory in Wheeling, West Virginia, for fifty years. Wright studied with John Crowe Ransom at Kenyon College (B.A. 1952) and with Theodore Roethke at the University of Washington (Ph.D. 1959), and was selected as the Yale Younger Poet for 1957 by W. H. Auden. With Robert Bly he began a series of translations of the work of Georg Trakl, César Vallejo, and Pablo Neruda. Although he taught at Hunter College in New York until his early death from cancer, Wright remained one of the few poetic voices of the American midwest — the gritty, bleak, and depressed places of his youth. His *Complete Poems* appeared in 1990.

Credits

A. R. AMMONS. "Hardweed Path Going," "Reflective," "Apologia pro Vita Sua," "Mountain Talk," "Clarity," "Hope's Okay," "Transaction," "Treaties," "The City Limits," "The Eternal City," "Grace Abounding," from *Collected Poems, 1951–1971*, Copyright © 1972 by A. R. Ammons. "Sphere" (excerpt) from *Sphere*, Copyright © 1974 by A. R. Ammons. "Bonus" from *Selected Poems*, Copyright © 1977, 1975, 1974, 1972, 1971, 1970, 1966, 1965, 1964, 1955 by A. R. Ammons; "Essay on Poetics" (excerpt) from *Selected Longer Poems*, Copyright © 1980, 1975, 1972 by A. R. Ammons; "Easter Morning" from *A Coast of Trees*, Copyright © 1981 by A. R. Ammons. All poems reprinted by permission of W. W. Norton & Company, Inc.

JOHN ASHBERY. "Some Trees" and "The Painter" from *Some Trees* (The Ecco Press), Copyright © 1956 by John Ashbery; "These Lacustrine Cities" from *Rivers and Mountains* (The Ecco Press), Copyright © 1966 by John Ashbery; "Soonest Mended" from *The Double Dream of Spring* (E. P. Dutton), Copyright © 1970 by John Ashbery; reprinted by permission of Georges Borchardt, Inc., and the author. "As One Put Drunk into the Packet-Boat" and "Self-Portrait in a Convex Mirror" from *Self-Portrait in a Convex Mirror*, Copyright © 1972, 1973, 1974, 1975 by John Ashbery; "Street Musicians" and "Syringa" from *Houseboat Days*, Copyright © 1975, 1976, 1977 by John Ashbery; "Many Wagons Ago," "A Love Poem," "Landscapeople" from *As We Know*, Copyright © 1979 by John Ashbery; "Drunken Americans" from *Sharon Train*, Copyright © 1980, 1981 by John Ashbery; "At North Farm," "The Ongoing Story," "Down By the Station, Early in the Morning," "Never Seek To Tell Thy Love" from *A Wave*, Copyright © 1981, 1982, 1983, 1984 by John Ashbery. Some originally published in *The New Yorker*; all reprinted by permission of Viking Penguin, Inc., and Georges Borchardt, Inc.

JOHN BERRYMAN. Thirteen "Dream Songs" from *The Dream Songs*, Copyright © 1959, 1962, 1963, 1964, 1965, 1966, 1967, 1968, 1969 by John Berryman. Reprinted by permission of Farrar, Straus and Giroux, Inc., and Faber and Faber Ltd.

FRANK BIDART. "Self-Portrait, 1969" and "Another Life" from *Golden State*, Copyright © 1973 by Frank Bidart; reprinted with permission of the publisher George Braziller, Inc. "Happy Birthday" and "Elegy" (excerpt) from *The Book of the Body*, Copyright © 1974, 1975, 1977 by Frank Bidart; reprinted by permission of Farrar, Straus and Giroux, Inc.

ELIZABETH BISHOP. All poems from *The Complete Poems, 1927–1979*, Copyright © 1983 by Alice Helen Methfessel; Copyright © 1939, 1940, 1947, 1949, 1952, 1955, 1957, 1971, 1972, 1979, by Elizabeth Bishop; Copyrights

from *Dear John, Dear Coltrane,* Copyright © 1970 by Michael S. Harper; "Nightmare Begins Responsibility" from *Nightmare Begins Responsibility,* Copyright © 1975 by Michael S. Harper; "Tongue-Tied in Black and White" from *Images of Kin,* Copyright © 1977 by Michael S. Harper; reprinted by permission of University of Illinois Press.

ROBERT HAYDEN. All poems from *Angle Of Ascent, New and Selected Poems,* Copyright © 1975, 1972, 1970, 1966 by Robert Hayden. Reprinted by permission of Liveright Publishing Corporation.

LANGSTON HUGHES. "The Negro Speaks of Rivers," "I, Too," "Harlem," Copyright 1926 by Alfred A. Knopf, Inc., and renewed 1954 by Langston Hughes, Copyright 1951 by Langston Hughes; reprinted from *Selected Poems of Langston Hughes* by permission of Alfred A. Knopf, Inc., and Faber and Faber Ltd. All other poems from *Montage of a Dream Deferred* (Henry Holt & Co.), Copyright 1951 by Langston Hughes, renewed 1979 by George Houston Bass; reprinted by permission of Harold Ober Associates Incorporated and Hughes Massie Ltd.

RANDALL JARRELL. "Losses" and "A Lullaby" from *The Complete Poems,* Copyright © 1944, 1948 and renewed © 1971, 1975 by Mrs. Randall Jarrell; reprinted by permission of Farrar, Straus and Giroux, Inc., and Faber and Faber Ltd. "The Woman at the Washington Zoo" from *The Woman at the Washington Zoo,* Copyright © 1960 by Randall Jarrell; reprinted with the permission of Atheneum Publishers, Inc., and Faber and Faber Ltd. "Next Day" from *The Lost World,* Copyright © Randall Jarrell 1963, 1969; reprinted with permission of Macmillan Publishing Company and Eyre & Spottiswoode Publishers Ltd. (Methuen).

ROBERT LOWELL. "Where the Rainbow Ends" from *Lord Weary's Castle,* Copyright © 1946, 1974 by Robert Lowell; reprinted by permission of Harcourt Brace Jovanovich, Inc., and Faber and Faber Ltd. "Sailing Home from Rapallo," "Waking in the Blue," "Home after Three Months Away," "Skunk Hour" from *Life Studies,* Copyright © 1956, 1959 by Robert Lowell; "For the Union Dead" from *For the Union Dead,* Copyright © 1960, 1964 by Robert Lowell; "Waking Early Sunday Morning" from *Near the Ocean,* Copyright © 1963, 1965, 1966, 1967 by Robert Lowell; "The March I" and "Death and the Bridge" from *Notebook,* Copyright © 1967, 1968, 1969, 1970 by Robert Lowell; "Harriet," "Mexico" (excerpt), "Obit" from *For Lizzie and Harriet,* Copyright © 1967, 1968, 1969, 1970, 1973 by Robert Lowell; "History," "Down the Nile," "Watchmaker God," "Stalin," "Reading Myself," "End of a Year" from *History,* Copyright © 1967, 1968, 1969, 1970, 1973 by Robert Lowell; "Fishnet" from *The Dolphin,* Copyright © 1973 by Robert Lowell; "For Sheridan," "Shifting Colors," "Epilogue" from *Day by Day,* Copyright © 1975, 1976, 1977 by Robert Lowell. All reprinted by permission of Farrar, Straus and Giroux, Inc., and Faber and Faber Ltd.

JAMES MERRILL. "The Broken Home" and "Days of 1964" from *Night and Days,* Copyright © 1966 by James Merrill. "Matinees" from *The Fire Screen,* Copyright © 1969 by James Merrill. "In Nine Sleep Valley" and "Syrinx" from *Braving the Elements,* Copyright © 1972 by James Merrill. "Lost in Translation" and "L" and "Z" from "The Book of Ephraim" in *Divine Comedies,* Copyright © 1976 by James Merrill. Excerpt from Book 9 of

Index of First Lines

Index of Titles